Borderle Behavior Analytics

Who's Inside? What're They Doing?

Saryu Nayyar
CEO, Gurucul Predictive Security Analytics

Contributors:
Jerry Archer – CSO, Major Financial Services Company
Gary Eppinger – CISO, Carnival Cruises
Gary Harbison – CISO, Monsanto
Leslie K. Lambert – CISO at Large
Robert Rodriguez – CEO, SINET
Joe Sullivan – CSO, UBER
Teri Takai – CIO at Large

Senior Contributing Editor – Patrick S. Barry

BORDERLESS BEHAVIOR ANALYTICS
Who's Inside? What're They Doing?

For more information contact:
Gurucul Predictive Security Analytics
www.gurucul.com

Publisher: Ankur Chadda
Managing Editor: Tom Clare
Graphics: Raghunath Sontakke
Cover Design: 99 QUEEN

ISBN: 13: 978-1535152655

"There are only two kinds of companies.
Those that were hacked
and those that don't yet know they were hacked."

Popular Cyber Security Credo

"The world has changed.
Security and data will be something
that goes on for hundreds of years in the future.
We are at the beginning of that stage."

Tim Armstrong – CEO, AOL

BORDERLESS BEHAVIOR ANALYTICS
Who's Inside? What're They Doing?

CONTENTS

ACKNOWLEDGMENTS

Nilesh Dherange, Craig Cooper,
Jim Routh, Renee Guttmann-Stark,
Devin Bhatt, Jairo Orea
Tom Clare, Ankur Chadda, Craig Kensek

Foreword

Being happily married for close to thirty years, my wife has shared with me her experiences of a job from her teens, with the kind of fondness that only decades of time and selective memory can provide. Her job was as a cashier at a local independently owned grocery store in her neighborhood. There, she would manually identify the price of each item on the checkout counter with one hand and punch the price into the cash register with the other, while carrying on a conversation with each customer, all with perfect cadence. I asked her what she did when the item lacked a price tag or sticker. She would simply make up what she thought the price of the item actually was and punch it in to avoid breaking the cadence in her conversation with the customer. This technique was highly valued by the supervisors and store manager, despite the occasional pricing mistake along the way, as only a small family-owned business can appreciate. My wife moved at the speed of the customer and adjusted her techniques, based both on her skill at doing three things simultaneously and her ability to demonstrate interest in the customer.

I hadn't given this professional experience much thought recently until I read this book which you're embarking on now. Then it dawned on me: what moving at the speed of the customer meant then and what it means today. Forty years ago, it meant demonstrating the ability to carry on a conversation while sorting groceries and punching the prices of each item into the register. Today, it means models or algorithms. Yet it is clearly infeasible to fulfill customer needs online without some level of data science applied to both order fulfillment and managing risk. This is an invitation for the CISO or CSO to be part of the design of the consumer interface where the consumer's behavior will determine the level of risk of fulfillment performed in close to real time. I read another book recently where a large retail organization made specific decisions for online order fulfillment of electronics (flat screen TVs), choosing models to make a commitment to the online customer in under 14 milliseconds to avoid losing a sale. That's customer speed and it requires more than automation, it requires intelligence delivered through algorithms. That same CISO can apply the same principle of customer speed to one of the most important components of any mature cyber security program today, the privileged user.

The privileged user (domain administrator, workstations, tech support, engineer, database analyst, etc.) all have a higher level of privilege to get things done in the administration and support of enterprise technology. They are also highly popular, not with customers, but with the threat actors attempting to gain privilege to execute their malicious intent. The most mature cyber programs today use models, or algorithms, to make real-time decisions on providing access to sensitive data and applications by comparing actual online behavior with models of past behaviors, spotting potential anomalistic events and taking action in real time. The provisioning and the de-provisioning of privilege happens with no human interaction in real time, enabled by a base technology platform categorized as user and entity behavior analytics (UEBA). For security professionals, that changes everything. Data science is now as much a part of security as are data lakes, puddles, ponds, etc. Unlike other highly innovative technology components, several behavior analytics solutions are implementable for an enterprise new to model-driven decisions, completing the first time through without extensive scar tissue. My enterprise is using machine learning models for privileged users today and all enterprise users tomorrow. Models are performing continuous authentication for consumers based on their patterns of behavior in real time, alerting applications how much functionality and access to data is appropriate based on the behavior risk of each user. Model-driven security has arrived and none too soon for the sophisticated threat actors that are using data science to attack enterprises.

This book is a collection of thought-provoking content from industry luminaries presenting practical guidance based on expertise essential to the impact of models on identity and risk-based security maturity, for enterprises large and small, moving at customer speed. Welcome to the future of cyber security coming soon to an enterprise near you!

Jim Routh
CSO, Aetna

Jim Routh is the Chief Security Officer, leading Global Security for Aetna and the Chairman of the NH-ISAC Board. A former board member of the FS-ISAC, he also served as the Global Head of Application & Mobile Security for JP Morgan Chase. Prior positions include the CISO for KPMG, DTCC and American Express. He has over 30 years of experience in information technology and information security as a practitioner, management consultant, and leader of technology, analytic and information security for global firms. He has won numerous industry awards including: the 2016 Security Alliance Award for Innovation, 2016 ISE Luminary Leadership Award – the Northeast, the 2014 North American Information Security Executive of the Year for Healthcare, the 2009 BITS Leadership Award for outstanding leadership of the Supply Chain Working Group (in collaboration with NIST the U.S. Dept. of Treasury), and the 2007 Information Security Executive of the Year for the Northeast. He is a co-author of the FS-ISAC white paper on 3rd Party Software Security Controls and several other industry white papers.

Introduction

With the advent of ubiquitous mobility and ever-expanding cloud adoption, humanity has crossed the threshold into a brave new world, yet not everyone knows that or understands the implications. This passage simultaneously represents profoundly exciting possibilities delivering empowered productivity and enhanced cost savings, but at the same time ushers in sobering trends in risk management. Those who understand this transition stand in a position to take advantage of the possibilities, as well as protect themselves against the perilous developments inherent in the journey. We have, in effect, left the comparatively safe confines of a modern suburban world and now find ourselves in something of a Wild West frontier, replete with the legendary gold rush where fortunes can be made overnight, or livelihoods are damaged from misguided actions based on uninformed perceptions and weak strategic decisions.

With the explosion of mobile devices, along with the IoT (Internet of Things) becoming integrated into the most intimate niches of our lives — from bio wristbands that count our steps and monitor our heartrate, to applications on our mobile phones that budget our calorie intake and keep us up-to-date with the inventory in our refrigerator — the massive amount of human data has ballooned to staggering proportions. Experts forecast this digital exhaust will reach 44 zettabytes by 2020. ABI Research estimates the global wireless connectivity market (excluding cellular), will exceed 10 billion integrated circuit (IC) shipments annually by 2021. This ocean of data, and data delivery nodes, is not only growing rapidly to gargantuan proportions, but the unique and complex segments in which data resides is expanding and evolving as well. Now in business, the same explosion of digital exhaust from mobility and cloud adoptions inside the enterprise is challenging human analysis capabilities. The security perimeter has blurred and for all intents and purposes, simply faded away.

Organizations are seismically impacted by this paradigm shift of cloud and mobility as they strive to adjust to the manner their employees and customers use and manage technology. The infusion of bring your own device (BYOD), high-speed internet connectivity and cloud-based applications is continually redefining enterprise networks, not through proactive planning and change management, but in an ad hoc reactive manner. The use profile is 24/7, global, instantaneous, and rich in consumer-driven IT. Everyone is going everywhere on the internet, all the time, and in a staggering volume of activity. At the same time, however, there persists a comparatively low awareness of access and activity risks, and their importance, among the general population of today's employees. This reality courts disaster, enabling more emerging undefined gray areas of risk than declarative defenses can address A new awareness of access and activity risks is urgently needed and one from a risk-based solution perspective which quantifies the severity of risk as quickly as possible.

Gone are the days when attacks on a system such as internet worms, email spam and opportunistic hacks were the prevalent security issues of the day, which could be addressed with firewalls, antivirus software and spam filtering mechanisms. Data no longer resides behind firewalls; that singular control point of protection is gone. Instead, there is a much more complex hybrid IT security challenge of on-premises environments being connected to a host of cloud applications and an array of mobile devices.

An enduring popular quote among security pundits is, "There are only two kinds of companies. Those that were hacked and those that don't yet know they were hacked." Now, however, attacks against any business are likely to be stealthier, targeted in a far more sophisticated manner, while always changing and evolving. Highly skilled individuals, sometimes IT professionals, who have vast and seasoned knowledge on the most effective way to attack companies' vulnerabilities, carry them out. They move quietly within organizations, sometimes for periods of years, rather than months, steadily acquiring everything they need for their malicious assaults. At the root of modern threats is the misuse and compromise of identity which gives the attacker access to the keys of the kingdom. Identity is the critical access risk and threat plane unacknowledged by far too many organizations. With identity-based access, attackers easily pass by current declarative defenses based on rules, signatures and patterns. Traditional defenses identify the known bads (red) and the safe profiles (green). Yet with identity as a primary risk, attention must now be focused on the vast gray areas between the red and the green. This is why a new form of risk management, with precise risk scoring form the context of big data, which moves from detective to predictive, has become so essential.

With most security traditional solutions dedicated on prevention, and some on detection, the impact of these emerging influences on these older security systems is profound. Firewall, security information and event management (SIEM), intrusion detection systems (IDS), intrusion protection systems (IPS), data loss prevention (DLP), vulnerability assessment, sandboxing — were all primarily designed to look for, to detect, the known, often from the outside. While this has been effective for preventing and detecting a specific class of external attacks, these techniques cannot catch the malicious insider because they have approved access. And the majority of organizations' access is far too over-provisioned. Industry experts observe that most Fortune 500 companies have 50% or more of privileged access risks outside their lists and vaults as hidden unknowns. Gurucul's direct delivery experience has observed a large enterprise where they discovered over 70% of the privileged access risks were often hidden entitlements, including application privileges and were unknown privileged access.

To make matters more concerning, insider attacks are on the rise. According to Verizon's *2016 Data Breach Investigations Report*, about 76% of network intrusions have involved employee identity and weak credentials. In addition, existing traditional identity management solutions were not originally designed to address this kind of challenge. They don't inherently provide insight into how access is used. Unfortunately, these solutions have been eclipsed in their standalone ability to manage identity and access effectively. The scale of unmanaged access often represents millions of entitlements that an organization must contend with. An influence on this troubling trend has been Sarbanes-Oxley requirements, resulting in rubber stamping of broad swaths of access certifications and the practice of access cloning. As a result, excess access has become institutionalized, a default organizational process.

Years of investment with traditional security approaches have not changed the outcome. The CyberEdge Group's *2016 Cyberthreat Defense Report* states that 76% of organizations were breached in the 12 months before the survey, a distinct rise over the preceding year. This represents a disquieting and rising upward trend. Yet with the factors described above, what are security teams trying to detect? Known bads? Or unknowns?

With over 72% of cyber security defenses spent on prevention (*2016 SANS IT Security Spending Trends*), this traditional investment is not delivering results. Organizations find they don't have all the tools they need to assure the security of their environments. What's required is an ability to tighten the identity access plane that modern attackers are leveraging through phishing and social attacks. The discovery gap of unknown privileged access entitlements must be closed with the awareness gap of how access entitlements are being utilized for an effective identity and access management program. As well, an integral part of the risk management strategy should include an ability to provide visibility into all instances of access entitlement, to monitor what access is being provided and how it is being used, and to have the capability to assess those instances with timely and reliable risk-based scores.

Security leaders should assume attackers are inside and that they must be detected. The most effective way to detect them and to find high risk is through their behavior. What we need to be looking for, and seeing, in the future, is the unknown, most often from the insider. The question is what is their behavior and what is that behavior's risk?

Yet within a growing sea of digital exhaust the scope of the challenge now lies well beyond manual human capabilities. Without a precise predictive behavior analytic solution, driven by advanced machine learning and drawing from big data for context — identifying the threats in near real time — the task to identify and stop these attacks, only with human capacity, becomes simply impossible.

The awareness for this need to identify these unknowns is growing within circles of forward-looking security leaders. This approach represents the only realistic path to analyze the surface area of identity for access risk, while detecting behavioral anomalies from advanced machine learning baselining. We call this solution approach 'Borderless Behavior Analytics'.

In this book, we have assembled thought leaders from a range of different industries — from financial services, transportation, agricultural biotechnology, manufacturing, cutting-edge social media, government, hospitality and more. They have seen this landscape change and have delivered solutions to address it. We share their experience, and their lessons learned, so that others following similar paths might benefit, and possibly avoid wrong turns. We also draw from industry analysts, leveraging as well the deep bench of seasoned expertise at Gurucul, to share insights into how data access and use are changing, to offer a resource that might help assure the success of your organization's future.

By reading this book you are joining a journey of discovery which defines the evolving future of cyber security and the robust challenges of addressing access and activity risks. We hope to help make your journey a productive one.

Saryu Nayyar
CEO, Gurucul

Impact of Cloud and Mobility
for Identity

The Evolution of Urgency for Change

So how did we get here? How did we arrive at this kaleidoscopic world of security challenges?

About ten years ago, the traditional chief information security officer's strategy for companies was to have a hard outside shell and a soft inside, something like an exoskeleton. This paradigm was established in the 70's and 80's. During that era, many mainframe set-ups maintained their data centers in central locations and built their security to protect these monoliths of data.

With the advent of technology developments in business that delivered more convenience and productivity, security teams were compelled to move to more of a distributed and open security policy. Business demanded that. Over the last six years, with the widespread use of the multifunctional mobile smartphones in business and companies experiencing the expanded BYOD (bring your own device) demand, the relevance and value of these original traditional security perspectives and strategies were coming to an end. Concurrently, the advent of cloud adoption had been expanding. A paradigm shift for security of this evolving technology was at hand.

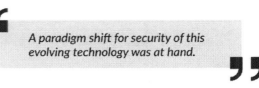

A paradigm shift for security of this evolving technology was at hand.

Cloud adoption first began as a shadow IT activity, beyond an IT organization's supervision. The trend started with small pockets of users using different software solutions that were easy to set up, and often free, to share files, instant text, post professional profiles, and more, (Box, Dropbox, Skype, LinkedIn, etc.) for their perceived advantages. These were completely outside IT's visibility. This usage took root across business units where employees resolved challenges which IT was unable to address in a timely, responsive manner, by accessing easily available cloud-based applications. Unsanctioned employee-driven IT had established itself in the business setting and this raised security concerns. While these solutions delivered enhanced productivity and flexibility, they did not focus on availability, scalability or security concerns. Then, a number of companies began to offer tools to provide visibility into what applications were being used within an organization's environment.

This ease of use and heightened efficiencies, however, led to expanded offerings and utilization of cloud applications. Organizations also witnessed groups within the corporate structure adopt top-down applications like Salesforce, with its sales force automation capabilities, to meet their business goals. This trend represented a growing migration for enterprise applications. Organizations would adopt a software as a service (SaaS) solution from the internet, the pattern of corporate adoption would expand — both within an organization and across the marketplace — eventually manifesting into the wide array of public and private cloud applications we see today. Migration of corporate information had moved outside the firewall, again without IT's official sanction. These popular cloud business applications included Zoho for enterprise business applications, as well as DocuSign for secure document signature management, and others, all delivering robust productivity within their specialized niches. The kaleidoscopic world of security challenges was well on its way.

Salesforce.com became acknowledged as the first widely adopted cloud business application. Their SaaS solutions originally offered portal access for different customers. Over time, they expanded and productized their solution to the point where it became a standard for sales organizations within a broad range of companies. More cloud solutions proliferated, offering new modes of productivity enhancement and other advantages. And as cloud gained in popularity, more and more data moved outside the perimeter.

In the recent past, organizations' adoptions of more comprehensive cloud solutions, such as Amazon Web Services, Rackspace, Office 365, Box, Google Apps, and other cloud solutions, have subsequently become standards. Business was dictating to IT: "We're going in this direction." This wholesale migration began about five to seven years ago as business applications like this came into more widespread availability. At that point, with broad sets of data residing in the cloud, the question for security leaders was: "Is it secure?" Demands for assurance of security in this newly evolving IT hybrid environment moved to the forefront, and rightfully so. Today, trends reveal the growing preponderance of specialized cloud adoptions in larger companies, where 82% of enterprises larger than 1000 employees have a multi-cloud strategy, with 71% hybrid cloud (*RightScale 2016 State of the Cloud Report*), all trending up from the previous year.

One of the advantages that cloud solutions provided was that they did not have legacy application and infrastructure to integrate into their solutions and the majority designed environments with security built in from the beginning.

An early driver for establishing policies for security and the protection of privacy was the Security Breach Statute – California Senate Bill 1386 (SB-1386, July 2003). This was the first piece of major legislation mandating that if a company lost any customer information, and it was not encrypted, then the company was required to report it to the customer. The statute also stipulated that *"...any business that violates, proposes to violate, or has violated this title may be enjoined."* So any enterprise representing themselves as being responsible for handling or managing sensitive customer information would be subject to a mandate requiring that customer information must be protected in a secure and standardized manner. Transparent and timely disclosure of any serious change in security status was a strict requirement. To do otherwise would be a risk for any business with paralyzing and costly legal sanctions.

The appearance of the chief information security officer (CISO) title on IT org charts, and the accompanying official roles and responsibilities, evolved in the early 2000's. The CISO's job was to protect a company's revenue producing business and the constituent sensitive pieces of data which support that objective. Yet with all a given organization's important data in the cloud, and with business applications on mobile phones, tablets, etc., being used 24/7 from everywhere, the burning question for security leaders had become: "How am I going to manage the risk with all these devices and applications — both on and off the cloud?" Data was no longer behind the firewall. That single security control point was gone. The border was gone. The data was no longer safe inside the fortress, because there was no fortress. The data resided in multiple locations outside the enterprise.

> *The data was no longer safe inside the fortress, because there was no fortress.*

Since the complexity of this usage trend was often initiated by business leaders in organizations outside the chief information officer's (CIO's) sphere of responsibility, some CISOs found their mandate at cross-purposes, generally taking a reflexive 'Dr. No' position on these productivity enhancing innovations. Earlier, instead of threat hunting, the traditional security tools from five to fifteen years ago involved the process that would entail placing a constraint, but only if a potential threat was understood. Of course, if an organization shut everyone out, there would be no threat, but without access, the business operations would cease. Yet the challenge remained that "we don't know what's coming at us next" concern. Nevertheless, successful CISO's generally recognized the importance and value adopting a consultant and partner-like role with the rest of the business, and helping them understand what best practices were required to assure effective security in their rapidly evolving hybrid IT environments. That meant CISOs needed to raise their game and take responsibility for all the new complexities an enterprise was taking on, or considering to take on.

This brave new evolving and complex networking world has represented a serious challenge for businesses. At first, organizations provided limited transparency. Then, to comply with government mandates, security teams had to know if data had been breached. They needed to identify what tools they possessed to assess the magnitude and direction of a breach. Yet traditional firewalls and other security applications were all designed to detect breaches coming from outside of the network and via known attack vectors. They were weak at detecting threats emanating from the inside. Security information and event management (SIEM) solutions had delivered value for over a decade of centralized visibility, mainly for compliance and operations, yet only recently provided selected threat hunting capabilities. Intrusion detection systems and intrusion protection systems (IDS/IPS), as well as data loss prevention (DLP), were designed more for awareness, than protection, resulting in event and alert input into SIEMs for more context to lower the noise factor. These tools, however, could not address the persistent risk of malicious insiders, which security experts recognized was on the rise and showing no signs of abatement.

Several years of escalating breaches were delivering an alarming quantity of alerts, creating fatigue among security staffers, with far too many futile false positives. Declarative defenses were not managing the challenge. New attack trends could not be fingerprinted when they were analyzed, because many attack signatures were unique due to massive polymorphism. There was surge of cybercrime beyond the scope of signatures, patterns and rules in declarative defenses. The complete breakdown of the perimeter had become manifest. This sobering observation ushered in the realization among CISOs that they no longer had effective controls to address the urgent evolving challenge. They recognized that a serious systemic threat to their organization's livelihood was at hand.

> *This sobering observation ushered in the realization among CISOs that they no longer had effective controls to address the urgent evolving challenge.*

Accentuating that realization of pandemic exposure, numerous events occurred between 2009 and 2012 that served to heighten security leaders' concerns, which included Operation Aurora and Stuxnet. Launched by a group affiliated with the People's Liberation Army of China, Aurora involved a series of cyber-attacks conducted against a host of American companies, including Google, Adobe Systems, Juniper Networks, Rackspace, Symantec, Northrop Grumman, Morgan Stanley and Dow Chemical. The objective was penetrating security and gaining access to the crown jewels of these high tech, security and defense contractor companies. Stuxnet was a targeted worm virus, alleged to have been developed by Israeli and U.S. groups. It was used to paralyze Iran's nuclear program by targeting Siemens computer systems which controlled Iran's nuclear centrifuges, of which one fifth were ruined. This event demonstrated that even physical assets could be compromised or destroyed (by changing the speed of the centrifuges) through cyber-attacks. The Stuxnet breach methodology also included leveraging four zero-day attacks, where just one zero-day exploit itself is highly valued. On a wider scale, a swarm of other zero-based events proliferated in the cyber world and continued to rise in frequency. A new alarming era of exposure had arrived.

Organizations saw that a new awareness and paradigm were required — a new way to look at, assess and strengthen the security of a business's crown jewels, their data. Sarbanes-Oxley certification requirements were in place. Earlier attitudes treated compliance reporting as an afterthought. Now, a number of larger organizations approached this requirement in a similar way service providers had with service level agreements (SLAs), a serious requirement of due diligence, giving this reporting a much higher priority. Conversely, some organizations sought to circumvent the meticulous requirements, and falsified their certifications. Meanwhile, enterprises recognized that intellectual property (IP) theft was on the rise from insiders. Cases included groups of employees and contractors at high tech companies, sometimes disgruntled, who moved to other companies taking their work with them, feeling unfounded entitled ownership of the intellectual property, despite employee contracts to the contrary. The complexity of exposure and risk for enterprises both outside and inside the organizational framework continued to unfold and amplify.

More recently (between 2012 and 2015), an evolutionary development of SIEM took place representing a functional amplification of the solution set, fortifying SOC's (security operations centers) capabilities with enhanced solution features such as the 'single pane of glass' concept, providing a centralized view of all system events and alerts. This further enabled forensic security capabilities that delivered insight into the pattern of an attack and how it happened. This meant SOCs could generate and manage their own threat intelligence. During this period, solutions like FireEye's advanced persistent threat (APT) detection appliances and sand boxes became more common. At this stage of security evolution, organizations were developing their own security intelligence, taking ownership of understanding the steps in the cyber kill chain (1-7) and developing a deeper awareness of how attack methods evolved. During this time, however, the declarative statement method to assess cyber security maturity was being challenged for the increasingly constrained value it delivered to security.

To respond successfully to this challenge, businesses needed to initiate a new perspective on the focus of identity, access and entitlements. Everyone should

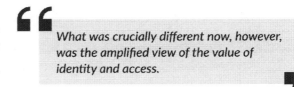

What was crucially different now, however, was the amplified view of the value of identity and access.

have their own ID, everyone should have their own set of permissions and credentials for the systems and applications they interface with. Otherwise, traceability would not exist. What was crucially different now, however, was the amplified view of the value of identity and access. Before, like compliance reporting, these elements were secondary in security priority. Now, they were becoming elevated to a crucial strategic role. How business and security viewed the role of identity and access in an organization defined how successful an organization's security strategy would be.

Yet, there was now too much data in the SIEM, and it was doubling every year. Any serious prospect of managing security analysis solely by human means was quickly becoming futile. Around this time, the misuse and compromise of identity emerged as a serious threat plane. Mismanaged with outdated legacy policies and rules, identity became an easy attack plane to compromise over-privileged accounts. Effective identity management was impaired. While its access enabling function remained important, its ability to actually see what identities were doing in the environment were piecemeal at best. Vast gray areas of activity anomalies remained unknown, and they were growing. Behavior was a blind spot. The behavior of activist insiders like Edward Snowden, and disgruntled employees, elevated the profile and visibility of the insider threat, highlighting the potential for severe negative impact on organizations. The perimeter was officially gone. A reliable new approach in security, capable of evolving with the changing environment was needed. This entailed effective behavior visibility and monitoring.

Identity and access are core components of a classification process to achieve the best method to define normal and abnormal user and entity behaviors. If a threat actor wanted to steal data from a network, they would need access to that data. The threat plane is comprised of identities and their associated credentials. That's the basis of access and the direct route to anything in an organization's network. With the evolving challenges, and sobering lessons learned with from recent high profile data breaches, the importance of identity and access was now better understood and perceived much more strategically by forward-looking security leaders. Security teams needed to know who was in their environment, what they had access to, and what were they doing there.

The threat plane is comprised of identities and their associated credentials. That's the basis of access and the direct route to anything in an organization's network.

These undefined activities represented gray areas of unknown risk. Addressing this challenge requires a comprehensive, accurate and timely measurement of the risks that lurk in the uncharted gray areas. Within that requirement is a recognition that visibility of privileged access accounts and entitlements risk is at the forefront of concerns, because a majority of privileged access within an organization is simply unknown at the entitlement level and within applications. This risk-based assessment capability has undergone various phases of evolution, based on need, while harnessing state-of-the-art technology capable of developing and delivering next generation security monitoring.

The first generation of information security professionals was generally comprised of forensic investigators who could discover and define the kill chain. They thrived on solving the mystery of how a threat actor broke into their system, from where and what method was used, and then closing the security hole. Over time, however, as environment complexity and the number of endpoints grew, it became too cumbersome, time-consuming, and expensive, to do a deep security dive. In addition, this approach did not improve security teams' abilities to stop these attacks.

During this time, an industry-wide awareness of this challenge grew. By 2008, the Center for Internet Security (CIS) and the SANS Institute had been participating in a public-private partnership with the NSA. This ultimately expanded to a wider consortium, which included international participation to examine the problem more holistically. An important outcome of this initiative was refining a list of security controls (*CIS Critical Controls*) that were most effective in preventing known attacks. These controls were widely adopted and continue to be periodically revised, encouraging shared continuous diagnostic investigation. A new proactive security framework had begun to evolve, promoting a structure for constructive security. Prescriptive advice began to show up in the role of security, along with fundamentals of security hygiene and best practices. Recognizing the need to target identity and implement behavior monitoring had begun during this phase of security evolution. This requirement, however, would also need to address more complex environments, demanding the application of new perspectives.

A new risk challenge emerged — 'dwell time' — the average time between intruder infection and detection. It was far too lengthy, by industry estimates, with the average often exceeding 200 days, and more recently just below 150 days. Attackers were spending months inside an environment undiscovered. SOC team effectiveness declined markedly, and became a major concern, even as new versions of SIEM were unable to improve the detection rate. Using a compromised identity, malicious attackers would move unimpeded, laterally, inside an environment. A risk-based solution was required to comprehensively address the myriad of challenges plaguing security teams dealing with account compromise and misuse, plus unknown anomalies based on access and activity in their hybrid environments. The era of user and entity behavior analytics (UEBA) and identity analytics (IdA)* security solutions had arrived, and none too soon.

Filling the gap of SIEMs, UEBA delivered identity-based behavior analysis of access and activity for new data sources including SIEMs, directories and applications with insight beyond what technical experts had previously been able to view with log access files. As well, IdA helped close the discovery gap of unknown access risks, with a

---

* While IdA, as standalone class of solution, has been available for years from select UEBA vendors, Gartner Research coined the term in early 2016, identifying it as an essential component of advanced security analytics.

special emphasis on the vast threat plane of privileged access. Now the prospect of preventing data exfiltration, detecting insider threats, as well as compromise and misuse of identity through phishing and social attacks, had become a realistic goal. These solutions delivered a new effective method to leverage and monitor an identity to establish what's normal and what's not. Finally, security analysts could answer, "What access risk does this user have? What activity risks does this user have?" and "What is the context of these risks?" This provided granular insight into how an identity's access and activity behavior was different from what their peer groups were doing, in all the different variables of: who, where, when, how, what action, and how these actions correlated with baseline definitions of established normal behavior.

The essential component of a successful and best-of-breed UEBA and IdA solution model involves machine learning. Drawing from big data for context, across all environments, machine learning delivers the mechanism to enable a broad range of issues to be managed, to find the red herrings, to discover what's going on and what's different or out of the ordinary. Advanced machine learning is designed to recognize that just because a behavior is different, it doesn't mean it's bad, and it eliminates potential red herrings from consideration.

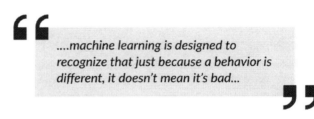

....machine learning is designed to recognize that just because a behavior is different, it doesn't mean it's bad...

Ultimately, a mature UEBA-IdA solution would furnish businesses with a centralized easy-to-use single view that encompasses all the users and entities in the hybrid environment. UEBA then provides holistic monitoring of access and activity where various levels of users and solutions leverage predictive risk scores to reduce access risks and detect unknown anomalies. While SOC teams will likely leverage risk scores within a UI, bi-directional API integration with solutions enables risk scores to drive automated risk responses. Forward-looking organizations finally have a cost-effective, efficient and reliable approach to address the urgent security priorities in their global environments, 24/7.

In this brave new world, there are, of course, early adopters who have traveled the road of integrating UEBA and IdA solutions and faced the challenges they represent. Each organization and industry segment has their own influences, challenges and requirements. In this book, we are proud to present to you CISO leaders from a range of business sectors who share their own insights and experiences on the UEBA and IdA journey through Borderless Behavior Analytics, facing the challenges of today's new evolving hybrid IT environments. They also discuss their strategies, goals and objectives of next-generation-facing UEBA and IdA solution requirements.

While the introduction and this chapter position UEBA and IdA via machine learning from the context of big data as an answer to cyber security challenges, the journey in the forthcoming interviews is rich with wisdom and experience beyond any possibly perceived promotional partiality.

Our first expert, Gary Eppinger has served in a broad range of industries, and arrived at a setting he calls a 'hyper-hybrid environment'. The challenges he has faced are unique, and his perspectives on the solutions required to address those challenges draw from his extensive security experience in a number of different vertical markets, from finance, manufacturing, retail, health care and more.

BORDERLESS EXPERT INSIGHTS

Gary Eppinger, CISO *
Carnival Corporation

Global VP, Chief Information Security and Privacy Officer for Carnival Corporation, Gary Eppinger conceives, implements, and leads technology solutions that protect corporate assets, increase organizational capability, and advance productivity for Fortune 100 companies. He is recognized globally as a highly valued resource with an exceptional ability to build and develop IT teams that deliver critical business objectives in companies within transformation. Ranked 24th in ExecRank's "Top Security Executive Rankings," Gary is an active speaker on IT and cyber security. He also assists numerous companies serving as a valued board advisor.

A member of Gurucul's Board of Advisers, Gary has provided valuable guidance in the company's evolution through the complex path of challenges facing the company's emergence in the field of UEBA security. He shares some of his seasoned in-depth insights into the challenges of hybrid cloud security and behavior analytics' place in it.

Overview

Eppinger begins with his observations on how data access is changing today's environments. He provides insights on the symptoms that reveal security defenses are a problem today, and then discusses the business vulnerabilities of a compromise leading to a breach. The critical drivers around the importance of insider threats are examined, as he notes the growing concerns about privilege misuse. Drawing from his unique Carnival Corporation experience, Eppinger shares insights on the impact on security defenses with a constant flow of insiders and customers traveling on ships, to land locations, or in combination. This systemic view incorporates environments around the world, across different on-premises locations, in the cloud and on the sea, and includes the profound impact on this exceptional hybrid environment's security requirements. The new role of identity-based access and activity risks, and how they tie together, are explored along with the key solution components required to address the needs of constantly changing security conditions. This topic also expands into the handling of the vast and growing scale of data for security analysis. Eppinger shares his perspectives on machine learning and predictive security analytics adoption in the environment and within his industry vertical. Finally, he provides his distinctive perspectives of security evolution through the wide range of vertical markets he has worked in which has shaped his approach to work in one of the most complex hybrid environments imaginable, something he calls the 'hyper-hybrid environment'.

---

* The views and opinions expressed by Gary Eppinger in this book are his own, and do not necessarily reflect those of Carnival Corporation, or any of his previous employers.

How data access is changing today's environments

Carnival Corporation's strategy for managing data has changed over the last few years. Originally, we were primarily a corporate holding company. Each of our ten brands was a standalone cruise company which we ran independently. They competed for customers internally, as well as with external competitors. Carnival just happened to acquire them and put them under the same umbrella.

Separate siloed views of data. This meant from a data perspective that corporate and customer data, the fuel of the company, was separated and isolated from each particular brand. For example, the information on customers for Carnival Cruises, AIDA, and for Princess, were all stored and accessed independently. When Gary Eppinger cruised on ships from all three lines, we were only capable of seeing that information associated with him separately, in each silo of data, with no correlation whatsoever.

Phased migration to a centralized view. We have worked to concatenate and bring that critical data together in phases, and over the last two years we acquired two more of the consolidated views of our customer data. This means if I am a customer of all three of those brands, corporate Carnival can now see all this in a single repository. As well as that, we market to customers differently because we can now correlate and use this information effectively and have insight into the preferences a customer has established on any ship and cruise line. More consolidated cruise brand views are in the works.

We have worked to concatenate and bring that critical data together in phases...

Centralized identity value. An example of the advantage this new visibility provides is if I sailed on Carnival fifty times, Carnival has a great deal of value data and information on me as a cruiser. When I go with Princess and Costa one time, I may look like a new customer to them, with no history. Now we can add visibility into these fifty Carnival cruises. They now know what food I like, they know if I'm a spa person, the types of spas I prefer, and the types of rooms that might make sense for me. So my identity represents great value information that can be leveraged to make my vacation a great experience.

New capabilities in risk management. As we bring that data together, it also gives us more of a capability to detect a higher level of risk to the information. As the data becomes concatenated into a single place, we know more effectively if it's compromised, a higher risk, or not protected properly. When it was spread between ten different brands, and two hundred different locations, it was much harder to get to and monitor properly. Now that it is coming together, it also raises the bar of what we have to do to protect that information.

The symptoms revealing security defenses are a problem today

No longer is it an environment where a CISO might have fifteen branches and a fixed number of connections, along with access and users connecting into their environment. That was manageable then. Today, however, there are millions of customers, millions of entry points, millions of devices connecting into our environments all over the world. That's millions of connection points we're responsible for. Now it's no longer possible to rely only on the entry point into our network, into our environment, to provide security assurance.

> *Today... there are millions of customers, millions of entry points, millions of devices connecting into our environments all over the world.*

Moving security closer to the data. Generally the closer you can put your controls to the data, the better you are. If you think about the traditional approach CISOs took for the last twenty plus years, we originally built the walls as far as we could from the data, just at the network layer, and then this model was no longer viable. In response, the focus moved to the application layer and data was controlled at the ERP (enterprise resource planning) level with multiple applications together. Finally, the objective became to move the security focus to the database level.

Maintaining the right controls on data. Today, it's a multi-tiered approach where you need to have appropriate controls across all the different channels and/or layers to make sense. Yet at the same time it includes sustaining the objective of maintaining controls much more closely to that data, no matter where the data resides, as well as how that data flows and where it flows to. Some of these controls need to go along with the data as it moves to its destination because data does not reside within the servers of an isolated DMZ all the time. It's continuously being leveraged, moved and adapted from system to system. In addition, you need to think about your controls based on location or point of time.

Technology evolution and new security perspectives. With technology and data use patterns continually evolving and changing, the old strategies of manual security monitoring have become unrealistic. This clearly indicates that an era of information security has passed and that the new age will require entirely new perspectives and solutions on how to achieve the same original goal of twenty years ago: to protect the information.

> *This clearly indicates that an era of information security has passed and that the new age will require entirely new perspectives and solutions... to protect the information.*

Security driving business value

Carnival protects a great deal of critical information — from credit cards, passports, driver's licenses, to health records, and more. This, of course, includes massive amounts of critical information for a huge number of customers who sail with us every day. Millions of customers entrust us with that information because it's essential for us to be able to deliver a high quality vacation for them. We take this responsibility very seriously. The prospect of damaging that trust represents a threat to our brand reputation. Without our brand reputation, customers' loyalty erodes and people simply choose other vacation destinations.

A range of security concerns. Anything that could damage our reputation is, of course, a serious matter, but data exfiltration, customer hacking, or customer information threats are all top priority critical concerns for us. We also think about safety and security at the highest level of importance to the company and to our employees. From our perspective, in an industry which services so many customers traveling through the world, our focus includes anything that involves the physical safety, or the perceived safety of an individual. Anything that might harm a customer, or one of our employees, is a foremost concern and priority. Therefore, any issue that could create a question over whether someone might somehow be physically harmed is paramount. This is all part of our DNA. It's part of what makes us successful and differentiates Carnival.

The focus on financial protections. Following very closely, of course, is the mandate to protect against any kind of financial threat. Here, the range of risk, which could translate into financial threat, is varied and wide. The theft of money itself, the theft of IP, the misuse of assets that incurs financial damage, and brand damage, are all part of this perspective. This expands to include other concerns as well, such as protection of onboard medical records and more.

A broader set of requirements than most enterprises. In addition, any issue concerning the proper running of our ships and the systems that control them are also our concern. This includes the medical centers, navigations systems for the ships, the computerized operations that run system safety checks and all those unseen processes that are taken for granted by the public. These remain our sacred trust to ensure their integrity is assured. The scope of security responsibilities for us is much broader than traditional land-based corporations. It's what I call a 'hyper-hybrid environment'. Within this complex world, the core essence of our information security mandate is: protect your people, your information and the finances.

Facing the prospect of insider threats

Businesses run on the concept of entrusting their employees to do the right thing with their access to the environment, access to the data, and access to their customer's data. It's been said many times: employees are our biggest assets and are our biggest risk exposure — so insider threat is a big deal to us. Of course, it is often the case that an outside threat first appears as an insider threat to a security analyst because of a compromised identity. However, either way, these people may be using the data inappropriately, not for its intended use, nor to the benefit of the company or our customers, and quite possibly to the advantage of our competitors.

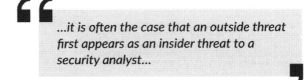

...it is often the case that an outside threat first appears as an insider threat to a security analyst...

A range of risk from breaches. The serious damage from insider threats can impact any and all of the areas of business vulnerability. These include brand reputation, customer trust, along with liability, loss of position in the market against competition, or fines, and the list goes on from there. While protecting the financial well-being of Carnival is a top concern for us, along with the well-being of our customers and our employees, the potential of an insider breach remains an equally important security mandate.

Growing concerns about privilege misuse and compromise

Privilege misuse is an issue that scares me relentlessly. This is especially the case with employees who have the higher privileged accounts and capabilities. As my colleagues in the UK say, it's "The Keys of the Kingdom" – and that's the last place you want the bad guys to be able to get to. From there, with the right HPA (high privileged access), and without the right safeguards in place, they can exploit your environment with impunity.

...it's "The Keys of the Kingdom" – and that's the last place you want the bad guys to be able to get to.

A fundamental security requirement. Understanding where those accounts and entitlements are, how to maintain them, how to restrict these privileges, and how to limit the risk and exposure, is critical for every company, no matter what their size. These proficiencies must be fundamental capabilities from the security perspective. In addition, as we expand our utility of predictive security analytics and machine learning, enhancing and empowering these objectives for our HPA accounts, security is at the center of our priorities to achieve.

A constant flow of insiders and customers on ships, land locations, or in combination: The hyper-hybrid security environment

The security of our hyper-hybrid environments must be adaptable to these different changes of user behavior based on location, on high volume, or based on need. We're in the process of implementing a long-term strategy to enhance our identity capabilities to be able to meet these new demands; it's a high priority.

A single view of identity is needed. Our employees and customers are included in this planning where their identities must be managed at a much higher level, enabling a holistic unified visibility of the individual. It's a highly complex challenge, especially with our customers. As a model, consider the type of individual who has one or two banking accounts, a car loan, and credit cards. They have multiple financial companies that they deal with every day, all with different identities. All must be managed separately. That's very complicated, even for individual accountability. So how do you do this across multiple companies within a corporation? Resolving this challenge is our objective.

The complex journey to achieve a single view of identity. While we may have the same customer on our different lines, we do not yet have the singular centralized view of them, and this is where the industry is going. From the Carnival corporate perspective, with our ten different companies, we are working through phases to achieve that goal, most recently with the first two consolidated brands clustered and migrated into a single view. It's important to understand where it all began as well. We've made decisive strides away from the time when cruisers sailed with all ten different companies, and would have ten different identities, which had ten different configurations, forcing Carnival to interface with you as a single person in ten different ways. Our ultimate path forward will be a single path, a single way of managing this as a single identity across all environments. The magnitude of all this information, originally residing in ten separate silos of different architectures and levels of maturity, is a considerable factor of the challenge.

Systems around the world, on-premises, in the cloud and on the sea: The impact on hybrid environment security

One of the things we talk about as we look at our security model, and strategy, is the level of maturity in our security capabilities, now and in the future. In doing so, we try to maintain as realistic a perspective as possible when we talk about what solutions we need in place to assure security in the future. We also know once we get there, because of the rapid evolution of technology and the cloud, that it will probably no longer be completely adequate.

A realistic view of phased progress. With this understanding of constant evolution in technology, we don't need to take a solution to what some might consider an ultimate world-class level. We do need take it to a level of reliable functionality. With that perspective, we maintain the strategy of continuous development and improvement, not adopt some monolithic solution that might be outdated as soon as it is finally implemented. For security, solutions must be light and flexible, capable of evolving in the same way, to integrate and grow with the various phases, and with all the complex variables. This is where user and entity

...we maintain the strategy of continuous development and improvement, not adopt some monolithic solution that might be outdated as soon as it is finally implemented.

behavior analytics and identity analytics represents the potential for productive growth with us at Carnival.

Integrating analytics and machine learning through phases in the environment. Of utmost importance, we have focused on the level of complexity required to move a global organization, which has data and information, as well as processes on-premises, off-premises, at sea, in the cloud, and across ten different brands. These were originally at different maturity levels, along with the varied applications, systems and infrastructure. From the start, we've dealt with a massive level of complexity. The goal we maintain is to drive the unified maturity of all our brands, to that same level, no matter where the data resides. This is especially true now that we have so many different places we have to be monitoring to assess risk and assure security. As we consolidate our views of the different businesses, machine learning is part of that integration process, which provides a strengthening of defenses at each phase by identifying risks and unknown threats.

Robust machine learning required for comprehensive security. It boils down to that old adage; we are as strong as our weakest link. If we're strong within the on-premises, and the cloud protection is weak, then we're collectively weak. If we're strong within the on-premises, at corporate offices, but weaker on the ship, then we're all weak. How do you identify that weakest link? As we view the challenges holistically and consistently across all of our stationary environments, as well as the constantly moving elements of our global environment, this is the focus of our strategy. Because of this wide-scaled environment, with increasingly high data volume to analyze, we needed big data and behavior analytics to find those weak links.

Because of this wide-scaled environment, with increasingly high data volume to analyze, we needed big data and behavior analytics to find those weak links.

Adjustments required to assure security in hyper-hybrid environments

It was a challenge for me to adapt at first. As a traditional professional who believed in risk management, and in the security principles that developed over so many years in the space, experience in the evolving complexities of the hybrid world has shown me a new reality. This is not an uncommon realization for CISOs to experience today.

A new normal of viewing security. I now have the perspective of, "It's not *if* I get compromised, it's *when* I get compromised." More importantly, upon reaching that recognition the priority then quickly becomes, "How do I determine exactly when it happens so I can react in the most efficient way to bring the environment back into compliance and ultimately stability?" These priority concerns center on resiliency. Keep in mind, you still need all of the preventive controls discussed earlier, but you also need the balanced detective and responsive controls in place as well.

Strategies for strong recovery following a breach. Because of this new perspective on today's security realities, we've changed our paradigm. We're no longer saying "if". By implementing a prescribed selection, along with a number of controls and declarative defenses, we know certain security events are managed. Yet, now we're also saying that when it happens, how do we know it happened and what was the magnitude? That's critical to know the extent of the compromise and the proper remedial steps required to prevent further attacks of this nature. This also leads directly to how we react to that breach as it is happening and bringing the system back into compliance and a maintainable state as quickly as possible.

The new role of identity and access: How they tie together

Identity and access have been around since the beginning of network security. However, that essential commissioning capability companies have had in the past must migrate to a higher level, delivering security assurance and enduring value. CISOs begin with the perspective that they want to assure their employees, contractors, partners, customers, and vendors, have the right access at the right time. This includes no more access than is required, with access ending when it is no longer needed. This is a fundamental business objective and absolutely important. But if you think about an employee – or a customer – along with their lifecycle of access requirements, they have changed. The access control objective hasn't changed. What has changed is our ability to assure the right access at the right time, at the right location, based on legitimate need.

Perpetually fluctuating user access. Specifically from the employee perspective, an example of the challenge is we have a range of accountants with Carnival Corporation. One may be working on one of our ships, and their use profile and requirements might be distinctly different from an accountant who is working in our corporate office. Then we might have an accountant who is traveling from the corporate office, or to Asia, or is onboard one of our ships. Their access life cycle might be very different, as well, and may change periodically, based on their legitimate work role requirements. The challenge becomes how we make sure they have the right access at the right time. Of course, behind all of that is the need to assure the right person has gained that access.

Risks with limited visibility into a wide range of users and access requests. The variables of these circumstances are accelerating or deaccelerating perpetually based on the needs at a particular moment. That's where serious risks occur. If you don't know who your users, your employees, and your customers are, then you have no chance of ensuring you're giving the right access at the right time. Multiply that user environment by the amount of employees, partners and customers, and the magnitude of complexity and risk reaches staggering proportions. It's this next layer of identity that determines the importance of solid solutions for access and identity that are essential to the success of security.

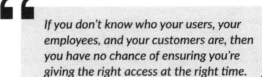

If you don't know who your users, your employees, and your customers are, then you have no chance of ensuring you're giving the right access at the right time.

Key solution components required for constantly changing security conditions

Elements we have initiated include identity lifecycle management tools with the ability to integrate the identity in the cloud, versus on-premises, versus any one of our environments. The other initiative we are integrating is machine learning analytics capabilities and tools. We have also flattened our network from an active directory perspective. We originally had many active directories and then integrated them into one, flattening the network down to a single tree. This makes it possible for us to have complete individual visibility.

A challenging orchestration of solution elements. We're also working on embedding role-based security principles into our strategy from an identity perspective. However, the challenges continue as we investigate how we integrate the entire application layer. Incorporating application security and application capabilities into our roles, and into our identity manager, are key objectives for us. Those are some of the solution elements we are leveraging to give us a heightened level of capability so we can connect them gaining optimal visibility and controls. Without machine learning, none of this would be possible.

Handling the overwhelming scale of entitlements for identity management and security

Dealing with the huge scale of big data is the ten million dollar question for us. There's an evolving challenge with scale we've seen building over the last several years. Traditionally, we try to develop our solutions from a people, process and technology perspective. The days of just throwing people at a challenge to solve the problem are over, especially for companies with our size and complexity.

The staggering scale of big data. When organizations continue to adopt cloud solutions to improve their business flexibility and amplify productivity, they generate huge amounts of data to sift through – the digital exhaust of big data. From the complexity, size and demand perspectives, it's dramatically more complicated. We need to process increasingly larger amounts of data that must be adjudicated quickly in order to be able to get answers and to insure we're providing the right visibility for access as needed. This requirement can no longer be guaranteed through manual processes. That puts the organization's welfare at risk.

This requirement can no longer be guaranteed through manual processes. That puts the organization's welfare at risk.

Traditional approach does not scale for complexity. Running security analysis, threat hunting and manual efforts on growing amounts of data in the traditional way becomes exponentially difficult. Add to that an identity perspective and there is simply no realistic way enterprises can scale internally to these demands. There needs to be a drastic game changer. It's something where you must leverage the cloud, big data, and machine learning with predictive security analytics solutions with UEBA and IdA models and use cases.

The equalizing impact of UEBA and IdA. With a balanced approach of people, process and technology, woven together, we're driving to address the scalability problem that is growing faster than we ever imagined. We see all three of these elements coming together with cloud based providers that help us from the perspective of scalability. That's where solutions like UEBA, integrated with IdA, can help level the playing field for customers like us. UEBA and IdA combined is easily capable of running on this kind of a scale, with productive and actionable risk-scored results.

...we're driving to address the scalability problem... That's where solutions like UEBA, integrated with IdA, can help level the playing field for customers like us.

People, process and technology benefit from UEBA and IdA. By using this solution, technology organizations leverage the computational capabilities of machine learning drawing from big data for context. This helps in terms of scaling, addressing security and identity challenges. From the perspectives of analytics processing, the systems are running more efficiently with fewer false positives. From the people perspective, the highly qualified security analysts are being freed from time-consuming manual investigations and able to focus on higher business critical tasks supporting the evolving needs of the security group. UEBA and IdA change and adapt the business process in a measurable way, integrating and optimizing a combination of people, process and technology.

How past behavior is predictive of potential future anomalies

When monitored effectively, some past behaviors provide a great indication for predicting future security issues. Timely, accurate data and context are the key. Yet because of the vast amount of data in today's environments, it can't be processed effectively without the robust reinforcement of machine learning. With that enhancement supporting the analytics, we have much more data that can be processed properly to deliver the all-important context which enables us to understand more of those future predictable scenarios with anomalies that arise. These anomalies will be undetected without the analysis of large amounts of data made possible by machine learning.

Increasing quality of results over time. The potential to uncover those anomalies through user behavior analytics will increase over time. First, the bigger anomalies and some of the obvious ones will surface. But as the learning process refines, and the baselines become more comprehensive, that number will double and triple six months or a year from now. Five years from now this number will be increased by a factor of five hundred. As we and the machine learning solution continually learn, we connect more of the dots. We continue to improve the evidence, and with it our ability to accurately predict at an increasingly specific level.

Identity management in a silo. We must assure the issue of identity is properly addressed. Too often, identity management from a security standpoint is in its own siloed IT framework, separate from security. A result has been that many times in the past organizations would perform certifications in separate systems. They would be unsuccessful in identifying anomalies, as they would possess an extremely limited visibility of the access risk plane.

Un-siloed identity is critical for useful analytics. When you flatten out the environment and examine this entire big behemoth of access data, then you can recognize the need to focus on identity, and then from there run

> This is often access that was in fact there, sometimes for many years, but because of the siloed segmentation, it was invisible.

identity analytics on the data. This will give identity access management teams a much richer context, where they can pick out the excess access and access outliers which otherwise go unnoticed. This is often access that was in fact there, sometimes for many years, but because of the siloed segmentation and human effort, it was invisible.

Machine learning adoption in the environment and industry verticals

It's interesting how some security people used to look at analytics very narrowly where they would have to come up with a rule or a query. This is great if they know exactly what they're looking for. However, this reliance solely on rules and queries limits security assurance and misses the critical issue of the unknown unknowns. Security analysts can't possibly think of all the ways an attacker might try to get into their environment. While they may try to think from their attacker's perspective, they can't reproduce every scenario. They have to be right every time, while the attackers only need to be right once. That's why user and entity behavior analytics and identity analytics are critical in today's environments.

Big data and machine learning lowers false positives. We're comparatively early into the adoption of machine learning. We're learning from some of the initial successes. First, we needed to confirm how well the solution characterizes normal behavior and then see how well we could detect abnormal behavior. The more we learn, the better we understand the wider capability of leveraging user behavior analytics to take us to the next level and understand how much of the detection would be false positives. We're improving on filtering the false positives as we get deeper context from our peer group baselines and mining the big data more effectively.

We're improving on filtering the false positives as we get deeper context from our peer group baselines and mining the big data more effectively.

Analytics and machine learning models of other verticals. If you examine some of the early adopter industries, such as banking, their models show us the immediacy of what we'd like to have in our environment. For example, my credit card gets used in three different locations all within two minutes and my cell phone goes off. This is the kind of analytics capabilities we're working to achieve for security controls that match the quality of that particular customer process. These other vertical solution capabilities are continually evolving. Today, there are probably fifty different scenarios which are triggers for the banking space that they didn't have two years ago. We intend to achieve the same kind of growth potential in our predictive security analytics solution within our own unique vertical.

Adoption trends for machine learning within the cruise line vertical

From a cruise line perspective, we're beginning to see early adoptions. The industry is recognizing how the unique challenges of their hyper-hybrid environments require unique solutions. With complex environments along with the element of ships constantly in movement around the world, hosting a range of technologies and users – some of it going through satellites — predictive security analytics is a solution that fits with their needs, goals and security objectives.

Visibility delivered with each integration phase. Specifically with Carnival, we're still in the early design and implementation of bringing all of our systems together into this integrated environment. We see huge upsides for us. We're now able to do things that previously would have taken us weeks, if not months to accomplish, or we couldn't do at all in the past.

Perspectives of security evolution through a range of verticals

After working over twenty-five years in a range of verticals, primarily with a security focus, my career path brought me to Carnival. Originally beginning as a programmer analyst for the Federal Reserve Bank of Cleveland, my work involved disaster recovery of systems, including old mainframe security systems, before moving into IT security. Positions in steel manufacturing, and healthcare with Blue Cross Family followed. After working in healthcare insurance, my work in the field led to medical imaging products manufacturing for GE HealthCare, where my responsibilities included building and managing a global security team. During that time, my portfolio broadened as the quality leader for the corporation responsible for Six Sigma across the global organization. Finally, just before joining Carnival, I held the CISO position at SuperValu, a large distribution and retail conglomerate grocery store chain.

Carnival hosts an array of businesses in one model. My position at Carnival is unique in that the organization contains a multitude of businesses that I worked within through the years, as well as a few new ones. Carnival is many things. It is like a corporation with a collection of small floating cities. It is a conglomerate of a huge supply chain organization, a transportation/people moving business, a hotel, restaurant and entertainment services enterprise, and a retail store chain that sells product all over the world. We have the largest collection of casinos afloat and a dedicated casino vertical. Carnival also has a medical services component. All of our ships have medical clinic centers, which carries a security perspective for the protection and control required for the clinics and

Carnival is many things. It is like a corporation with a collection of small floating cities.

their healthcare records.

A global operation with thousands of customers. Carnival has the traditional physical environment, with the corporate offices needing to protect IP. In addition, our security model must include some of our ships with over 4,000 customers and 1,000 plus crew. That translates into over 120,000 employees, of which 70% are on the ship at any given day, across the world, versus traditional corporate offices with locations that don't move. Add to that our responsibility for over one hundred ships around the world, all with moving data centers, which also need to be able to run off satellites when far off shore. It's a new layer of complexity of how to deliver IT services specifically to the customer as well as to the employees who run the ship.

Witnessing the road of security evolution with big data and machine learning. As I have witnessed the trends in the security industry evolve from the traditional on-premises to the hybrid cloud, and on to what I call Carnival Corporation's hyper-hybrid environment, I have come to recognize and appreciate the continuous state of evolution and development required to keep pace with the challenges, the new threat planes and development in technology. For the foreseeable future, predictive security analytics and machine learning driven by big data will be part of that evolution.

CONCLUSIONS & TAKEAWAYS:
Recognizing the urgency for change in security

Gary Eppinger's hyper-hybrid environment is a unique model of security challenge, contending with the complexities of environments on-premises, in the cloud, at sea, and in constant motion. Any one of the separate business verticals within Carnival Corporation's multifaceted umbrella environment would represent a full slate of demanding responsibilities for many enterprise CISOs. As Eppinger improves his security environment, and concatenates his company's ten brands into one view, along with developing the required security solutions to wrap around his hyper-hybrid environment, he observes the importance of maintaining flexibility with growth, and phased solution evolution. This contrasts with some monolithic solution approaches that entail 'rip and replace' which are often outdated upon completion of implementation.

Balancing people, process and technology, Eppinger calls out the objective of achieving reliable functionality over perfection with each phase. Perfection is virtually impossible to achieve since technology is perpetually evolving. This phased strategy includes the integration of risk-based predictive security analytics and capitalizing on the short-term benefits, while refining the long-term goals and increasing the critical mass of quality over time. Eppinger's objectives include bringing unique and separate siloed environments under one centralized management approach. His strategy also includes moving security closer to the data itself, with the right controls.

At the core of this strategy is the holistic need for centralized identity, which optimizes the capabilities of risk management through robust identity analytics. None of this would be possible without the implementation of machine learning to leverage the burgeoning scale of big data in today's evolving hybrid environments.

The devil, of course, is always in the details. To achieve their security goals, security leaders must constantly update their understanding of a broad range of factors, including the importance of emerging trends in the misuse and the compromise of identity to keep in pace with their responsibilities for Borderless Behavior Analytics. This will be explored in the next chapter. For some high tech executives, however, an understanding of security risks should not be taken for granted. We'll see this in the following *Borderless Breach Flashcard*. These one-page case studies featured at the end of each expert interview section highlight the wide range of breach scenarios that security leaders face in protecting their evolving environments today.

BORDERLESS BREACH FLASHCARD	
High Tech CEOs in the Crosshairs	
CATEGORY	Social media password theft, account breach, by foreign powers.
WHO	**The target:** Various C-level leaders in tech companies, along with other social media customers.
WHAT	Prominent high tech executives had their Twitter, and other social media accounts, breached. On a wider scale, many more customers were impacted.
WHEN	2016
WHERE	USA.
WHY	Economic greed, market control.
HOW	A Saudi-based group of hackers sent a Tweet which read: *"Hey, it's OurMine Team we are just testing your security, please send us a message."* Many people responded, including Mark Zuckerberg, founder and CEO of Facebook, Evan Williams, co-founder of Twitter, and Mikkel Svane, CEO of Zendesk, a software tech support firm. Ryan Holmes, CEO of Hootsuite, a social media security management company was included. Hootsuite's IT team confirmed the hackers used Foursquare, an 'app authing' application, to get information to help gain access to the social media accounts. For Holmes, the Foursquare account had been unused for years. Dormant accounts are a prime avenue to access users' accounts in private and corporate use. With Zuckerberg, hackers took advantage of a weak password, unchanged for years: *dadada*. Over 32 million Twitter hacked logins were put on sale on the Dark Web.
HOW BAD?	Individual damage was minor. The image of high tech leaders being susceptible to cyber-attacks like these underline the casual attitude some execs adopt toward the importance of security in technology. Social media phishing is a main threat plane for malicious attacks. The damage could have been much worse.
HOW COULD IT BE AVOIDED?	Whether in personal or business accounts, ignoring unverified social media messaging is a key best practice. Using two-factor authentication on Twitter and closing unused dormant accounts are also best practices. If the tech leaders' companies had a UEBA-IdA solution, this might have been averted. Visibility into unusual account access, including social media from locations or devices outside normal patterns, could have raised risk alerts, facilitating timely SOC response. The execs could have avoided the embarrassment of ignoring basic online security rules.

The Compromise and Misuse
of Identity

Recognizing a new reality in security

Is the problem of compromise and misuse of identity really that bad? How can we really know for sure?

Verizon's 2016 Data Breach Digest – Scenarios from the Field, shares a credential theft case study in this area of concern. A law enforcement agency came to a company while investigating malicious activity that had a connection with the company in question. The company was informed that a number of its externally facing IP addresses were associated with the criminal activity under investigation. The law enforcement team provided the company with a list of the suspected IP addresses associated with the company that they had found during the investigation. In response, the company engaged the Verizon RISK team as part of their incident response (IR) escalation process.

Examination of forensic evidence in the suspected compromised systems included numerous web servers, domain controllers, along with administrator and end user systems. Analysis revealed the systems were riddled with an array of malware variants. The scale of compromise far exceeded the list originally identified in the investigation. Continued examination of network log data uncovered that several other systems had been communicating with an external malicious IP address as well. The more the investigation progressed, the more bad news came to light.

The forensic investigation revealed that the initial compromise occurred on one of the victim's web servers several months earlier than indicated by the law enforcement investigators. Using a web shell, the threat actors had gone undetected for several months during which they had broad access of the network. This compromise was not the ultimate objective. Malware capable of dumping passwords, stealing credentials and performing exfiltration of data were all uploaded via the web shell. The ultimate goal of the malware: to penetrate deeper into the network using malware specifically designed to leverage existing credentials.

The ultimate goal of the malware: to penetrate deeper into the network using malware specifically designed to leverage existing credentials.

The threat actors successfully compromised numerous administrator accounts using password dumping, password cracking and keylogging. The scope of the credential theft was even greater than originally thought. A deleted spreadsheet containing more than 100 usernames and passwords associated with a particular high privileged access administrator was subsequently discovered. This set of compromised credentials led to access for gaining even more credentials and ultimately provided the threat actors with access to numerous network locations, including several domain controllers. Given the amount of time the adversary had dwelled in the environment, the volume of data at risk was severely critical.

As a standalone story, it's sobering. But unfortunately this kind of event is not a rarity. Citing the Verizon *2016 Data Breach Investigations Report* (DBIR), the new upward trend this year is Web application attacks for the financial services sector. Here the attack kill chain involves credentials compromised to obtain more access credentials to log back into the financial services websites to commit financial fraud for these stolen accounts. This trend now ranks at 82%, whereas it was only 31% the previous year.

The compromise and misuse of identity expands beyond employees to business partners and even customers. The kill chain starts with the compromise of employees to get the account data. Quoting the DBIR in relation to this trend: *"These breaches, uncovered through the forensic analysis performed on several C2* (command and control) *servers, tell the tale of phished customer > C2 > Drop Keylogger > Export captured data > Use stolen credentials."* Given this significant increase in threat activity, prudent banking and financial customers are investing heavily in new identity-based defenses to stop this trend.

Given this new perspective, a better question to ask at the beginning of this section might be, "Do I have the right tools and solutions in place for visibility of compromise and misuse of identity, and am I prepared if it's really that bad?"

Answering this question requires acknowledging that identity is the easiest doorway into your network. It's also the quickest pathway to the enterprise's kingdom of valuable assets. An identity consists of the user or entity, their accounts and entitlements. Gaining access to these is the root cause of most data breaches and theft. Recognizing this, and having solutions in place to manage this comprehensively is key to establishing detection early in the kill chain with predictive security analytics for identity compromise and misuse.

...identity is the easiest doorway into your network... the quickest pathway to the enterprise's kingdom of value assets.

Part of the challenge facing organizations today lies in the functional gap that often exists between IAM and security teams. While security is focused on malware detection, finding threats, and delivering responses, IAM teams are focused on providing access, often in excess. They are too often working at cross-purposes regarding critical elements of the same access risk and threat plane. Herein lies the dilemma. For success to occur, IT and SOCs must agree that the compromise and misuse of identity are at the core of modern threats and they need to collaborate effectively. Identity is an access risk and threat plane that must have its surface area reduced and then monitored for compromise and abuse.

Identity consists of users, or their accounts, access entitlements and activity, both on-premises and in the cloud. Identity issues include excess access, access outliers, orphan and dormant accounts, as well as, unknown privileged access risks. Security teams especially must have a high awareness and detailed understanding of the concept of identity as a threat plane and its prioritization. On the IT side, awareness of how group and role proliferation are part of the problem is needed. Unfortunately, IAM has had been increasingly constrained by inflexible and inefficient manual processes for compliance with legacy rules to define roles. If identity is core to modern threats, how do we deal with flexible access to data?

Who can forget the 2013 Target nightmare? Unfortunately, too many forget exactly *how* it happened. Partner credentials were the doorway for this data breach. Identity is the new attack vector for everyone. Protecting identity is also the key to the future in the cloud/mobility world. If that isn't concerning enough, organizations must look beyond employees to partners and customers. Plus, more than just data, 'safety' is now part of the game for everyone. CISOs need to know how important identity and access are for their business partners in relation to their own organization's security and safety.

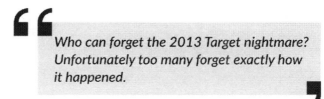

Who can forget the 2013 Target nightmare? Unfortunately too many forget exactly how it happened.

While account compromise and misuse remain a concern for all organizations, it's all a matter of prioritization and focus. Our expert contributor Jerry Archer, CSO of a prominent financial services enterprise, draws from a vast range of first-hand experience in information security since its earliest days. He shares his seasoned insights on the evolution of security with a special focus on the financial market vertical, along with the outcomes of employing big data machine learning for user and entity behavior analytics (UEBA) and identity analytics (IdA) in that space.

BORDERLESS EXPERT INSIGHTS

Jerry Archer, CISO*
Major Financial Services Company

As CSO of a major financial services enterprise, Jerry Archer's responsibilities include securing and protecting all of the organization's systems and offerings, and for security initiatives across the company. He has more than 30 years of experience at other leading companies and government agencies, including Intuit, Visa, and the CIA. He is a founder and board member of the Cloud Security Alliance; a fellow at the Ponemon Institute; a member of the Advisory Board for George Mason University International Cyber Center; President, Security Adviser Alliance; serves on the Security Innovation Network (SINET) Showcase steering committee; and is a member of numerous industry and corporate advisory boards. Archer was also named the 2011 North American Information Security Executive of the Year by Information Security Executive® (ISE).

As a member of Gurucul's Executive Advisory Board, Archer has provided critical guidance for the company's strategic growth and evolution in the UEBA-IdA field of machine learning and big data. He draws from his firsthand and seasoned insights into the inception of the first generation of security strategies, where he has continued to work through evolving developments in cyber security and machine learning for predictive security analytics.

Overview

In this chapter, Archer begins by observing the dynamic between CIO and CISO objectives of productivity versus security and discusses the symptoms of inadequate security defenses. Part of his insight includes the recognition that security data volume exceeds manual processing capabilities. Archer provides insights on the requirements for detecting account compromise and misuse and he also observes aspects of risk in maintaining a status quo security strategy. While the importance of monitoring the endpoint remains constant, impacting factors of traditional security perspective versus those in hybrid environments are reviewed. Archer then explores the importance of insider threats, the drivers of this threat, and the need for establishing a single identity for users in both on-premises and in the cloud. This includes requirements for coordinated security measures against insider threat and privileged access abuse. Leveraging analytics to improve the identity access side of security is a key to success in this objective. Archer observes factors influencing UEBA and IdA adoption as a

* The views and opinions expressed by Jerry Archer in this book are his own, and do not necessarily reflect those of his current, or any of his previous employers.

supplement to security strategy. He then discusses early and long-term objectives for UEBA implementation, as well as the benefits of UEBA. Archer concludes with insights into the growth and evolution of security strategies he has observed during his decades in the field.

Productivity versus security: The dynamic between CIO and CISO priorities

There will always be a natural tension between the CISO and the CIO. This dynamic is determined by the fact that the CIO is driven to provide more and better services at lower costs, while a CISO's job is to protect everything, the data, environment, transactions, and to maintain the assurance of confidentiality, integrity availability and safety. Every one of those attributes is potentially contrary to what the CIO wants to do, at least in the fundamental technical sense.

The partnership of common goals. While there is this natural tension between the two, it is in their common interest to cooperate and collaborate with an eye on the organization's goals, objectives and needs, as well as facilitate safe productivity and profitability. It is important to recognize that the CISO of the future must understand much more about what's in the cloud and how they can take advantage of this world of empowering possibilities. As the cloud creates issues around security, the cloud also provides solutions. Security provided through the cloud is an important element in the IT mix.

Big data's place in today's security. A great deal of the work performed today in security revolves around big data. Security teams now use the cloud for security purposes to do analytical work that could in no realistic way be performed if the cloud was unavailable to do it. This advantage is both from a cost, as well as a human resource bandwidth perspective. The evolution of security solutions — as is exemplified by new versions of SIEMs (security incident and event management solutions) — is now becoming heavily based on big data. This is where mature UEBA vendors like Gurucul help to support both the CIO's and CISO's goals. Gurucul in essence is a big data analytical engine that leverages the low cost and productivity enhancing capabilities in the cloud and hybrid environments. This represents a real boon to the security community. For a CIO and CISO, it represents the best of both of their worlds.

Symptoms of inadequate security defenses

There have been two factors in today's environments that revealed defenses could not keep up with the rising trends of security threats. One has been the rapid mutation of malware. If you look at the number of new malware instances occurring yearly, there's a new variant of malware being created every 200 milliseconds. These attack scenarios which cyber criminals have been using continue to evolve so quickly that it's virtually impossible for anything signature-based to contend with them. Organizations must be right every single time as a defender, but the perpetrator only has to be right once to succeed. As a

...a number of organizations are moving to a solution which is not searching for predefined specifics, but looking for actors doing something nefarious.

result, a number of organizations are moving to a solution which is not searching for predefined specifics, but looking for actors doing something nefarious.

Evolving requirements for security monitoring. The second problem was that most malware today comes into the environment and it doesn't even have a payload. SOCs don't know what its intent is until someone downloads the payload into a piece of malware to execute a command directed at stealing credentials, penetrating sensitive data, injecting ransomware, and so forth. Ultimately, the only way to effectively defend the environment is to monitor behavior with an ability to alert security teams if there's something wrong with the system or the end user.

Overwhelming majority of threats at the endpoint. Monitoring behavior effectively in the environment represents a complex challenge. For example, many companies employ network activity analysis solutions which are used extensively to look for advanced threats on the network along with malware and bad actors throughout the network environment. A closer investigation of the problem, however, indicates that probably 60% of the threat problem exists at the endpoint.

Rapid threat change through the human interface. While CISOs have been very effective defending their networks at the front end, with their interfaces to the internet, the hackers — logically — have moved to the endpoint, the weakest point, which is where humans are. The human interface into the environment is by far the one being attacked the most today. Looking at it from this perspective, signatures can't accomplish the task, because the threat model changes so rapidly.

Solutions detecting abnormal behavior. In response to this challenge, a growing number of organizations are adopting a behavior analytics system to detect what is normal and abnormal behavior in the environment, then to have the ability to flag the abnormal behavior and take action on it as needed. As a number of CISOs have witnessed the natural evolution of the attack scenarios and strategies, their logical response with UEBA adoption has also been a natural evolution of defending against those attacks.

Transformation realities: Security data volume exceeds manual processing capabilities

In 2012, as part of the response to the new challenges in defense, security architects targeted analytical work around Web log files, which became a significant initiative. Yet it was quickly discovered that in order to produce anything resembling useful data output, a Hadoop environment was necessary to perform the data analysis. At that time, security experts were already seeing the impact of digital exhaust which necessitated a form of outsourced services to do analytical work around big data.

At that time, security experts were already seeing the impact of digital exhaust which necessitated a form of outsourced services to do analytical work around big data.

Scalability for crunching today's security data. Machine learning is different from artificial intelligence (AI). Machine learning looks at routine and being able to describe incidences that occur, so the machine can understand them in a useful way for analytical purposes and then flag the legitimate behavior anomalies. Machine learning is well on the path to performing that functionality with robust results. Security analytics are not yet close to AI, however, where SOCs can look for completely unforeseen kinds of anomalies. That will come over time.

False positive reduction via machine learning. The ability to crunch the numbers and deliver tangible results through machine learning is already here. It can be done today with negligible constraints. What the security community sees coming out of its analytical work is quite solid, with machine learning computational capabilities for the scale of data needed with the coverage required in a growing number of use cases. What machine learning is achieving today is very good and getting better, delivering fewer false positives. The key is getting rid of the false positives in a measurable way, and machine learning is getting increasingly better at that.

Experienced insights into behavior analytics requirements. Organizations that have arrived at this milestone in security for understanding the need and the importance of big data are very likely to be in a stronger position to see the advantages of a mature UEBA solution to supplement the security strategy for their environment. In addition, as each environment is unique, the challenge becomes defining the custom requirements for any enterprise considering a UEBA solution's function, fit and breadth of use cases.

Requirements for detecting account compromise and misuse

Most environments contain sensitive, customer or corporate information. It's extremely important to be able to detect misuse, misuse of credentials, and misuse of accounts — any activity that correlates with trying to get at sensitive data. Most companies today have an intensive focus in terms of the use, as well as application and storage of sensitive information. It's a high priority to be able to detect account compromise and misuse.

Visibility on the weakest point. To be successful at that requirement, however, demands that security analysts must have effective visibility to monitor the endpoint. That's now the weakest point and the target that most hackers are attacking. It remains of the utmost importance to protect that information at the endpoint. If that is not achieved, a business's viability is at risk. This mandate is not just about protecting the information. It also includes maintaining secure systems

...security analysts must have effective visibility to monitor the endpoint.

from both a regulatory perspective, and a customer trust perspective.

Vulnerabilities in the status quo security

In most companies, the vast majority of the workforce performs the same routine task every day. They access the same data and generally the same amount of data. Their behavior, day-to-day, month-to-month, and year-to-year, is fundamentally the same.

Past behavior defining normal context. The concept of past behavior being a predictor of future behavior holds a great deal of truth. As a result, it's easy to look at that behavior, and it quickly becomes apparent when someone is doing something different. That immediately becomes a flag since an employee's behavior is typically routine.

Challenges with depth and focus of visibility. As soon as an intruder gains access to someone's credentials, they start exploring the environment, yet in a manner unlike the valid credential owner. Utilizing a user behavior analytics solution which identifies such anomalous behavior, it in turn generates alerts for analysts to investigate. The challenge also relates to the depth and focus of visibility and monitoring within the environment.

Closer monitoring capability of the endpoint required. Network activity and analysis solutions work well on the network backbones and major trunks, but are not as effective down toward the endpoints and in the last links. There are simply too many of them. While monitoring traffic on the backbone remains constant, at the first level on the network, someone could still explore the environment. Visibility at the endpoint is essential.

Invisible attackers persist without the right solution. As long as an attacker remains on the device, as long as they stay with what's available to that person through their credentials, and unless we have something on the endpoint to monitor, we can't even see the breach and observe nefarious activity happening.

Impacting the endpoint: Traditional security perspectives versus the complexity of hybrid environments

The cloud presents an entirely new set of problems for any organization's security team. One is the ability to gain visibility into the cloud, which is for the most part opaque. Cloud providers, particularly in the public cloud space — will not allow customers to look at detailed nuanced behavior within their environment. They provide some visibility. However, it will be by necessity limited visibility.

Enduring endpoint criticality in cloud expansion. It's difficult to get into the environment in a way that was done in traditional on-premises environments, where organizations owned the infrastructure. So the ability now to use some sort of a behavior analysis on the endpoint is much more important. The next element of this challenge is the fact that we now have cloud providers communicating on our behalf to other cloud providers, and then to other cloud providers, and so on. As a result, organizations will continually struggle to effectively manage the communication between elements in their environments. And, in many cases, that will be managed by cloud providers themselves.

Shifting workload models change security strategies. As the challenge factors progress, CISOs must find ways to look at security that doesn't involve placing devices in-line, in communications streams, between cloud providers, or between environments, because they will evolve, they will move. Essentially, workloads will become fungible and facilitate the ability to arbitrage between cloud providers, particularly as containers evolve. As a result, there will be a seismic shift in security, away from the perimeter-based models.

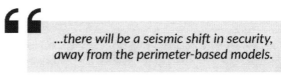

...there will be a seismic shift in security, away from the perimeter-based models.

Evolving cloud security frameworks. Different kinds of solutions we'll call IPS or firewalls will be involved in this next generation of cloud security options. However, they will be virtual. They'll be more microscopic in nature and operate more like a microservice. An application will have its own firewall, its own IPS system. Endpoints will need to be more protective of themselves. Tools will have to be developed for the endpoint and security teams will monitor that endpoint, regardless of where it's being driven from.

Data origins uncertain in the future. As the cloud evolves, in the future, you won't even know where the data is coming from. It can come from any place, from any provider. That's a pressing problem to solve for data governance and integrity.

Impacting the traditional perimeter: Emerging factors of hybrid access

The perimeter is, of course, quickly disappearing. Even today most organizations simply cannot draw a

The reality is that the perimeter will shrink to one individual, one application, or one small set of applications.

perimeter around an entire environment because of the adoption of some form of cloud solution. CISOs create what we call boundaries and within them are various systems, but those systems have broad access and broad capabilities. So in reality these boundaries are more of an abstraction, something like a conceptual drawing. They're not real. The reality is that the perimeter will shrink to one individual, one application, or one small set of applications.

New challenges define tomorrow's solutions. Solutions like containers, microservices and built-in security, will become more the norm than what we have today, which is trying to place a lot of appliances in line to cope with the challenge. Until those become widely available, the current state-of-the-art security solution for today's environments must include some form of a mature monitoring and a behavior analytics solution to assure 24/7 global visibility at the granular level of the endpoint.

The importance of insider threats

Breaches due to insiders represent a significant percentage and are not going away. The insider threat problem is one of those situations where, as the defenses continue to improve, one of the key areas attackers will target is the insider because they have knowledge and they have access. Account compromise is the goal for these attackers. Ultimately many security leaders expect the insider threat will become the biggest threat. Today, it's probably less so, because the avenues to get into an environment are still relatively easy enough, so that attackers don't need to go and recruit insiders.

Trends moving to the insider threat. Over time the threat will evolve. As the perimeters are tightened and additional security policies are applied to people who access from the outside, we'll see trends moving more toward the inside with the insider threat problem. What a majority of security teams look for now is not so much an individual going bad, or rogue, but instead they consider an individual starts acting badly because they have a piece of malware on their VDI (virtual desktop infrastructure) or their laptop. It's not really the legitimate insider; it's someone pretending to be one.

Monitoring for indicators of intrusion. The focus in effect becomes more on the technical perspective. This may entail looking for indicators of the intruder impersonating a real person versus the real person going bad. It could be an account compromise or hijacking in an environment which is a common path outsiders will use where they pretend to be a legitimate user.

Breach without system compromise. One of the most notable breaches was at E-Trade, a few years ago. Attackers had a Trojan that targeted high volume traders, and they simply put trades into the path of that stream.

It cost E-Trade over ten million dollars in losses without a single E-Trade system being compromised.

The hackers had first located the high volume traders using E-Trade. They then put a Trojan on the target workstations and they were simply injecting trades into the trade system that the legitimate users were performing. It cost E-Trade over ten million dollars in losses without a single E-Trade system being compromised.

Drivers for insider threat

There are two facets of the insider threat problem. If you look at the true insider threat where you have a rogue employee, it's typically due to the fact that a person is unhappy at work. They also believe they have something of value they can sell. There's a certain level of emotion. It could be desperation. It could be anger. That emotion drives people to feel they need or deserve something which does not belong to them, and it compels them to take that asset of value. The public and all security leaders are quite familiar with these scenarios.

Rogue employees versus irrational behavior. In most cases — and this brings us to the second facet of the insider threat problem — CISOs find it's someone doing something that's basically stupid. You can't stop stupid. You can't always eliminate stupid through training. Stupid exists in every company. Rogue employees are a minor problem when you stack them up against stupid. Stupid will find a way around just about anything. Remember Hanlon's razor: "Never attribute to malice that which is adequately explained by stupidity."

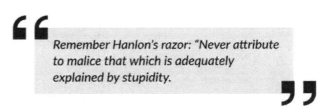

Remember Hanlon's razor: "Never attribute to malice that which is adequately explained by stupidity.

Severe consequences of irrational actions. The bluntness in the choice of the word describing this behavior is intentional. Because the severe consequences which result from this kind of anomalous behavior was originally initiated by good intentions and unintentional actions, some security leaders might place this vulnerability factor at a lower level of priority in their considerations. To do so would be to place their environment and their organization's welfare in jeopardy. Stupid behavior within the secure environment is real and a grave risk to any enterprise. It's only a question of magnitude. Take for example, in 2006, the head of AOL Research released a compressed text file on one of its websites containing 20 million search keywords used by more than 650,000 subscribers. While the file was intended for research purposes, it was mistakenly posted publicly. Customer confidence and trust in AOL were impacted as a result.

Priorities for establishing a single identity for users on-premises and in the cloud

A first priority for security leaders is establishing the segregation of duties and access appropriate to roles. This includes partitioning employees' access from information they don't need to do their job. Those measures are important today, and they'll be equally important in the future — perhaps more so. Being able to create a stringent identity around somebody and what they can do, and what they have access to, will become essential security hygiene.

> *Being able to create a stringent identity around somebody and what they can do, and what they have access to, will become essential security hygiene.*

Challenges of effective monitoring and segregation of duties. Successful segregation and partitioning represents something of a parent-child problem. How can I get the security information required by going through various paths? What options exist to achieve the visibility required? On some level, security analysts must be able to look at the endpoint to determine what applications and data content the endpoint is accessing. In the process of achieving this kind of monitoring, it's critical to make sure the entire segregation of duties model has not been subverted, or to fail granting appropriate access.

Security measures against insider threat and privileged access abuse

One of the biggest problems is if organizations have an insider who goes rogue with privileged access. That's basically the Holy Grail cybercriminals seek. Generally, enforcement of many policies and numerous processes that don't involve machine learning identity analytics is the primary model for management. They relate more to the segregation of duties, the segregation of accounts, a strong auditing of accounts, and similar procedures to make sure an insider with elevated privileges can't act out in some malicious way.

> *One of the biggest problems is if organizations have an insider who goes rogue with privileged access.*

Machine learning's critical role monitoring privileged access. A solution like Gurucul definitely comes into play in terms of detecting or alerting when a privileged user is doing something strange, or outside the range of 'normal'. There are several security approaches today, in addition to Gurucul, which also look at what this individual is doing, including strong audit trails, not using the same IDs, or specialized accounts that don't have internet access — all of those types of measures that seriously tighten down the controls on privileged users. Assuring complete discovery of all privileged access entitlements is also critical, and very few PAM (privileged access management) solutions can manage the complete inventory of an organization's instances of privileged access entitlements. A small selection of mature UEBA vendors like Gurucul also offer identity analytics (IdA), drawing from big data and empowered by machine learning, to address this discovery gap.

Deep monitoring capabilities. UEBA and IdA — and more specifically solutions with the maturity of Gurucul — provide the needed tools that deliver the capability of seeing into the network to the endpoint. Moreover, doing this delivers a granularity of monitoring into who has access to what. UEBA and IdA don't replace existing capabilities, they supplement them. Without them, there would be a serious gap in the security model. As the industry is continually making improvements to security solutions, Gurucul is there as well, advancing its machine learning models and use cases.

> UEBA and IdA don't replace existing capabilities, they supplement them. Without them, there would be a serious gap in the security model.

Leveraging analytics to improve the identity access side of security

Regular monitoring of access log files has become essential. This can be leveraged to not only see who has access to what, but also to see who is accessing the data. One of the functions traditional identity management tools don't really perform is looking at activity: who's accessing the data. On a deeper level security analysts are able to get insight into: What are their access entitlements? Have they looked at the data? Do they have access entitlements they don't need? Those kinds of details security teams can now see with an identity analytics tool that could not be seen efficiently with the typical identity management tools which would require a much more labor-intensive effort. Many critical nuances around identity management are becoming available which have not been seen before.

Precise access controls. This solution set also solves much of the parent-child problem. This means that, because an IT department gives someone access, to system A, the system A path gave the user access to data in system B, which the security team did not want them to have. The problem is obviously much more complex than the A and B scenario, but it articulates the general idea. This has been one of the most difficult problems to solve in identity management, which is giving someone direct access to data unintentionally when they shouldn't have had it. Organizations usually find out about the consequences only when something bad happens.

Policies for managing excess access. As it relates to excessive access, contrary to companies in other verticals, financial services focuses heavily on access appropriate for role without excessive access. This means if someone transfers, this person only gets the access associated with the profile associated with the job. If they wanted anything other than the assigned profile access, it would be an exception, which would require approval, and have a time limit on it.

Zero baseline access policy. Essentially every time someone transfers to a new position, their access is brought to a zero baseline. All of their access is eliminated and IT then gives them back only what they need. Financial services companies probably suffer less of the excess access issue than other industries.

Quarterly certifications ensure zero baseline adherence. Excessive access is generally identified during certification processes. It's difficult for someone to accumulate access, because every manager is required to attest to the fact that every one of his employee's access is appropriate to their role. Financial services companies must demonstrate zero-baselining for all access.

Factors influencing UEBA adoption as a security supplement

Financial organizations have leveraged a number of security controls, through network activity and analysis, automated threat forensics, and dynamic malware protection against advanced cyber threats into the network, and into their email streams. From there, moving to a UEBA environment fills an important gap in the security strategy. For many organizations, it is simply a next logical step in the buildout of a resilient defense model.

...moving to a UEBA environment, fills an important gap in the security strategy. For many organizations, it is simply a next logical step in the buildout of a resilient defense model.

Cloud's rapid evolution and forward-thinking adoption. Added to the gap UEBA filled, is the fact that the world of cloud and technology is evolving at such a rapid pace that UEBA is important to have in place. Some security leaders see user and entity behavior analytics adoption not just part of a recognition of addressing a new reality and security requirement. It has actually become something of a goal for them to achieve because of the value they can extract from it on a daily basis.

Early and long-term objectives for UEBA implementation

One of the primary uses of UEBA is to characterize normal behavior. Then security teams can detect abnormal behavior and understand how much of the detection would be false positives. The next step is to refine processes to gain richer and deeper context from user baseline profiles to reduce false positives.

Simple evolution of the tool utility. A UEBA-IdA solution adoption starts off simply, by reducing excess access, dormant and orphaned accounts, and unknown privileged access risks, with IdA, thereby drastically reducing the surface area of the access risk plane. From there, a natural evolution is using the tool to look at segregation of duties, access appropriate to role, and to limit access to data users shouldn't have. This facilitates optimal UEBA monitoring for anomalous behavior, which follows. In addition, identity analytics can evolve to become an adjunct to identity management for automated risk response.

Broader applications of UEBA. An important focus CISOs are also looking at now is much more in terms of a broad-brush view of identity access and the behavior of an identity in terms of meeting true holistic security needs and supporting compliance requirements. That entire area of access certification, access appropriate to role, segregation of duties, risk associated with access to systems, all of these requirements are now part of the whole process of which UEBA-IdA is becoming a critical part.

The benefits of a UEBA solution: A first-hand view

The primary benefit most enterprises experience is that UEBA reveals abnormal behaviors which were invisible to security analysts in the past. It empowers a SOC team to say, "This person is doing something abnormal and we have to go find out why."

This translates into the ability to discover things going wrong in the environment which had not been possible to see before. It delivers a critical visibility into those kinds of issues.

...UEBA ...empowers a SOC team to say, "This person is doing something abnormal and we have to find out why."

Discovering solution advantages. There are the two big benefits CISOs traditionally see at a comparatively early state of the solution adoption. The first is expected — the ability to see abnormal behavior in the environment — and the second is being able to use UEBA-IdA for a risk-based approach for identity and access management. In addition, the capability of being able to use the solution as a strong tool for identity and access management is a key utility which becomes more apparent as the use of the tool matures.

UEBA and the value of a self-audit solution

The self-audit is a solution that uses a singular user identity view across all environments and applications where UEBA analyzes all activities of that end user in an organization and generates a regular report. It can be sent as a periodic email statement, usually weekly, with customizable levels of abstraction. It's something like a credit card statement, which says, "This is what we see in terms of your risk-scored access and activity on your account."

Virtually no false positives. Employees review the report regularly to see if there's anything off balance. If they see something's wrong, they report it. This results in virtually no false positives and allows the end users, or employees, to become deputized into the security solution. Organizations as large as 60,000 employees have successfully adopted this kind of self-audit solution.

Evolution of security strategies

My experience over the last 30 years suggests that security strategies are ever-changing and that tools and technologies drive this change at an increasing rate. Adaptation to that change is necessary and essential to maintain an adequate defense. While a CISO must deal with the problems at hand, he must also keep an eye to the future to surf the wave and not be drowned by it.

Change targeted on future requirements. Recognizing the need to adopt productive change in a timely manner, striving to stay ahead of the curve, to understand what's happening in environments in the present, and to anticipate what will be happening two to three years from now, are key mandates for CISOs. To do so successfully, means to stay current with trends and to listen to the right people who understand the deeper details of technology. With this perspective — as opposed to implementing any seismic or comprehensive replacement of systems — it appears that at times a layered or phased approach to security solution evolution is the most sensible strategy.

Flexibility needed in security solution evolution. This concept speaks to the recognition that as the hybrid cloud evolves, organizations have a requirement to evolve with them. Having the flexibility to execute on that strategy can be better achieved if the environment has the capability to evolve. Adopting a wholesale institutional infrastructure changeout rarely has the capability for that kind of flexibility. Security solutions that are able to be part of that evolution, that have the compatibility to work with an array of best-of-breed solutions, have the best chance of success in helping an organization move to the next level of dynamic productivity coupled with reliable security.

> Security solutions that are able to be part of that evolution... have the best chance of success in helping an organization... with reliable security.

Priorities for security in the hybrid environment

Looking at any organization's strategies and tactics for security is, in effect, a snapshot in time. Years ago, strategies were focused on the perimeter. With the rapid expansion of the internet, and then the hybrid cloud, strategies changed again and evolved. Currently, the idea behind a resilient defense model is important. It centers on developing strategies to live with an active breach, because those are the realities of the future. Being able to establish defensive models with various perimeters of isolation, so organizations can continue to function, is at the very heart of this objective. Best practices centered on that top priority is what industry experts see moving forward.

The importance of metrics. One related area organizations are increasing their focus on includes metrics. Boards are now more interested in cyber security. They need to see measurable specifics. Being able to effectively communicate with management and the board of directors is important. Resiliency after a breach and metrics are probably the biggest areas of focus security experts see today.

Resilient defense and UEBA securing the environment

One key to building a successful security program is resilient defense. This consists of protecting against inbound threats, but also implementing equal amounts of measures to deter unauthorized outbound activity. So even if an intruder can get into the environment, and they can get access to data, it is difficult for them to exit with it. User and entity behavior analytics is one way to support that objective. This is part of an implementation of an array of different systems and tools to stop people from exfiltrating the data.

A critical focus on outbound. The idea is to focus as much on outbound as you do on inbound. The reality is that a hacker will get into an environment if they're determined enough. Getting into the environment represents an infinite number of paths. But once someone succeeds, and once they steal something, they then need to exfiltrate it. On the security side, security analysts know what the target data looks like, where it's located and that the hacker wants to exit with it.

The advantage of knowing the attacker's target. The key is to know what they want and what they're going to try to steal. Then they have a payload they must carry on their way out of the intranet. This slows them down. This also means that the activity, whatever they touch, generates telltales and digital exhaust. It creates evidence. When they're carrying a payload, they're clearly less agile on the outbound side as they were on the inbound. It's easier to detect and that's to the SOC's advantage. As a result, security teams can be well-prepared for exfiltration prevention capability. It's an easier job to defend against the outbound side than the inbound side.

When they're carrying a payload they're clearly not as agile on the outbound side as they were on the inbound. It's easier to detect...

Deep monitoring of all priority points. A major element of that ease of defense has to do with UEBA, which facilitates monitoring with the highest priority for the exact points that CISOs know are sensitive and represent the primary targets attackers want to penetrate. Every aspect of activity and access interacting with these priority points can be monitored, empowered by machine learning and leveraging big data for context.

Not all environments benefit from the same strategy. It's important to observe that different organizations have different environment architecture configurations and resources that must be protected. In a financial institution, the attackers' targets are straightforward, financially based, and easier to prepare for since security teams know what they're after. However, it's much more challenging for an organization like an engineering company, for example. It's hard to characterize what their intellectual property looks like. It's harder for companies that have this very difficult challenge to tag sensitive data effectively since by its nature, it's more complex and it is generally not as well structured. It doesn't have any real telltales to it. It's harder to discern. Having a mature UEBA solution would be a critical part of any large engineering company's portfolio to help address these kinds of challenges for defending their environments.

Anticipated long-term utilities of UEBA and IdA

As hybrid cloud challenges and attackers' sophistication evolve, there is an evolution of security into more of a microservice type function where user and entity behavior analytics risk scores and analytic response codes would provide something like a holistic security wrapper that goes around an end user which is continuously updated. The possibilities expand from there.

UEBA and IdA evolving with the environment. One can envision all kinds of things UEBA-IdA could do for an organization. I would expect it to evolve as the environment evolved to perform many other functions such as risk-based intrusion protection, intrusion detection, and more. With IdA's ability close the awareness gap between access provided and activity, and to fill the discovery gap in identifying unknown risks in privileged access entitlements, a full holistic view of identity and access in the environment is now possible.

CONCLUSIONS & TAKEAWAYS:
Optimizing new realities in security

Jerry Archer's tenure in security at the early development of the internet provides him with a seasoned, holistic and nuanced perspective on the ever-changing nature of requirements needed to ensure an organization's security. His observations of the various symptoms of inadequate security defenses, including that a new variant of malware is being created every 200 milliseconds, might be alarming for new professionals in the security field. This acknowledgement also includes his observation of rising threats on the endpoint, where 60% of the risk resides. Solutions to address these and others in emerging hybrid environments can no longer be managed with manual security solutions. This challenge is complicated by the evolution of hybrid cloud access and the plethora of devices, a majority of them mobile, which malicious actors take advantage of. Security data volume exceeds manual processing capabilities as anomalous behavior continues to rise. The overwhelming scale of false positives can only be reduced through machine learning and mature behavior analytics. These must also incorporate the holistic use of identity analytics to reduce access risk. This solution set delivers comprehensive visibility and monitoring of both physical and hybrid environments.

With this new paradigm of security solutions in place, detecting account compromise and misuse becomes a realistic objective. This is an important requirement, since the emerging factors of hybrid access are continuing to grow and evolve, with no sign of abatement. At the core of this requirement is addressing a new risk trend, the insider threat. Leveraged as a user, or entity account with entitlements, or through partner access, identity compromise and misuse is the root cause of most data theft and breaches. Whether actual insiders within an organization, or attackers posing as insiders with compromised identity, the risk associated with this trend can be a systemic threat for organizations. This underlines the urgent need for a single identity risk profile for users both on-premises and in the cloud.

The problem of excess access, access outliers, and orphan or dormant accounts is widespread among enterprises. The gap between IAM and security teams, however, is a challenge as these groups in some organizations are working at cross-purposes. Archer observes the benefits of cooperative strategic partnerships with CIOs and CISOs. Archer endorses a security strategy of resilient defense, making it as difficult as possible for attackers to exit with the data they seek once they have gained access to the environment. Like Eppinger, Archer observes that the phased approach to implementing complex changes in the environment has proven be both cost-effective and strengthens the assurance that the solution is delivered in synch with the original solution requirements.

The next chapter will examine more closely insider threats, account compromise and data exfiltration. These lie at the core of a security team's responsibilities: to protect the data. Heeding the signs of sobering consequences of the potential for security breaches, however, is not a forgone conclusion. In the following *Borderless Breach Flashcard*, one healthcare organization suffered three security breaches over the course of a few years. While one might be understandable from a physical security standpoint with a missing laptop, the second remains under investigation, and the final breach could most likely have been avoided with the right predictive security analytics solutions in place.

BORDERLESS BREACH FLASHCARD	
An Inside Job	
CATEGORY	Insider, former employee exfiltrates key patient information.
WHO	**The target:** Sutter Health, California, regional healthcare provider.
WHAT	A former employee gains access to sensitive billing information on 2,582 patients and emails it to his private account. Patients' social security and driver license information were compromised.
WHEN	2013
WHERE	Northern California.
WHY	Potential economic gain.
HOW	After two serious security breaches, a third breach occurred. The pattern began with a high profile breach two years earlier, with the data for over four million patients stolen from a lost laptop. A multi-billion dollar class action lawsuit resulted. Later, an unrelated police arrest revealed a cache of stolen patient data, forcing Sutter Health to notify 4,500 patients of a possible compromise. Finally, due to reports of a former employee's alleged illegal activities, Sutter Health's IT team discovered the employee had sent sensitive billing information to his private email. The individual had originally worked in Sutter Physician Services, with billing for Sutter Health's physician medical foundations. Multiple instances of patient data compromise were confirmed.
HOW BAD?	Sutter Health offered free credit monitoring services to all patients impacted. The actual monetary damage in this case is comparatively, low due to the minimal volume. The brand damage, however, is inestimable. Sutter Health already had a reputation for faulty security. Customer trust erodes as a result. With Accenture forecasting cyber-attacks will cost hospitals over $305 billion in the next five years, where one in 13 patients will have data compromised by a hack, Sutter Health must take notice. Operating 24 hospitals, 27 ambulatory care facilities, home healthcare and hospice services in Northern California, with a network of over 5,000 physicians, Sutter Health must consider itself a primary target of enterprising hackers and future attacks.
HOW COULD IT BE AVOIDED?	First with C-level awareness, as a government mandate on standardized electronic records thrust healthcare into the digital age, leaving security strategies behind other businesses'. With a UEBA solution in place, the emailing of sensitive billing records to a private email address would have likely triggered an immediate alert, followed by remedial action.

Insider Threats, Account Compromise and Data Exfiltration

The enduring challenge of the insider threat

Is steady incremental improvement of security systems a standard operating procedure for organizations?

In 2008, the Carnegie Mellon University (CMU) Software Engineering Institute CERT (Community Emergency Response Team) Program, along with the U.S. Secret Service, analyzed 150 insider cybercrimes across U.S. critical infrastructure sectors (*The 'Big Picture' of Insider IT Sabotage Across U.S. Critical Infrastructures*). Additional research by CERT involved more detailed group modeling and analysis of 30 cases from the 150 total cases of insider IT sabotage in the report. The researchers made a number of observations, one of which has an enduring criticality as it relates to Borderless Behavior Analytics. That was that the lack of physical and electronic access controls facilitated these attacks. More concerning, 93% of the malicious insiders in the cases studied exploited inadequate access controls. Of these, 75% of these insiders created or used access paths unknown to management to set up their attack and conceal their identity or actions.

> **"** *...93% of the malicious insiders in the cases studied exploited inadequate access controls.* **"**

In 2012, the CMU CERT program published its fourth edition of the *Common Sense Guide to Mitigating Insider Threats*, outlining nineteen best practices, all of which are aligned with mature security frameworks. With this body of well-established institutional understanding and insight in place from CMU CERT, as well as equivalently important findings from a host of other industry and academic experts providing additional security wisdom, one would hope the security communities in enterprises today had taken notice of the original risks noted above and adopted appropriate incremental measures to address them. Hope, however, is never a plan for success.

One industry observation puts that concern into perspective. Craig Cooper is Gurucul's COO, and former financial industry information security officer. He observed that currently, most Fortune 500 companies have more privileged access risks outside their IAM (identity and access management) and PAM (privileged access management) vaults, than inside. That means more than half of the most prized access entitlements hackers seek to compromise are not even on these organizations' radar screens for access management. That's an unmanaged access risk plane of sobering proportions.

> *...more than half of the most prized access entitlements hackers seek to compromise are not even on these organizations' radar screens for access management.*

Why has this concerning trend been allowed to occur? Tight budgets and prioritization of security and IT initiatives, limited to what was perceived to be the most urgent and pressing issues, accounts for some of it. In addition, access management and security in the evolving environments of today has not kept pace with the growing challenges. A driver for security since 2003 has been compliance, which resulted in rubber stamping and user account cloning. This, in turn, created excess access and access outliers. Over time, security leaders at many organizations came to face entitlement levels which often went into millions. Yet managing this mass of data, and to understand it at a detailed level, was futile for humans. Only recently, in 2015, have industry analysts identified the urgent need to see what the risks are at the entitlement level. However, due to the massive amount of entitlements involved, it was not possible without the advent of machine learning. Now, with the right identity analytics solution, it had become possible to clean up these excess and outlier entitlements, where too much access had been given out, resulting in high risk. Effective discovery of access as a risk plane was finally available. Widespread adoption of this solution capability, however, is in the early adopter phase.

Compounding the challenge CISOs face, is the rapid growth of the access risk plane by virtue of cloud adoptions, with BYOD, IoT and global access to systems, and the originally employed security strategies designed for traditional on-premises use. Moreover, that term 'traditional' represents a potential CISO mindset gap for today's emerging requirements in assuring comprehensive and holistic security assurance.

As Gary Eppinger observed in the first chapter of this book, it was not an easy transition away from his old school security perspectives and strategies. These were originally built on solid thinking at the time, based on well-established principles. Traditional security tactics, like threat hunting using rules, patterns and signatures, still have a place in SOCs. However, that's the issue. It's only part of the solution, and over the long-term, an increasingly smaller part of the big picture. While using rules, patterns and signatures is an important resource for lowering the signal to noise ratio for known threats, this approach in no way addresses the unknown unknowns. For forward-looking security leaders, that's the elephant in the room.

Detection continues to be popular, but it is limited to what humans know. Today, most organizations only detect what they know about with signatures, patterns and rules. They have hit a wall for prevention. After decades of declarative defenses, the continuously growing volume of big data underscores and defines the requirements for the new frontier of security. Dwell time (the time between compromise and breach detection) remains near 150 days, with some breaches only being discovered when the attackers themselves declare it. The recently revealed 2014 breach at Yahoo with over 500 million accounts compromised — some experts say, the largest in history — is a case in point.

How do you detect what you do not know? Where do you start? How do you ensure you cover all the bases? Limited skilled resources, budgets and time for detection are a constant challenge for security leaders. Those who understand the problem know that just throwing more humans at the security problem will not solve it. Humans are not the solution, because the scale and complexity of the unknowns is far beyond human capability. A force multiplier of these efforts is required. It must facilitate the ability to ingest the big data, to process it accurately, to minimize access risks and detect unknown threats across all environments in an organization's infrastructure. That's where machine learning provides an optimal and cost effective answer to the challenges of insider threats, account compromise and data exfiltration.

Machine learning, with context of big data for UEBA and IdA, find the unknowns on the identity access risk and threat plane. This puts security teams back in control of protecting their environments with confidence.

> ....the scale and complexity of the unknowns is far beyond human capability. A force multiplier of these efforts is required.

While some traditional security leaders maintain the status quo, others have forged on into the new frontier of the hybrid environment to discover the broad range of requirements and challenges facing them. Our expert contributor Joe Sullivan, CSO of

Uber, with a vast range of first-hand experience in information security will share his experience with the growing evolution of behavior analytics, machine learning and big data. He will also highlight the benefits they deliver to Borderless Behavior Analytics.

BORDERLESS EXPERT INSIGHTS

Joe Sullivan, CSO*
Uber

Joe Sullivan is the Chief Security Officer at Uber where he is responsible for all aspects of safety and security—rider and driver safety, data security, physical security, and investigations. Before joining Uber in early 2015, Joe was the CSO at Facebook where he led their information security, product security, investigations, and law enforcement relationship teams for 6 years. Prior to joining Facebook, Joe spent 6 years working in a number of security and legal roles at eBay and PayPal, culminating in managing PayPal's North America legal team (and for a time serving as Acting General Counsel of PayPal). Before entering the private sector, Joe spent 8 years with the United States Department of Justice. As a prosecutor in the U.S. Attorney's Office for the Northern District of California, he was a founding member of a unit dedicated to full time investigation and prosecution of technology-related crimes, including the technical aspects of the 9/11 investigation. Joe was appointed by President Obama in 2016 to serve as a commissioner on the Presidential Commission on Enhancing National Cybersecurity. Joe has also volunteered his time with a number of organizations that promote internet safety and security, including the National Cyber Security Alliance, the Action Alliance for Suicide Prevention, and the Bay Area CSO Council. He serves on the External Advisory Committee for the Center for Long-Term Cybersecurity at the University of California at Berkeley. He has also served on the advisory boards of a number of startups, including AirBnB, BlueCava, Gurucul, and RiskIQ.

A member of Gurucul's Executive Advisory Board, Joe has provided his insights and stewardship for Gurucul's growth and evolution in developing next generation solutions in the field of UEBA and IdA security disciplines. He shares insights from his broad experience with the challenges and solutions of UEBA and IdA for hybrid cloud security.

Overview

In this segment, Sullivan begins with comparing the CIO and CISO's perspectives, which segues into his insights on the symptoms of today's environments struggling with unknown threats. His discussion observes the need for new approaches to address gaps in traditional non-identity based security solutions. He then explores cloud and mobility's impact on visibility and the security challenges in hybrid network environments. This investigation brings a deeper look at the challenge of effectively

---

* The views and opinions expressed by Joe Sullivan in this book are his own, and do not necessarily reflect those of Uber, or any of his previous employers.

monitoring and analyzing security data in global organizations in the midst of big data and cloud scalability. Sullivan then cites the challenges with detecting account compromise and misuse, along with observing the patterns of insider threats, privilege misuse and data exfiltration. This brings into focus the critical challenge of confronting the unknown unknowns while addressing attackers' constant innovation. While coping with budgets and limited resources and the impact on CISOs' goals and priorities in security solution adoptions, Sullivan observes the logistical implementation priorities for prospective predictive security analytics customers. He then shares his insights on CIO and CISO preference trends within machine learning solution adoption. He concludes with his forecast of security solution requirements for the next two to five years.

Comparing the CIO and CISO perspectives

The head of security's mission is to manage and reduce risk for the company. The CIO's goal is to enable the business to move fast through technology to mobilize and empower their workforce and optimize their productivity. That's why they're both moving in the direction of the varied cloud solutions. Yet they don't want to create friction for employees in the way that traditional identity management frameworks work. Their approach to security strives to produce as little friction as possible for good employees doing good work. This ideal strikes to the heart of a CIO's sense of balance. They want to be able to satisfy the risk management folks, while optimizing the efficiency and effectiveness for their employees. Any solution that allows employees to go fast is a good solution in their eyes. The CISO, however, needs to keep an eye on the threat factors, wherever they may lie.

CIOs drive solutions into a borderless world. A CISO's focus is still to try to facilitate the new cloud-driven advantages while assuring the protections and coverage, and at the same time, to enable optimal productivity of the workforce. Some CISOs will be left behind if they don't embrace solutions like this, since the CIO is already moving to a borderless world and building an approach that will allow all employees to have access to all the data they need. The CISO must align with the program and implement solutions that manage risk in this new environment.

Maintaining an optimal balance is key. The challenge between CIO and CISO priorities can be tricky, of course, especially for the CISO, because they must support the speed and productivity of the programs. However, if there is any breach in the meantime, or the security solution is not in step with where the solutions are going, then it's a problem for the CISO. That's the nature of being a CISO.

Symptoms in today's environments struggling with unknown threats

Most of the existing security defenses have been built for a model of an enterprise technology architecture that no longer exists. If you look at a castle, you can build a moat around it. This has been the basic approach enterprises have taken to securing their technology stack by establishing a moat-like perimeter or layer between the company and the internet.

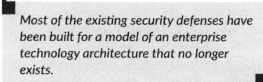

Most of the existing security defenses have been built for a model of an enterprise technology architecture that no longer exists.

Traditional defense models no longer adequate. Originally, and at the highest level, that model was generally effective if you could work around that barrier and focus your defenses on the perimeter. That's why enterprises have network security, VPNs, and tools that monitor all the identities and traffic that comes from the outside world, to control who is allowed inside the corporate network. The fundamental problem is that modern companies no longer have that architecture.

Business units adopt cloud solutions outside IT's purview. In varying degrees, all enterprises now have a hybrid or effectively borderless architecture. That's the trend in modern companies. The corporate IT department is being left behind as a result. It used to be that security teams would ride on the coattails of the IT team, where the corporate IT's team was responsible for all of an organization's technology. Today, more frequently, the corporate IT team doesn't even know about what technology is being used, as other business units adopt cloud technologies, circumventing their IT department.

New normal: Decentralization and fragmentation of environments. In every context that used to be managed internally — whether it was email, customer relationship management, data storage, computation, customer support, product development — today it's being done in a much more fragmented way, decentralized and outside the original network set of contexts. As a result, you can no longer build a moat, or set up the kind of monitoring around your perimeter in the traditional sense. An unintended consequence of this is that a new set of risks have manifested themselves. This new norm is where security defenses must now be evaluated.

....you can no longer build a moat, or set up the kind of monitoring around your perimeter in the traditional sense... a new set of risks have manifested themselves.

The need for new approaches to address gaps in traditional non-identity based security solutions

For my colleagues and me, the growing awareness of the borderless side of network security began around 2012. Three years before that we also recognized the need to have an identity-based anomaly detection engine solution. This approach involves seeing how our employees worked and viewing the data they were accessing.

Responsible control of employee access to customer data. At my prior company, our business model involved enabling people with their own choices in how to store and share their information online. That meant a good percentage of our employees needed access to some of this information at certain times to do their job to support the customers. It didn't mean every employee in the company needed access all the time. We also had to articulate to regulators how we oversaw responsible employee access to user access data.

Controlling access for legitimate use only. Everyone in our security group realized a traditional role-based approach to access control would be insufficient. While we recognized some employees would always need to have access to celebrities' accounts to help them manage their pages, that didn't mean the employees should feel entitled to be voyeuristic in exploring those celebrities' accounts. Therefore, we needed to build a solution to facilitate our monitoring and understanding employees who were authorized to look at these accounts. We also needed to manage access, and control it if a particular instance of access was not for a legitimate purpose.

Everyone in our security group realized a traditional role-based approach to access control would be insufficient.

Recognizing future trends of big data requirements. It was in this context where I began to appreciate that organizations needed more than just the traditional role-based access. Access needed to be tied to specific legitimate uses. We knew of no solution that addressed this challenge at the time. That's when I began working in this area of security. At my prior company, we began building a custom solution to support this requirement. And as I researched it more deeply — seeing that every company was storing increasingly more data — I came to realize that the future was in big data. That was when I first spoke with Gurucul. They seemed to be one of the only vendors out there at the time building something similar to what we had tried to build on our own.

...as I researched it more deeply... I came to realize that the future was in big data.

Aligning customer challenges with behavior analytics solutions. Gurucul was already dealing with customer challenges similar to ours. In one case, they had a customer in a consumer-based environment who wanted to cross-correlate what customer support calls were coming in and what accounts the customer support representatives were opening. The issue of concern was that in opening a customer account, the support reps had access to everything. Since a call could come from anywhere in the country, they needed the ability to have global access to anyone's account to service the call. The fact that all those accounts could be looked at was considered a critical risk. Gurucul's customer wanted to cross-correlate what access was being initiated and ensure it was tied to specific customer support responsibilities. Another concern was that this enterprise also had celebrity customers. Gurucul's customer needed to ensure their people were looking at these and any other accounts only for legitimate reasons.

Machine learning use case models with wider applications. This concern and use case models for machine learning behavior analytics extends into other verticals as well, for example, with financial institutions and bank tellers. The leading banks have a majority of the entire population of the country covered. More often than not, most will have celebrity accounts accessible from any bank branch. Yet if an employee is looking at this information just for entertainment, or to misuse this data for malicious intent, then organizations must be able to recognize this quickly and have the monitor, alert and response capabilities in place to effectively stop this kind of behavior quickly.

Cloud and mobility's impact on visibility: Security challenges in hybrid network environments

Cloud and mobility's impact on visibility is profound. Companies are putting an increasing amount of sensitive applications and data in different cloud solutions. This use pattern will only grow and broaden going forward. The challenge of reliable visibility within the hybrid cloud is complex and a top concern of many CISOs.

The need to address the complexities of hybrid environments. In response to cloud and mobility's impact on visibility, organizations must have an identity management framework and anomaly detection system that incorporates all the attributes found in a traditional old network security. It requires the objective for the solution to work just as well, if not better, than those original systems. However, that's where many of the traditional security tools have fallen short. They're just not flexible enough to be able to expand into that more complex hybrid environment.

Account provisioning limitations. Part of the visibility challenge includes provisioning, deep provisioning, as well as activating and deactivating all those accounts. The timing of these procedures is especially critical with the recognition of new employment models in play, as organizations adjust to terms and the conditions of the emerging gig economy. People may now work with a company as contractors or partners, not for years, but instead for weeks or months.

Cloud accounts outside of IT's control or responsibility. Managing the timely and precise activation and deactivation of those accounts is critical and challenging. Moreover, when an employee is terminated, how do organizations ensure the termination successfully includes severance of their access to a myriad of different cloud environments that a company is trying to manage? This wide array of cloud solutions outside of IT's responsibility and involvement complicates the challenge of keeping on top of these accounts and maintaining comprehensive and reliable visibility. Complicating this challenge, a number of cloud environments do not always provide the visibility required. Application program interface (API) standards for the visibility required with cloud applications are still evolving. Many cloud applications don't have an API, so the data needed for visibility is simply not always available, leaving customers lacking the data they need for machine learning models in identity analytics. As a result, many companies struggle with the situation of keeping their cloud solutions managed effectively.

New requirements for security defenses in the hybrid environment

Instead of tracking a network perimeter, SOCs must now track the individual, and build a program tied to the multiple components, the employees, business partners, and the applications. The challenge is that the applications are fragmented all over the place, and employees are fragmented in dispersed locations as well. As a result, security teams need to develop tools aligned with securing those key elements in an insecure world.

The challenge is that the applications are fragmented all over the place, and employees are fragmented in dispersed locations as well.

Solutions required to track both employees and applications. An important component of this requirement is fulfilled with a mature UEBA solution that also incorporates comprehensive identity analytics (IdA) across application access and activity for all employees. Both UEBA and IdA employ fuzzy logic as a critical characteristic of machine learning. For IdA, this provides a risk-based approach for identity access management, reducing excess access and access outliers. For UEBA, the objective is to detect compromised identity and suspect activity from behavior anomalies of normal baselines and peering which would remain unknown without this type of security monitoring.

The challenge of effectively monitoring and analyzing security data in global organizations

With security today, it's about anomaly detection and determining if a person should be allowed to cross the bridge and into a particular environment, at a certain time, for a specific purpose. Companies can't hire enough security engineers and analysts to keep an eye on a hundred thousand employees, using twenty thousand applications, scattered across an array of different public and private clouds. The bandwidth requirements are staggering. Instead, enterprises must rely on technology, have a good faith foundation of identity, and maintain good tracking of the applications. They require a system that reviews and brings state-of-the-art identity management into this world.

> " *Companies can't hire enough security engineers... to keep an eye on a hundred thousand employees, using twenty thousand applications, scattered across an array of different public and private clouds.* "

Three-part security program. Identity management systems that service the old networked environments are role-based and blunt. They don't allow for today's flexible workforce where employees are frequently shifting roles and responsibilities. To address this challenge, a three-part security program is required. One part is to secure the applications. The second is to lock down identity. The third involves looking at how the authorized identities are using the applications, or behavior analytics.

> " *Identity management systems that service the old networked environments are role-based and blunt. They don't allow for today's flexible workforce where employees are frequently shifting roles and responsibilities.* "

Growing multi-tiered data expansion and proliferation. The other reality of today's applications is that much more sensitive data is in them. It's being stored in many more places, and accessed by many more employees, for an increasing amount of legitimate reasons. Where one technology expert might say, "Every company is becoming a software company," it now appears the statement "Every company is becoming a data company" represents the next generation's reality. Every company now has sensitive data which may include intellectual property. It also might be where companies are storing more of their customer data and recognizing that half of their employee population may need access to some of this data.

New realities in big data require new strategies in security. As every company becomes a data company, trying to get insights about their customer, using artificial intelligence to perform customer support, and big data machine learning to figure out which customer should get what — there must be different expectations around data storage and security. Traditional identity management systems don't scale in these new environments. In fact, in many cases they suffer from a severe discovery gap in privileged access risks at the entitlement level within applications. This represents a serious and growing access risk plane. To manage the vast scope of analysis required, a new approach must be adopted, one that integrates identity management, with identity analytics from machine learning models analyzing both access and activity data.

Exponential data generation and cloud scalability: Challenges with detecting account compromise and misuse

To enhance protection and response, and to confront the unavoidable rising challenges in today's environments, security teams must adopt advanced machine learning analytics solutions, drawing from the value of big data. Within this funnel, a proven behavior anomaly detection engine can monitor users' behavior and evaluate what unknown risks might exist. To manage identity risk and access entitlements beyond current IAM and PAM capabilities, a next-generation identity analytics solution would reduce access risk. Collectively, they form a funnel of integrated analytics providing risk scoring at each layer that ensure security assurance in today's environments. In the graphic below, data flows down the left side, while analytics and risk scoring flow up on the right side.

Big Data Analytics Funnel
Figure 3.1

Surfacing anomalous behavior. A scenario of when access and threat analytics would be applied is with a product development team that might have a hundred employees, and all of them work consistently with a particular data set for specific purposes. Then, for some reason, one employee starts interacting with an entirely different set of data. That's the kind of behavior anomaly security teams must surface and then assure an analyst individually reviews it

> *...the more of this qualified anomaly identification that can be performed with technology, and the less the security analysts have to surface for manual review, the better.*

or compares it to what the employee's project work has been. Another example might be a customer service representative responsible for a particular region who begins interacting with data on customers outside their regional domain. Considering the vast volume of data a security team must contend with, the more of this qualified anomaly identification that can be performed with technology, and the less security analysts have to surface for manual review, the better. This frees up security analysts' time to deal with other priority issues.

Leveraging specialized solutions and qualified expertise. When security teams can leverage the computing power of machine learning with scalability of today's hybrid and cloud solutions, for the increasing amount of constantly expanding big data, they are better able to manage the needles in the haystack. It's no longer realistic for a security leader to just plan for his team to log all the data and mandate his data science team to build a specialized kind of capability, homegrown within the environment. Instead, an experienced CISO will likely rely on outside companies, preferably best-of-breed, with proven expertise in data science and behavior analytics, to build that system for them. These solution partners who provide these security analytics tools should also have acquired a comprehensive understanding of the range of threats and risks across industries.

Quality and breadth of data assures monitoring value. In the world of anomaly detection, it is critical to have incredibly large data sets incorporated into this kind of machine learning. This facilitates predicting and identifying legitimate versus anomalous behavior. Within this data framework, having a rich set of true positives to build out an effective data science approach is required, which a mature UEBA solution provides. In addition, security teams can add and incorporate their organization's own historical data. With this data, individual baselines of all users' past behavior are created and correlated with their team's baseline behavior. This raises the level and quality of good data which is crucial for the information to be effective and actionable. It further empowers a SOC team's ability to detect nefarious anomalies. This quantity and quality of the data is essential to reduce the amount of time it takes to pinpoint what's going on in the environment.

Rich context lowers false positives. The biggest challenge in setting up a security program with the objective of either detecting a compromised insider account, or malicious insider, is that you must go deep into the data to examine the behavior. Too many of the existing systems utilize a

...you must go deep into the data to examine the behavior. Too many of the existing systems utilize a security approach that delivers a high volume of false positives.

security approach that delivers a high volume of false positives. No security leader wants to have a situation where his team takes an employee in a room and starts asking pointed questions without being completely sure of the issue. What's needed, and what a mature UEBA solution provides, is context. Even when there's an alert on something an employee has never done before — or that no one on their team has ever done before — you have a lot of context provided. The result is that an analyst will possess that deeper understanding which provides critically defining additional feedback and insight.

Patterns of insider threats and privilege misuse

When employing an identity-based solution, you're working on detecting two different primary threats. One is where the insider's identity has been compromised. The other involves the insider who has a malicious intent. Yet from most security leaders' perspectives, that almost doesn't matter. Companies traditionally have a high trust of their inside employees. However, when they have worked at detecting a malicious insider, the processes that were implemented and proved the most valuable at detecting them also revealed compromised accounts as well. These attackers aren't just coming through a firewall to find all their target data. They're entering under the guise of a trusted insider.

Double benefit of three-sided security strategy. The three-sided security program referenced earlier — which focuses on strong identity, strong application security, and the identity-based solution that monitors who's using what — is the foundation of this detection capability. Most modern attacks involve some kind of privilege escalation. When attackers gain entry to an enterprise, it involves compromising the identity of an employee and then using their permissions to gain access. This is what so many modern attacks involve: a bad guy using a good person's identity, versus a good person turning into a bad person. Yet they're basically doing the

Most modern attacks involve some kind of privilege escalation... This is what so many modern attacks involve, a bad guy using a good person's identity...

exact same things. This approach to security has a double benefit, when even the outsider threats end up being detected first as an insider threat, where someone who is on the inside is there because valid credentials were being stolen and misused by an outsider.

The criticality of focusing on insider threats. Any good security program must care about both threats. Focusing on insider threats is important because it's been documented extensively that people leave companies and try to take company intellectual property with them. People are bribed, have pressure put on their families, or realize they can monetize internal data or intellectual property. Employees also get disgruntled and want to hurt the company because they feel the company hasn't treated them well. There are many different reasons why someone originally hired as a good employee could ultimately become a risk to the company. It's important to think about threats from both standpoints.

A compromise UEBA could have caught. One perspective related to this type of breach — noted from the recent *Verizon 2016 Data Breach Digest* — is the story about an employee who actually outsourced his own job to Asia. He would go to the office, give his token to the engineer in Asia, who would then log in using the employee's credential. That person would then do the employee's job. The employee paid the engineer in Asia out of his pocket, at a much cheaper rate, and was getting great yearly performance reviews. This activity went undetected for years before discovery. So in this case the behavior was not intended to steal anything, but the employee decisively compromised the integrity of the company's security solutions, which were set up to protect the data. If a user behavior analytics solution had been in place, it would have detected this compromise much earlier than any of the traditional security solutions that failed for years.

An attacker's first target once inside the environment. Another pattern security experts typically see is when a real outsider gets into the network using a privilege escalation approach cloaked as legitimate insider activity. If an organization allowed a red team to assess and challenge their network's security plan, the team would quickly inform them that one of the first things attackers do when they get inside a company's

environment is to search for insiders' usernames and passwords. They also look at org charts and information which specifically tells them who inside the company has the best credentials they should try to leverage for the next step in their attack.

> ...one of the first things attackers do when they get inside a company's environment is to search for insiders' user names and passwords.

Data exfiltration in hybrid environments versus traditional environments

In the traditional environment, you would have a network TiVo solution (network flight recorder) that allowed security teams to look at all the data passing out of the network. They could tell what data was leaving or what data someone was trying to take out. That network pipe no longer exists. The network perimeter security solutions – whether it was DLP, or advanced firewalls, NetWitness, network TiVo — don't help now with hybrid environments. They can't provide all those logs in a viewable way or in real-time. These outdated security approaches cannot cope with the emerging challenges networks face today.

A new perspective and strategy is required. Beyond this old framework of options and approaches, CISO's must look at new and adjusted solutions to deal with the new kinds of threat planes found in hybrid environments. These adjusted solutions must be much more flexible and robust to address the challenge. A growing majority of security experts feel that the answer lies in a mature predictive security analytics solution with big data.

Confronting the unknown unknowns: Addressing attackers constant innovation

Security teams must leverage other attacker's true positives to help create a probable threat terrain. For example, how do signature-based antiviruses (AV) work? They count on having seen a specific malware attack before. When deploying basic antivirus, it looks for signatures which are a known bad. To a certain extent, every company is on a quest to identify all the known bad patterns or signatures of known attacks. More advanced AV solutions may also rely on heuristic analysis of commands and execution.

Known bad attack signature repositories. The problem is most companies, both large and small, don't have the ability to aggregate all the known bad patterns or signatures of specific malware. That's where collaborating with a qualified and best-of-breed anti-malware solution vendor comes in, along with their repository of known bad signatures, which are constantly being updated. Organizations should choose a solution product that has ingested a large volume of known bads from a wide range of contexts so when that signature of a bad appears in their environment it can be keyed on effectively.

Machine learning keys off known bad patterns. Where UEBA technology has improved, is in defining the specifics of what to alert on as risk-scored anomalous behavior. In the traditional antiviral context, it entailed watching for code, or a known signature, executing in a particular way. The technology is now moving toward identity-based anomaly detection, which is not examining code executing in any particular way, but instead looking at human behavior executing in an anomalous way from known baselines and peer groups. For this aspect in the big data machine learning approach to work there must be patterns of known normal and bad behavior to key off of, learn from, build on, and model against.

Exact attack signatures not required. The good thing in this case is you don't actually have to see the exact attack signature with UEBA. With the traditional antivirus software, the known signature, or precise code, has to operate in a specifically exact profile for it to be flagged. With UEBA and big data machine learning, however, you no longer need that concrete a set of specifics. What is needed is a significant volume of true positives, big data context, to build on and to learn from. Also, if bad behavior exists when creating a baseline, the use of multiple peer groups will identify the anomalous behavior for the user or entity. This is in contrast to a common misconception about behavior analytics.

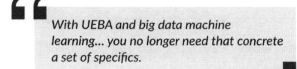

> With UEBA and big data machine learning... you no longer need that concrete a set of specifics.

Attacker innovation is perpetual. Always keep in mind that innovation is taking place on both sides, on the solution side, as well as with the people trying to get into your environment and breach your data. Originally, phishing emails were so common and typically easy to recognize because their messages were poorly crafted and cast such a broad net. That's changing. Recently emails have become more personalized, where the email might explain that they found the phishing target on a specific industry website which was familiar to the recipient. That familiarity encourages the impression the email is legitimate. These attackers have found ways to automate this whole process, finding the first non-advertised search result to come up when a phishing target name is put in a search engine. That detail adds to the credibility of the email. If it compels the recipient to click the link, their job is done. Mission accomplished. This is all part of the innovation bad actors are performing, and for which security teams must remain constantly on alert. Meanwhile, social engineering continues to get more sophisticated.

Budgets and limited resources: The impact on CISOs' goals and priorities in security solution adoptions

There's currently a talent drought in security. Qualified security analysts are in short supply. According to Forbes.com, as of September 2016, there were over 209,000 unfilled cyber security openings in the US, and over one million worldwide. Security engineers are paid at a premium compared to traditional software engineers and numerous published articles document this fact. Some companies in Silicon Valley pay security engineers up to 20% more than a typical engineer. Indeed, all engineers who meet a high quality bar are hard to find and the law of supply and demand is in effect.

Bandwidth and headcount cannot handle the challenge. No company can hire and staff up with the number of security engineers they actually want and need to cover the volume of deep investigation required. The digital exhaust of big data is overwhelming. Small companies don't have a shot of getting the highest quality security engineers and their prime skill sets, so the challenge is widespread. Organizations must have alternatives for their comprehensive security coverage through technology.

> *Organizations must have alternatives for their comprehensive security coverage through technology.*

Logistical priorities for prospective UEBA customers

It's critical for any good UEBA solution to be easy to get up and running. The typical security team lacks the time, energy and technical resources to devote to a bespoke deployment of a new security solution. Therefore the more plug and play the new technology solution is, the better it will be for the adopting company. Having qualified resources from the solution provider to assist with deploying the solution in the customer's security portfolio is critical. Ease of implementation along with a high degree of accuracy for detection of anomalies is a key component of success.

> *Ease of implementation, along with a high degree of accuracy, are key components of success.*

Realities of solution requirements tied to custom environments. While having as much plug and play capability as possible, CISOs should also maintain a realistic perspective on this point. Traditionally many customer environments are multilayered and have evolved over time in distinct ways, often homegrown and customized, creating problematic issues where logging and event data are often incomplete. Also, these environments may have a unique set of variables and technologies, all of which represent complex sets of requirements to interface effectively. While plug and play may appear to be advantageous due to its simplicity, and ease of use, if the logging data produced is inadequate, the solution cannot provide real value in the long run.

The advantage of out-of-the-box UEBA plug-ins for established systems. A key delivery value for experienced and well-established UEBA solution providers is to offer packaged data connectors for the more common and established systems and data sources. This speeds the integration cycle, allowing the UEBA solution vendor to focus on the system components requiring customized data ingestion or API integration. The same holds true for new SaaS applications and silos of access and activity data to provide API access to behavior analytics solutions.

The importance of ease of use. Once the solution has been implemented, the ideal utility model is to deliver both robust capabilities and ease of use with accuracy. This precedent of utilization was established by much of the mobile-based technology which has demonstrated how a range of functions can be performed simply. If you have an application with less buttons or options, but just the important ones to perform the functions needed on a normal daily basis, then the user experience is enhanced and empowered and the security team's efficiency is heightened, delivering better productivity.

CIO and CISO preference trends for machine learning solution adoption

An important perspective to maintain is to recognize the effectiveness of having a large team of analysts performing at the same level. On top of that, there is value in understanding that organizations can use this technology to facilitate their security team's work more efficiently and consistently, raising their productivity and freeing them for more impactful and business-critical work. For example, when you have twenty analysts looking at cases, each person only sees what they alone see; they don't see what the other nineteen analysts see. But if you have a technology that sees what all twenty analysts would have seen, and it's ingesting data from many more different angles and perspectives, then everyone on the team is working at a much higher level of performance. The silos have disappeared. It also frees the security engineers up to perform more intelligent work required to address the evolution of growing threats in the environment. As a result, machine learning raises efficiencies in the organization.

....if you have a technology that sees what all twenty analysts would have seen, and it's ingesting data from many more different angles and perspectives, then everyone on the team is working at a much higher level of performance.

UEBA fulfills goals and objectives of the CISO. From a CISO's perspective of productivity goals, and security objectives, the result is to make the employees in the security group more effective with machine learning, where lower priority anomalies are filtered out, leaving only the highly critical cases which require more investigation. Productivity is increased and comprehensive security assurance is empowered. Effectiveness increases measurably on both sides of the equation. At the same time, UEBA can detect anomalies (and more quickly), that a team of analysts may miss entirely.

UEBA optimizing time and efficiency. Instead of looking at a UEBA solution as a method of reducing the staff, the more productive way to see this is that a security team's time is being utilized more effectively. Getting the most out of your analysts is key to a company's ROI on this valuable investment, achieving a great deal more with the same number of people. This is exactly what's needed to face the growing security challenges of expanding digital exhaust evolving in today's hybrid cloud environments.

Security solution requirements in the next two to five years

The CISO's domain will continue in the same direction is has over the last seven years and will eventually result in total fragmentation. Increasingly more employees will be accessing sensitive enterprise data and information from more and more fragmented devices, through fragmented paths. Everyone's going to be on mobile devices, accessing sensitive information over different kinds of network pipes, and it will all be in applications stored in hundreds of different places. That's the path we're on right now, and will continue to be on.

Levels of UEBA solution maturity. As any prospective organization considers adopting a UEBA-IdA solution to face these challenges, they must narrow down the field of qualified vendors as efficiently as possible and understand where a vendor sits within the hierarchy of UEBA-IdA maturity. UEBA-IdA solution offerings in today's market have three levels of maturity:

- ***First generation UEBA*** – Tools-based analytics, their functionality primarily focuses on entity link analysis across structured data with the objective of resolving and linking identities and entities. These solutions, however, are limited in capability and ill-suited to deal with the rising fragmentation and complexity in hybrid environments today.

- ***Second generation UEBA*** – Progressive data integration and early canned use case analytics are in this group. These offer automatically resolved identities and entities using proprietary fuzzy logic and data-matching techniques. The primary use cases offered by both first and second generation UEBA vendors address only forensics and the investigation of threats and risks which have occurred or are continuing. Extensive professional services are usually required to maintain these solutions. Their ability to evolve with hybrid environments is questionable.

- ***State-of-the-art UEBA-IdA*** – Advanced predictive security analytics for unknown threats and access risks are in this category. This next generation of UEBA-IdA innovation delivers predictive packaged analytics which detect and identify insider and advanced threats, plus excess access, access outliers, and orphan or dormant accounts. UEBA-IdA solutions in this grouping have exceeded the capabilities of the widely adopted security user monitoring applications like SIEM and DLP and often incorporate identity analytics (IdA). These mature UEBA vendors continue to innovate in the development of their predictive security analytic models. The applications will not be reliant on customer-driven analytics or inquiries of the data.

These are the best suited solutions for today's evolving network environments.

CONCLUSIONS & TAKEAWAYS:
Facing the realities of the insider threat challenge

Recognizing that enterprises are storing increasingly more data, and that the future is in big data, Joe Sullivan has been at the forefront of evolving security strategies for years. The challenge a majority of CISOs face is that most of the existing security defenses were built for a model of an enterprise technology architecture that no longer exists. This new reality is, in large part, the byproduct of CIOs' well-intentioned goals to make their employees and environments more nimble, productive and efficient, with the adoption of a broad range of cloud solutions and other applications. Sullivan shares two critical observations about this new reality in security: 1) the time has passed for security strategies based mainly on rules and signatures and 2) identity management systems servicing the old networked environments are role-based and blunt, rigid and inflexible.

This hybrid cloud trend empowering organizations opens new gaps in security, creating a host of risks, and a serious threat plane that CISOs must mitigate. As well, some of these cloud solutions are completely outside IT's purview. Sensitive data is being stored globally, in many more places, and being accessed by increasing numbers of employees, partners and customers. Sobering new realities dictate that this is a borderless world, becoming increasingly decentralized and fragmented, where traditional defense models are no longer adequate.

With limited skilled resources, budgets and time for insider threat detection, allocating more humans to security issues will not solve the problem. Sullivan observes the need for new approaches to address the widening gaps in traditional solutions, to control access for legitimate use only. This challenge highlights cloud and mobility's impact on visibility and the growing security challenges in hybrid network environments. At the core of his security strategy is a three-pronged approach to manage employees and applications. One part consists of securing the applications. The second is to lock down identity. The third involves monitoring how the authorized identities use the applications. To meet this challenge, Sullivan recognized early on that risk-based behavior analytics and identity analytics, powered by machine learning, and drawing from big data, were cornerstone requirements to achieve success.

Embedded in this strategy is the capability to reliably identify anomalous behavior which facilitates an automated risk response to attackers' constant innovation. Quality and breadth of data assures monitoring value where rich context lowers false positives.

This refined big data helps eliminate blind spots in the environment which represent serious unknowns and translates directly into serious access risks and exposing an unknown threat plane of unwieldy proportions. Building on true positives from big data, through self-learning and self-training machine learning models, behavior and identity analytics continue to evolve with their environments. This new generation of predictive security analytics is a fundamental requirement in security for a future holding accelerated fragmentation, decentralization and attacker innovation.

In the following *Borderless Breach Flashcard*, one company faced a virtual threat to its survival from the results of an insider breach, and then it got worse. Moreover, this initial breach took place after the company thought they had performed all the correct due diligence and taken all the proper security precautions. In the following chapter, the factors of identity, access risks and access outliers will be examined in relation to their critical importance in Borderless Behavior Analytics.

BORDERLESS BREACH FLASHCARD *Stealing the Wind*	
CATEGORY	Data theft, economic espionage by foreign powers.
WHO	**The target:** American Superconductor Corporation (ACC), wind turbine hi-tech component manufacturer.
WHAT	American Superconductor partnered with Sinovel, a small Chinese firm partly owned by the government. Sinovel manufactured the skeleton hardware for the turbines, while ACC supplied the proprietary sophisticated control technology and computer code to run them.
WHEN	2011
WHERE	USA, China, Austria, transnational insider breach, followed by cyber-attacks thru social media.
WHY	Economic greed, market control.
HOW	Already aware of China's reputation for theft of American intellectual property, ACC took extensive security precautions to protect their technology with encrypted protocols and kept the IP off the internet. Unable to reverse engineer the technology, the Chinese used classic entrapment spycraft and recruited an Austrian employee of ACC who had privileged access to the proprietary software. Once turned, the Chinese gave the insider a shopping list of items, including source code to the technology, and then put it into production. Later, when ACC engineers were testing the next-generation of software in the turbines in China, they discovered their new software was already installed. Once the breach was discovered, ACC brought a lawsuit against the Sinovel. In turn, the Chinese military's cyber-espionage Unit 61398 launched a phishing email attack against ACC. It succeeded and gave the Chinese complete access to all of ACC's legal strategies.
HOW BAD?	ACC lost their lawsuit against Sinovel. ACC's total economic loss is well over a billion dollars, with a workforce reduction from 900 to 300. Adding insult to injury, Massachusetts, ACC's home state, later purchased these windmills with the stolen software in it using U.S. federal stimulus funds.
HOW COULD IT BE AVOIDED?	If UEBA had been in place, it is likely that data exfiltration would have surfaced as anomalous behavior with unusual downloads of sensitive intellectual property. In addition, an unusual concentration of access requests targeted on the Chinese lawsuit within ACC's legal department would also have likely raised alerts the security team could respond to.

Identity, Access Risks
and Access Outliers

The Thresholds to Cross, The Gaps to Fill

How far must enterprises go to assure their access plane is risk free?

It is no longer enough for companies to merely shore up defenses against general dangers. Evidence-based knowledge — drawn from context, mechanisms, indicators, implications and actionable intelligence — can help leaders prepare for precise strikes against IT or information assets. Concurrently, forward-thinking CISOs recognize that identity — as a core element of access — represents a serious potential threat plane to the environment. Yet with that recognition, another reality rears its ugly head. Manual processes and legacy roles driving identity and access management (IAM) today leave far too many open doors. In addition, the ubiquitous advent of hybrid and on-premises data centers, integrated with a range of cloud applications, represents a widening surface area as the complexity of access increases with technology innovation.

> **It is no longer enough for companies to merely shore up defenses against general dangers.**

The practice of periodically rubber stamping certifications for compliance in no realistic way resolves access risks. Instead, it is an ineffective waste of time and broadens the access risk plane. Consider, for example, a small enterprise environment with *100* users, with *10* accounts each, plus each account has *10* entitlements (*100 x 10 x 10*). That totals *10,000* entitlements. Then consider compliance certifications are required quarterly, and you must manually manage *40,000* entitlements per year for only *100* users! That's just one slice of the access complexity beyond human capacity to analyze. Add to that all the other entities, devices and applications operating within the environment, and the magnitude of potential for identity-based access risks then expands to a sobering scale for any CISO.

These are access entitlements that IT is theoretically aware of, but there are also instances of privileged access entitlements that occur which are unknown to IT. Some experts say as much as 50%, or more, of an organization's privileged access is unknown. That's a lot of access. More accurately, that's a lot of unmanaged access and unknown privileged access. To manage risk across the access plane, how can an organization achieve that if it doesn't even know who has privileged access entitlements?

> *To manage risk across the access plane, how can an organization achieve that if it doesn't even know who has privileged access entitlements?*

A new approach to security is essential. Just as importantly, it must be a smart approach. It must have the right phases and steps that address today's known challenges, to effectively position an organization to manage the unknown threats of tomorrow, and to scale with the evolving requirements of the future. The core focus of the solution to this challenge lies in a functional merging of identity analytics (IdA) with UEBA (user and entity behavior analytics).

The disquieting discovery gap of access in privileged access in IAM and privileged access management (PAM) solutions is closed by the fusing of IdA and UEBA capabilities. For a UEBA solution to monitor and analyze privileged account abuse, it first needs to know where privileged access resides, and this comes from IdA. Legacy methods of identifying privileged accounts with tags, prefixes or other traditional approaches, have resulted in missing more than 50% of privileged access, much of it having been granted over time at the entitlement level via privilege escalations.

Compatible with IAM/PAM solutions, identity analytics improves with the ability to ingest and analyze data from their varied environments (including hybrid) to deliver a risk-based solution for identity access management from the analytics made possible by integration with UEBA. IdA removes rubber stamping and access cloning, provides risk-based certifications, detects access outliers, cleans up access for dormant and orphan accounts, and reduces workload with dynamic access provisioning.

IdA is a major evolutionary phase for empowering IAM/PAM. The leading IdA solutions reside in a few best-of-breed UEBA vendors that provide identity analytics through machine learning models. The advantages of a UEBA-IdA solution adoption for reducing risk within an organization's environment continue to become apparent.

For example, as a first empowering step, an organization can drastically reduce its identity attack surface area before integrating a UEBA component of the solution that will detect behavior-based anomalies. Gurucul's best practices for predictive security analytics solution installation recommends a discovery and deactivation process (using IdA) of targeting all inactive, orphan or dormant accounts and misaligned or excess entitlements.

In one real-world Gurucul case, a financial institution implementing this process reduced their potential internal access risk plane of accounts and entitlements by 83%. They took their world of identity-based access risks and minimized them in one straightforward and comprehensive project step. Only the required users and entities that remained within the enterprise had up-to-date access permissions and entitlements. At this phase in the adoption of predictive security analytics, using IdA first, the planned implementation of UEBA was measurably streamlined and optimized.

From this point in a solution adoption, the ultimate goal for security and risk teams implementing IdA would be to maintain risk-based access only when, where and how it is appropriate, to the right individuals. Then the enterprise would have a more effective UEBA monitoring solution to look for the unknowns, the behavior anomalies that might indicate a compromise and a possible breach.

By leveraging a risk based approach, access is no longer defined or constrained by hard and fast static rules of access control. The evolving challenge remains how to continually improve controls on access and optimize comprehensive 360-degree monitoring. How do you reliably maintain the surface area of access?

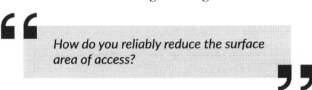

How do you reliably reduce the surface area of access?

One IdA solution component entails refining the context of access controls. For example, with someone working in a high tech R&D department, why might they need access to sensitive information while on vacation in Hawaii, unless they had indicated their plan to do so ahead of time? What kind of device might this engineer be attempting to access with? Is it out of the ordinary? This enhanced context insight into identity and access risk is empowered by IdA risk scoring. Making sure users and entities have access to assets only when and where they need it is a core mandate of IdA consolidated with UEBA. In the case with the engineer in Hawaii, their ad hoc access request would leverage risk scoring for approval.

With the implementation of IdA and UEBA — drawing from data science and machine learning, which supports the evolving and deep system knowledge behind every identity — the prospect of rapidly and confidently targeting access outliers and access risks on the identity risk plane becomes eminently more manageable.

Through baseline definitions built and defined for each identity, account, access and activity — analyzed against peer groups a 'living' persona of 'normal' is created to detect anomalies. It is performed through continuous self-learning and self-training machine learning models. This

> *With... IdA and UEBA – drawing from data science and machine learning, which supports the evolving and deep system knowledge behind every identity – the prospect of rapidly... targeting access outliers and access risks on the identity risk plane becomes eminently more manageable.*

comprehensive UEBA-IdA solution capability enables security teams to reliably spot privileged access risks, to proactively reduce access risks and monitor risk-scored behavior from a single view. This keeps access risks clean for the access rights provided, as well as providing monitoring for behavior-based anomalies and threats. The two sides work holistically together.

If a high-risk-scored behavior anomaly occurs, a SOC knows the exact details and avoids wasting time. For example: *what's* happening and *when* (e.g., an unusual volume of prioritized data is being accessed); *who* is performing it (actions that might be completely contrary to their user's identity use profile); *where* the action is taking place (which might be remote and unsanctioned); and *how*, on *what* device (an atypical one, which might also trip alerts).

A couple of practical use cases exemplify the utility, functionality, and value of a UEBA-IdA solution:

- A software development company needs to ensure an application developer has access to the production environment to do his work. The enterprise's leadership team is concerned that different developers with the same permissions can get into the same production environment and make changes in the code that are unwarranted or unsanctioned. IdA facilitates removing high-risk or shared access risks and provides intelligent roles for users based on the context of accounts, access and activity. Now controls are placed on particular files with risk-based access certifications on who can check them out.

- A company's payroll system contains sensitive information, and as a matter of course, issues can arise with its functionality. A help desk ticket is opened and the issue is forwarded to the support professional who is on call. By opening the ticket, the individual is requesting temporary access permission from a PAM system. IdA would validate the access is privileged when used and would provide a risk score on this access. As the support team member is given special access into the payroll system to work on resolving the issue, UEBA would monitor the identity, account, access and activity for abuse, compromise and anomalies during the workflow. When the support member has completed his work, he checks the ticket back in. With it, his access to the payroll system closes. The enterprise systems accessed by this support team member are only enabled in direct association with the help desk tickets he is assigned to and only for the period of the support action

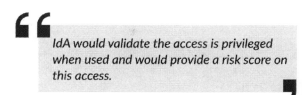

IdA would validate the access is privileged when used and would provide a risk score on this access.

response itself into which IdA and UBEA maintain full visibility.

None of this is possible unless an enterprise knows who the individual is, so that systematic assessments can be performed based what their defined roles are as well as the context of the activity by user. Clearly, modern enterprises represent a range of sizes and business models. As a result, they have different uses and requirements for UEBA and IdA.

In the following section, CIO Teri Takai shares her perspectives and insights from her broad range of experience in government and enterprises. They relate to how IdA and UEBA's predictive security analytics address the challenges of managing identity, access risks and access outliers in a broad range of emerging cloud and hybrid cloud network environments. Following this, we'll share additional observations on her insights about the Borderless Behavior Analytics story.

BORDERLESS EXPERT INSIGHTS

Teri Takai*
CIO at Large

Currently a Senior Advisor for the Center for Digital Government, Teri Takai recently served as the CIO and EVP of Meridian Health Plan. Prior to that, she served as the Department of Defense Chief Information Officer (DoD CIO). In this capacity, Ms. Takai was the principal advisor to the Secretary of Defense for Information Management/Information Technology and Information Assurance, as well as non-intelligence space systems, critical satellite communications, navigation, and timing programs, spectrum and telecommunications. She provided strategy, leadership and guidance, to create a unified information management and technology vision for the DoD. As Chief Information Officer for the State of California, she led more than 130 CIOs and 10,000 IT employees spread across the state's different agencies, departments, boards, commissions, and offices. Prior to these positions, she was a Director at the Ford Motor Company, serving the company for over thirty years.

A member of Gurucul's Executive Advisory Board, Ms. Takai has supplied instrumental support in the company's planning, development and strategy for the organization's solution development and market approach with a special focus on identity and access intelligence analytics and management. In this chapter she provides her expert insights on the challenges of identity access management with organizations facing the challenges of migrating from legacy environments into the cloud.

Overview

Identity is a new perimeter and threat plane that CIOs, CSOs and CISOs must address to reduce risk, protect resources and detect threats. Identity is a plane that intersects with virtually every data source within the IT infrastructure and its importance only increases with cloud adoption. Many organizations still rely on declarative legacy roles, rubber stamping certifications and manual processes to manage identities exposing them to excess access risks and access outliers. External threat actors compromise identities to evade detection from existing defenses while insiders work under the radar to access data for exfiltration. Analyzing access, activity and alerts with identity-centric behavior analytics provides a new defense for a new perimeter.

---

* The views and opinions expressed by Teri Takai in this book are her own, and do not necessarily reflect those of her current, or any of her previous employers.

Evolving perspectives on identity as a new perimeter

In the past, a first order of business for chief information officers was focused on protecting their data at the perimeter. Today, many continue with this traditional perspective and

> *It's quickly reaching the point... where it's impossible for organizations to keep up effectively with the threat vector.*

there are multiple ways of doing that. They have implemented new technologies in terms of next-generation firewalls, and other solutions designed to protect the perimeter, all of which remain a necessary part of the IT infrastructure. It's quickly reaching the point, however, where it's impossible for organizations to keep up effectively with the threat vector. CIOs, CSOs and CISOs must realize that a shift in thinking is in order to face the new challenges of what happens if someone is in their networks and how they then protect their data.

Recognizing a new reality of the perimeter. The second element of this new priority perspective is that as we migrate to the cloud, we're usually not taking our entire infrastructure to the cloud. Instead, organizations are using cloud providers that effectively support a particular area of the business but are nonetheless connected to their networks. That trend highlights this second vulnerability which is increasing and growing as it poses three crucial questions: What is the perimeter? What's protecting the perimeter? Is that protection effective?

> *What is the perimeter? What's protecting the perimeter? Is that protection effective?*

Risks posed by partners in the environment. The third priority involves the recognition that going forward, enterprises will need to engage with external partners on an expanding basis. While this trend is not new, its impact has become much more acute and the factors behind it are changing and evolving. Clearly, the notorious Target data breach of 2013 received a great deal of attention in headlines. However, it has not necessarily raised appropriate awareness of the serious security concerns behind that story. Many times in the past under legacy environment frameworks, partners engaged with file transfers. Now as use patterns move more towards APIs, and more active exchange ensues, this opens all the participating organizations to the vulnerabilities of all their partners.

The essentials of protecting the amorphous new perimeter. These new realities compel the security community to expand and reform their concept of what it really means to protect at the perimeter, which is continually changing. The essentials of this challenge boil down to two crucial certainties. The first point is that it's important for us to have tools that effectively show what is happening in our network. The second point says that relying on personnel to continue to manually monitor the networks is no longer a reliable security practice. The scope and volume of data, users, and systems is simply too vast. The only realistic approach now is to move into a machine learning

> *The only realistic approach now is to move into a machine learning environment where comprehensive visibility, monitoring and analytics can be set up, based on the behaviors observed and reliable effective alerts can be provided.*

environment where comprehensive visibility, monitoring and analytics can be set up, based on the behaviors observed and reliable effective alerts can be provided.

Insider risk, the hidden time bomb

The next element of delivering network security assurance centers on having a clear understanding of what constitutes the insider risk. This subject has been the topic of paramount concern in government circles, especially the Department of Defense (DoD) at the time the WikiLeaks challenge occurred. This was exacerbated by the 2013 Edward Snowden incident. What's critical to understand is that these cases did not necessarily involve threat actors who planned to do intentional harm. However, this is the way many traditional enterprise SOCs think of and approach the problem.

> *...these cases did not necessarily involve threat actors who planned to do intentional harm. However, this is the way many traditional enterprise SOCs think of and approach the problem.*

Unintentional bad behavior remains a serious risk. With the workforce changing, and being accustomed to having access to all types of information, it becomes increasingly difficult to ensure secure data. In many cases the insider risk turns out to be unintentional. Numerous organizations, including my own experience in state jobs, at the DoD, and also at a health care company I worked for, was to run drills to show people what would happen when they inadvertently clicked on links in emails they shouldn't have clicked on.

Valid and compromised identities represent risk. Identity is clearly a new perimeter. While compromises and breaches are not always driven by malicious motivations, they still represent a threat plane of serious risk for any organization. Security leaders should keep this in mind when planning the next generation of security assurance in their networks.

IAM controls access

Identity and access management (IAM) has been the main focus to control access, but traditional approaches no longer address the security demands of today's sprawling perimeters. A key requirement is to assure organizations have the analytics in place to be able to understand what activity is occurring in the network for the access granted. To achieve this, security leaders need to know about both what the next generation of identity is, as well as the next generation of identity management controls.

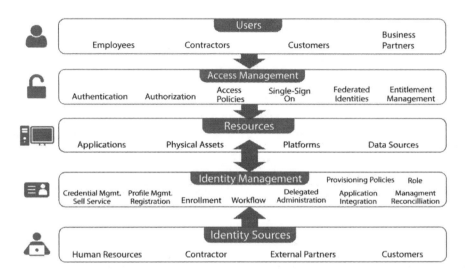

IAM Controls Access
Figure 4.1

Traditional identity management's increasing challenges. The illustration above depicts the identity and access management issues in greater detail. At the top, the user base itself represents a range of different issues and challenges with employees versus contractors, versus customers and business partners. Historically, in addition to protecting at the perimeter, IT teams tried to control access with access management policies through identity management solutions.

New complexities compound the difficulties. The security assurance problem is more clearly illustrated when you examine the details in the access management box. It calls out a range of security access processes. In the box above are the different resources, such as various applications and platforms. All of these come with an accompanying array of complexity. Network experts

...in the final analysis, all that manual control is prone to serious error.

logically ask, "How do you actually do that?" Managing this through provisioning, policies, registrations, and so on, can only be achieved if organizations commit a significant amount of headcount to manually control all that access. Yet in the final analysis, all that manual control is prone to serious error.

The urgency of recognizing new requirements in security. When one considers the number of applications, the number of legacy applications, as well as the systems administration rights — and the difficulty with being able to administer all of that across the numerous users and the various identity sources — it quickly becomes clear this requirement for reliable network access security can only be achieved with robust analytic support and machine learning. Recognizing the need to respond and adapt to this profound growth in network access risk is critical for the CIO's and CISO's organizational survival and success.

Data expansion in modern networks

Data continues to expand with increasing velocity and variety. This is the challenging new normal facing CIOs, CSOs and CISOs. IDC Research (International Data Corporation) observes that data is growing so quickly that it will reach 44 zettabytes by 2020. And an interesting fact conveyed from the recent PBS special — *The Human Face of Big Data* — cites that humanity ingested the same volume of data in their lifetimes during the 16th century as they would in two days of modern times. However, there's an important extension to these observations which impacts network security today.

Legacy systems facing evolving technologies. Even as one views the technologies of 2013, security experts recognize that a majority of legacy systems, both from government and commercial sectors, date back well before 2013. While it's interesting to look at the 16th century, the pertinent exercise is to view the mid-1900's, which provided the framework of thinking where so many of these legacy systems originated. The network architects' priorities at the time were all focused on mainframe, file transfers and controlled access to data. They could in no way anticipate, or account for, the sophisticated access and staggering data volume that IT organizations face today. They never conceived of their networks being accessed by the general public or by someone in a different geographical area. When you correlate that infrastructure model with the way data are growing, it clearly indicates there must be a new and different approach to how we're protecting that data.

> **"** The network architects... could in no way anticipate, or account for, the sophisticated access and staggering data volume that IT organizations face today. **"**

Government priority on revamping security. Today there's a great deal of focus in the federal government on what to do about securing legacy systems. The Federal

CIO, Tony Scott, has put a great deal of attention on the renovation of those legacy systems to ensure they are secure. Anyone can sign up for *Federal Computer Week's* daily email (https://fcw.com/). There, you can see the government's approach regarding how they protect their systems and how they achieve that with the old legacy systems still occupying a sizable footprint in network technology.

Data + Access = Threat Surface

When engaging in next-generation thinking beyond the constraints of traditional legacy environment perspectives, security leaders need to recognize the new challenges posed by identity. The first element is the existence of the insider risk. The second involves external partners who need to access an organization's data, in turn creating access outliers that may or may not be known by the system owner. The third component addresses the challenge of being able to keep up with this onslaught of data on-demand, to see, or allow others to see, the data safely and effectively to run the business. The complexity of these challenges centers on a pure and all-encompassing access management framework. Data and access are linked, opening up the surface area for access risks centered on these essential points:

- Compromise and misuse of identity is at the root of modern threats.
- Identity is also a perimeter with excess access risks and access outliers.
- Security cannot be assured unless organizations know: who has access, when was the access, and whether the identity should have access.

Complex access management requirements. While organizations must provide the access to whoever needs it, when they need it, as well as the level of access required, they also need to be able take it away whenever necessary. This is a key point. People within a company may be moving to other positions within the organization, and in doing so, no longer need particular access rights. Those unrequired (and fundamentally unsupervised by the original owner) access identities accumulate within an organization; the risk associated with each one grows as well. Access management policies and processes must be quicker to respond, to close the gap between what access is really needed and what organizations are continuing to allow reflexively.

Accelerating access complexities. Here's a case in point regarding the challenges managing access entitlements: Workforces have different access needs, at different times, plus levels of data management expertise. Identity aggregates multiple accounts and entitlements per user or entity. So if an organization had *1000* users with *10* accounts each, that would equal *10,000* credentials to manage. Then add in *10* permissions per account and that would equal *100,000* entitlements to manage. That's a considerable access risk and threat surface area.

Realistic controls on access required. This example, while seemingly dramatic, actually represents a reality within organizations. It encourages security leaders to step back and think about the number of users in a company, think about what these users (and entities) need access to, and even within that, what permissions they need. This highlights the challenge of how an organization actually manages that, and how that organization realistically controls what individuals have access to.

The consequences of failed access management

Organizations and their workforces face growing threats through breaches of their identities. Hijacked accounts enable intruders with full access rights of the employee. Security leaders

> *Security leaders must now assume that external actors are in their infrastructure. This urgently reinforces their prime mandate: protect your data.*

must now assume that external actors are in their infrastructure. This urgently reinforces their prime mandate: protect your data.

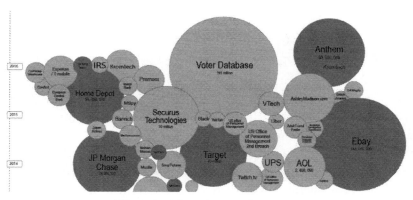

The World's Biggest Data Breaches
2014 to Mid-2016
(Source: http://www.informationisbeautiful.net/)
Figure 4.2

Breach trends growing. The illustration above provides a vivid example of how widespread data breaches have been over the last two years and the magnitude of the damage. While many are probably known to the majority of readers, seeing the range of impact within a correlating context is instructive. These breach trends are becoming far more visible to the senior management of organizations, up to the

> *...many organizations just feel overwhelmed and they don't really know what it takes to ensure they have the best security possible.*

board level. A problem, however, is that many organizations just feel overwhelmed and they don't really know what it takes to ensure they have the best security possible. This is a growing issue where the government may need to expand control and requirements of standards for disclosure. As well, there are contributing factors to these breach trends that security leaders should keep in mind.

Training is insufficient. Training is no longer adequate to address identity threats and account hijacking. As it relates to the insider risk and the insider management, while virtually every company does training and periodic drills, it's insufficient. We now live in a world, depending on the particular demographics of any company, where people are just used to being able to click on things and feel secure to do so. Attackers today are devising ingenious ways to encourage people to believe their email link is legitimate. It is highly unlikely that anyone reading this has never clicked on something at least once that they shouldn't have. So the takeaway is that it doesn't mean there shouldn't be training, but training alone will not deal with the dimension and the size of the problem.

Workforces change constantly. New hires, departures, part-time and remote workers are part of the constant ebb and flow of the modern workplace. These new, departing and terminated employees are high risk groups who require special focused analysis. In addition, high privileged access (HPA) accounts are also a high-risk group often with accompanying account sharing which compounds the risk element. Another element of the emerging workforce transformation that organizations are contending with is the use of a growing number of contract resources, some of whom may work remotely. While that contract resource may come in for days, weeks, months, or ultimately become a permanent part of the enterprise, the organization remains dependent upon whoever they have contracted, to ensure the access to the network is secure. This is a characteristic of the new gig economy, where more and more people will be serving for short-term engagements, and the trend will likely only increase over time. Moreover, access to the network often doesn't end with the end of the engagement. This may be unintentional, but the risk of this open access is real.

Unchecked expansion of a range of access. As organizations move into engaging that kind of broad range of individuals, while still maintaining a core employee workforce, it becomes increasingly more difficult to control access through our existing identity management solutions. If you consider the scenario mentioned earlier that resulted with a hundred thousand entitlements, think how that will change on a daily basis. It fully exacerbates the problem to the point where it is fundamentally uncontrollable.

The importance of detecting access risk or access outliers

If they haven't already, CIOs must realize that they will be breached. It's just a question of when, and how badly. In August of 2016, *IT Security Guru* cited a survey which reported that, "65% of IT leaders expect a serious data breach to hit their business within the next year." This is a frightening statistic. Whether that's on purpose,

> If they haven't already, CIOs must come to the realization that they will be breached. It's just a question of when, and how badly.

whether it's inadvertent, regardless of where it comes from, there will be individuals accessing information in networks who shouldn't. Particularly with the insider threat, that's an important concept for all security leaders to keep in mind.

The criteria of visibility. Once CIOs acknowledge the inevitability of a breach of some magnitude, it then becomes critical to ensure comprehensive visibility. This entails first being able to set ground rules around what SOCs want visibility of, then to have visibility of it. After this, and most importantly, they must have the machine learning capability to continually iterate on the data and context to facilitate threat and risk analysis, recognition and response.

The balance between human requirements and efficiencies. With these visibility objectives in mind, here's an example of the challenges many CIOs face with selecting and integrating new solutions into the security mix. In this case it relates to solutions we were considering at the Department of Defense. Many of the early user behavioral analytics tools required a significant amount of analytic time from individuals looking at data in order to detect the anomalies from false positives. We decided it was prohibitive to even think about implementing the tool, not because of the tool's cost, but because we couldn't afford the manpower to do the analyses with the tool.

Enhanced efficiencies with next generation UEBA. With the next generation of UEBA tools, the human resource requirement is changing. CIOs don't need the same levels of staff or high analytic expertise as before. A majority of the analysis can be done using the tool that will learn from itself. These advancements are exactly the advantages we were seeking at the Department of Defense. Unfortunately, they did not yet exist in a robust, mature and reliable form. However, the older generation of UEBA tools, which lack the efficiencies of real machine learning, are still also available on the market. Organizations must exercise prudence when considering an adoption of this kind.

> With the next generation of UEBA tools, the human resource requirement is all changing. CIOs don't need the same levels of staff or high analytic expertise as before.

The impact of cloud applications on IAM

Simply put, cloud applications change identity management dramatically. During my Ford Motor Company experience, one of the initiatives Ford performed over time, was to build our own very large application systems. We put in what we felt were very sophisticated identity management and access management solutions. These were ultimately linked to active directory and a common email.

Yesterday's environments working with tomorrow's solutions. Now CIOs are faced with two challenges. The first is they want to supplement their homegrown systems with a software as a service solution (SaaS), for example, a CRM (customer relationship management) tool, which sits outside the original network perimeter. The second is that the control and configuration of SaaS solutions are different. The CIO's desire is to integrate one of those CRM tools into the legacy systems that have information necessary to manage the customer. The current access management and identity management schemes, however, don't provide the control needed to ensure comprehensive security.

A multitude of access points. To begin with, the advent of cloud applications means CIOs are dealing with more than one access management approach. For one particular data access scenario, users must come through the SaaS provider, then they have to go to legacy data, or the legacy application identity management solution. That means it becomes increasingly difficult to accurately control that access and assess risk. Within this rising complexity, CIOs must be able to both control access and monitor the access in near real-time, to see where the anomalies are. That is why a tool like a mature UEBA solution integrated with identity analytics (IdA) is so important as a supplement to today's access management capabilities.

Visibility across the IT and SOC domains of responsibility. UBEA with IdA provides a holistic perspective addressing access risks and detecting unknown threats. Historically, CIOs might not have seen it that way, where the IT side of an organization would be responsible for access, while the security side looked for threats. In too many cases in the past, however, both sides considered them to be completely separate priorities. In doing so, they might have been missing a critical access risk aspect of the identity threat plane.

An old problem with new insights. While everyone's heard more about Target than they've cared to, there's still another angle to consider with this case. It's remarkable that there are organization leaders who don't understand the organized crime threat and how identity has been leveraged for malicious ends. They don't see that their data might represent an identity management access threat or a privacy concern. These adversaries have become

It's not just a national security threat anymore, it's become big business.

sophisticated in terms of being able to piece data together from different sources to produce lucrative results. It's not just a national security threat anymore, it's become big business. Organizations face a new form of competition, which is ruthless, unethical and targeted on the crown jewels of the enterprise: their data.

Surpassing IAM capabilities

With this evolving rich complexity of identities and access privileges, the ability to holistically control access through IAM has passed. Traditional declarative roles and groups lack the flexibility for today's needs. Active directory (AD) and other directories often have access conglomeration and group proliferation.

With this evolving rich complexity of identities and access privileges, the ability to holistically control access through IAM has passed.

IAM challenges include:
- Dealing with multiple identities
- Dealing with multiple accounts
- Managing many manual tasks
- Coping with ill-defined business processes
- Expectation to make the IAM a data synchronization engine for application data
- Getting all stakeholders to share a common view of solution objectives, priorities and responsibilities
- Lack of leadership and support from sponsors
- Deploying too many siloed IAM technologies in a short period of time
- Lack of consistent architectural vision

Manual management of identity is outdated. Any of the bullet points above represent a checklist of its own. There could be paragraphs of insight around what each means and why it exacerbates the identity management issue. But in summation, taking all of these factors into account, the idea of being able to deal manually with the multiple identities, accounts and access entitlements becomes virtually impossible. The only logical deduction you can arrive at is that a new approach is required.

Symptoms of struggling identity management

The first symptom that companies are struggling with identity management is rooted in the fact that a large number of organizations have an enterprise architecture that has become outdated, obsolete. Consequently, the value and utility identity management solutions deliver vary based on when they were adopted and their suitability to the context of today's environments. In addition, they are different at the platform level as well. As a result, the ability to standardize how an organization performs pure system administration at the platform level becomes a serious challenge.

Status quo equals status 'no'. Technology does not sleep, and of course, security leaders must keep their eye on an evolving market and the next generation of identity management. Hoping the current legacy identity management solutions will continue to serve an organization is unfortunately only a strategy encouraging eventual compromise and breaches which will likely be discovered only months later. This scenario benefits no one, including those on the IT staff.

> *Hoping the current legacy identity management solutions will continue to serve an organization is... only a strategy encouraging eventual compromise and breaches...*

Evolving technologies and growing challenges. Another symptom of struggling identity management is at the application level. CIOs remain hard-pressed to control the way applications are rolled out to ensure they have consistency of identity management across all their solutions. Add into this rich mix in the environment the newer technologies needing to drive through APIs along with enterprises wanting to accommodate external customers and business partners. These are all areas where these problems have grown significantly and they represent a major challenge for the CIO.

Accurate visibility of risk plane restricted by traditional tools. Too many elements of the hybrid environment are nebulous and changing quickly so that it is not humanly possible to manage them all. The resource cost is prohibitive. As a result, it is equally challenging for any CIO or CISO to be expected to know exactly what their identity access risk and threat plane is from the view available through traditional legacy access management. When you add to that the desire for businesses to have more control over who has access, where it's actually out of the hands of the CIO, the imperative to have a different perspective on this entire mounting problem becomes even more critical.

New solutions should support existing solutions. One key point to keep in mind, however, is this new perspective is not about replacing the identity management solutions organizations have today. There's nothing wrong with them within their functional context. They still service a crucial part of the environment. They just lack the comprehensiveness to close the awareness gap of what access has been provided and how the access is being utilized. They need to go to the next generation. However, until that next generation of identity management is fully developed and mature, which in many cases means replacing aging legacy systems, organizations need to supplement the system with identity analytics driven by machine learning. This means security leaders should have different tools and different approaches which deal with the access environment the CIO has today to be able to move forward successfully. Any mature

UEBA solution with identity analytics fills an awareness gap as an integrated part of the tool suite. It offers a risk-based approach of identity access management for organizations that was not originally provided by their solution framework.

How do CIOs and CISOs achieve security assurance? The pressing questions for CIOs and CISOs are: How do they get to where they are confident their long-term security decisions are risk-based? How do they use the right identity analytics to reduce excess access and access outliers, along with user and entity behavior analytics solutions to detect unknown threats, beyond rules, signatures and patterns? In this rapidly evolving world, most are recognizing they can't do it alone. Before, they only had to identify and manage the red and green — the bad and the good activities. Now they must also manage and monitor the massive amount of gray — the unknown unknowns — in their environments.

> Before, they only had to identify and manage the red and green – the bad and the good activities. Now they must also manage and monitor the massive amount of gray – the unknown unknowns – in their environments.

Partnering with solution providers who 'Get it'

Facing the imperative to implement productive change to ensure network security, CIOs and CISOs face a range of solution vendors. Many are quick to point out what's wrong with the CISOs' environments and what needs to be changed or replaced. More mature solution vendors approach this prospect and discussion from more of a partnership perspective that communicates, "Yes, in fact you have a problem with your legacy systems, but we understand replacing them is a long, lengthy and ugly process. Until you can replace them, how are you going to be able to understand who's accessing those systems, how they're being accessed and who's actually utilizing the information? We have that experience and customers who can verify that. We can help you." What this means is the solution must supplement, and perhaps modify the access security strategy, not replace it. These solution providers must be able to complement the current protection of the identity perimeter, and protection of the data, and delivering the ability to see who actually is accessing the data.

> What this means is the solution must supplement, and perhaps modify the network security strategy, not replace it.

Ease of use after adoption. When considering these security solutions, CIOs should also take into account their workforce's productivity. While some CISOs may believe they are adopting a technology that secures and manages access, if it is too painstaking to work with, it will result in employee frustration. Some of the workforce may even try to find a way to skirt the new system to make their jobs easier. This creates a new access risk and threat plane. Adopting organizations and solution vendors must take these factors into account together to assure the solution is one that can be institutionalized and supported over the long term by all involved. Lack of support will likely lead to solution failure.

Final perspectives on identity management and UEBA providing identity analytics

With the title of this book being *Borderless Behavior Analytics – Who's Inside? What're They Doing?*, the intended message is targeted at organization leaders and security professionals who do not necessarily see identity analytics and user and entity behavior analytics as being involved holistically to address access risks and unknown threats. Security teams often focus on detection and response within SOCs. However, if the identity access plane is loaded with excess access, access outliers and over-provisioned from years of rubber stamping certifications and access cloning, the reduction of these access risks is paramount to the success of the SOC mission. Add in industry's adoption of cloud technologies and we face a hybrid environment where identity is the attack vector. With this realization comes the recognition there is no longer a perimeter, there is no border. To achieve holistic security in this borderless environment, today's SOCs must now look at identities from the access risk side, the threat side, and integrate everything together for a risk-based approach to be predictive and eventually prescriptive in response.

Fundamental security objectives remain the same. With this recognition of a need for transformation, certain traditional security priorities and methods do not change. This means don't throw out what you have. For example, the firewall is important, but it must compliment the solution array to the point where it achieves the seamless and holistic coverage made possible by mature UEBA, identity analytics and machine learning. This is not a substitute for what CIOs are doing today. It's an augmentation that addresses a need that exists because of the evolving state of an organization's infrastructure and applications.

Patterns of complexity will grow. This insight also includes the acknowledgment that things are going in and out of environments much more often, as opposed to in the past, and this pattern will only continue to increase. It's almost impossible today to find an organization with zero cloud access. There would be some application hosted online, whether it's Salesforce.com, Box, Dropbox, an FTP server, or any of the document sharing facilities. Their presence in an organization all fortify the view that change is inevitable, and required, and stakeholders in this world must pay attention to this trend and its implications.

The new normal. While security leaders are continually trying to implement improvements, they are simultaneously and constantly being barraged by the technology landscape. They're constantly required to make those adjustments to that reality. Given their constrained resources, and the rapid pace of technology evolution, there's only so much they can do to protect their environments with status quo thinking. They *will* be breached. It's only a question of time and magnitude. There is access in their networks they don't know about. The question remains: What tool will they use to supplement what they have today, to be able to know what they control and who's in their network?

> There is access in their networks that they don't know about.

Essentials of identity analytics for identity management. The first priority is closing the awareness gap to understand who is in your network, what their access entitlements are and their associated activity accessing data and applications at any point in time. This awareness gap has been a serious challenge for IAM solutions. The second priority is for the user and entity behavior analytics component to have the ability to establish baselines via machine learning. They must then highlight anomalies with risk scoring, enabling a SOC team to inspect and potentially take remedial action.

Targeted and granular risk scoring capability. A popular use case is using UEBA to analyze privileged access abuse. However, you need identity analytics to learn and locate privileged access first as legacy methods to track privileged access are ineffective. Too often the status quo is at the account level using naming prefixes, tags or an access management solution that reports on what has been recorded. It is not uncommon for identity analytics to find 50% or more of unknown or hidden privileged access. They are frequently entitlements that have escalated to privileged access within standard accounts. For UEBA to be effective for privileged access abuse as a use case, it requires identity analytics to locate privileged access accounts and entitlements. The new mandate is risk scoring down to the entitlement level. This is a perfect task for machine learning and a futile one for humans.

Suitability of UEBA solutions and ranges of maturity. The requirements for sound identity management today are profoundly complex. Any identity management solution that has not incorporated identity analytics along with user and entity behavior analytics, and machine learning, into its security strategy is at a disadvantage. Expect partnerships between leading IAM and PAM solution vendors and UEBA solutions with identity

> Expect partnerships between leading IAM and PAM solution vendors and UEBA solutions with identity analytics to close the awareness gap... and discovery gap...

analytics to close the awareness gap between access and activity and discovery gap to locate unknown privileged access, migrating to a risk-based approach for identity access management. This enables risk-based certifications, detection of excess access, access outliers, cleanup of access for dormant and orphan accounts, and reduced workloads with dynamic access provisioning. In addition, intelligent roles replace legacy roles with reduced risk and more accuracy for users and peers.

The security leader's mandate. CIOs, CSOs and CISOs need to keep doing what they're doing, to be aware of where new developments exist, where innovation is going, with the realities of their organizations continuing to expand their world into the cloud. In addition, as business partners get savvier, they will want organizations to open up data in different ways than ever before. Through all this, security leaders must be aware of where the industry's going in terms of next-generation identity management and how IdA and UEBA augments confronting the challenge of identity as a new perimeter and attack vector.

CONCLUSIONS & TAKEAWAYS:
Critical strategies for filling the gaps in security through identity analytics

To reduce risk, protect resources and detect threats CIOs, CSOs and CISOs must recognize identity as a new perimeter, access risk and threat plane, a borderless perimeter. Insider threats, partners, customers, devices, entities and applications must be accounted for in evolving identity management strategies. CIO at Large Teri Takai shares the essentials of protecting this continually changing amorphous new perimeter. Addressing this challenge boils down to two essential points: 1) it's critical to have tools to effectively monitor activity in the network; 2) relying on personnel to continue to manually monitor the networks is no longer a reliable security practice. The scope and volume of data, users, and systems is simply too vast for human management. Within this challenge lurks the insider risk. Here, unintentional, as well as valid and compromised identities, all represent serious risk. Traditional IAM, as the conventional focus of access control strategies, no longer addresses the security demands of today's sprawling perimeters. Takai observes that security leaders must understand this next generation of identity and employ a new generation of identity management controls. Without that, the perimeter will continue to expand in unmanageable complexity, resulting in an even broader access risk plane of alarming magnitude.

As data and the multitude of access points expand in modern environments with increasing velocity and variety, identity is the singular plane that intersects with virtually every data source within the IT infrastructure. Its importance only increases with cloud adoption. *Data + Access = Threat Surface.* As workforces change constantly and the unchecked expansion of a range of access increases with no prospect of abatement, the importance of detecting access risks and access outliers resonates with increasing urgency. Privileged access abuse stands at the top of this hierarchy of unaddressed risks, where over 50% of organizations' privileged access risks are unaccounted for. One cause of this discovery gap in unknown privileged access risks is there are far too many entitlements for humans to manage or assess.

Realistic, robust and effective controls on access are required. Core requirements include comprehensive visibility across the hybrid environment into access and behavior. With the overwhelming volume of data, this has only been possible recently with advanced machine learning drawing from big data. With the advent of widespread cloud adoptions there is no other realistic option to manage risk effectively. Threats can no longer be considered the work of individual attackers. It has become big business, and the strategic objective of nation states. External threat actors compromise identities to evade detection from existing defenses while insiders work under the radar to access data for exfiltration. Analyzing accounts, access, activity and alerts with identity-centric behavior analytics provides a reliable new defense for an emerging amorphous perimeter. With these advanced predictive security analytics solutions in place, using risk-based analytics, organizations are more effectively able to provide the right level of access to whoever needs it, when they need it, and maintain the capability of taking it away whenever necessary.

All of the preceding chapters have led up to and supported the realization that we need a new approach in security, managing identity, and detecting unknown threats. The next chapter will explore security innovation in greater detail, along with the key drivers behind that imperative. The next *Borderless Breach Flashcard* highlights an instance in the growing trend of potential insider threats and the seismic impact these risks pose to organizations.

BORDERLESS BREACH FLASHCARD *For Sale: Keys to the Kingdom*	
CATEGORY	Hacktivism by a suspected NSA insider, or an alleged Russian operation.
WHO	**The target:** National Security Agency (NSA).
WHAT	The NSA's super-secret hacking tools appeared on an online digital auction, with samples of classified NSA documents, and were offered for sale to the highest bidder.
WHEN	2013
WHERE	Onsite or possibly cyberspace: Suspected NSA insider breach, while allegations of Russian espionage persist.
WHY	Political activism, economic gain, or alleged espionage.
HOW	In August 2016, a group calling themselves the Shadow Brokers stated that they possessed a "full state-sponsored toolset" of "cyberweapons," designed to break into computer systems and networks, and offered them online for auction via Bitcoin bid. A number of sample classified NSA files released by the group were deemed authentic by ex-NSA members of the agency's Tailored Access Operations (TAO), their elite hacking unit. The logical route for this exfiltration would be either through misuse or highjacking of insider credentials for high privileged access (HPA). While accusations of Russian involvement have been voiced, expert opinions refute that. They observed the logical likelihood of insider involvement, with the files dating back to five months after the Snowden breach and his escape to Hong Kong.
HOW BAD?	The damage includes the potential compromise of this cyber toolset, as well as a loss of confidence in the NSA's own security capabilities. More concerning is if the toolset was acquired by malicious actors. As long as the flaws that the toolset exploits remain unpatched, it enables attackers from anywhere around the world to gain access to countless critical computers to steal data, plant malware and cause chaos.
HOW COULD IT BE AVOIDED?	Alerted to the possibility of additional Snowden-like breaches, if the NSA had a mature UEBA-IdA solution in place, HPA account anomalous behavior would have likely identified unusual downloads of highly classified sensitive intellectual property. This would have enabled them to deny access and identify the threat actors.

We Need a New Approach:
Key Drivers

Recognizing a time of change is at hand

How do you recognize innovations in security that can advance your objectives and mission?

The annual *Data Breach Investigations Report* (DBIR) from Verizon is a much-anticipated release of critical findings for the security community. It's comprehensive, analytical and a bible of insights for security leaders to help them to understand their evolving worlds, to recognize new emerging areas of concern, and to help map the road ahead of them. They use this independent data to reference when developing their strategies going forward, and to have the metrics for known risk when proposing new security initiatives for their environments to management. Constructive change begins with one voice articulating the challenges at hand to management, accompanied by the severity of the problem, the solution options, the assessment of which solution is the best, along with the costs and logistics required to implement that solution.

The recent 2016 DBIR report (the ninth year of its issuance) shared the latest trends which highlights the importance of identity as a threat plane. The percentage of data breaches breaks down to 83% external actors and 17% insiders. This has remained consistent over the past three years. Insider threats are relevant and not going away soon. But there's more. A new trend in the financial services sector with Web App attacks involves credential compromise to commit financial fraud. It ranks at 82% where it was 31% the previous year. For threat action types, phishing leads the pack along with hacking, malware and social media as the primary methods of attack.

Hacking with stolen credentials ranks #2 next to malware for command-and-control (C2) communications (#1) and malware to export data (#3). What does this mean? We have financially motivated external threat actors using phishing attacks to steal credentials to install malware for C2 and data export. The burning question this brings to thoughtful security leaders is whether they focus on the polymorphic response for every changing malware, or, whether they focus on the account compromise and hijacking. If there are blind spots for access risks and identity misuse or compromise, how can they be detected?

> *If there are blind spots for access risks and identity misuse or compromise, how can they be detected?*

A number of industry leaders have observed the concerning number of privileged access instances which reside outside organizations' identity and access management solutions' purview. Gurucul's Craig Cooper, Chief Operating Officer is one of them: "Most Fortune 500 companies have more privileged access outside the vault than inside." That means those privileged access entitlements are unaccounted for, off the radar screen. That's a serious threat plane. Meanwhile, many organizations still rely on manual methods to manage privilege accounts and credentials through IT, without any coordination with SOCs. A number of accounts still have default passwords, and most organizations lack an approval process to create privileged accounts. Some security leaders are asking if they can live with these risks given identity is the new attack vector and the most valuable accounts to compromise are privileged. Others already know the answer to that question, and are actively seeking the solutions to a problem that is only getting more complex and acute over time.

The complexity and density of today's hybrid environments has grown beyond queries, filters and pivots to search for threats. With no current and future-proof security strategies in place to understand exactly who is in your network, and what their access entitlements are, how can there be any semblance of a prudent security policy in place? A number of solutions already in place should be assessed. Many IAM (identity and access management) and PAM (privileged access management) now need predictive security analytics support to maintain secure management of access. They can't do it alone anymore.

Returning to the *DBIR*, the statistics are discouraging:

- Time to compromise is getting faster due to phishing, credentials compromise and quick installation of malware for C2 and data export — all achieved in a matter of minutes.
- Time to detection is slightly better, but still remains a matter of months, and dwell time persists as a large time gap.

- Phishing effectiveness continues with 30% of recipients opening phishing emails, 12% clicking, and the median time for a first user to open was 1 min 40 secs, while the median time for the first click was 3 mins 45 secs.
- Only 3% of targeted individuals reported phishing emails.
- 63% of confirmed data breaches involved weak, default or stolen passwords.
- Privilege misuse ranked #2 for reported incidents and #4 for reported data breaches.
- Miscellaneous errors and privilege misuse are the two highest frequency items for incident classification.
- Stolen or default credentials are key to POS (Point of Sale) attacks where 97% data breaches featuring stolen credentials leverage legitimate partner access.
- POS vendors are a key target to then attack their customers using stolen credentials.

What does this mean? Humans click, passwords fail, time to infection is minutes, while detection takes months. Detecting account compromise, hijacking and misuse from an identity-based behavior perspective changes the game for defenses. New gray areas exist. It's no longer just good or bad. There are good people with inadvertent actions and misunderstood behaviors. While training is helpful to face the challenge, it is inadequate to resolve the overall problem. The goal for CISOs is to move to the front of the kill chain, to detect compromise, versus confirming the data was stolen at the end of the kill *New gray areas exist. It's no longer just good or bad. There are good people with inadvertent actions and misunderstood behaviors.* chain. Clearly there is a need for security innovation.

While a number of CISOs and CIOs have indeed recognized the sea change for security defenses and processes — a transformation is at hand — some nonetheless remain committed to the status quo of legacy perimeter defenses for various reasons. Our expert contributor Robert Rodriguez, founder and president of SINET, has hosted the annual SINET 16 Innovation Awards, which enlists a panel of CISO judges to select the top security innovations each year. Drawing from his vast range of first-hand experience in both the public and private sectors with the challenges of information security, Rodriguez shares his seasoned insights on security innovations and the context for user and entity behavior analytics and identity analytics. His observations include the influences behind solution adoption and the future of innovation in the cyber security industry.

BORDERLESS EXPERT INSIGHTS

Robert D. Rodriguez*
Chairman/Founder, SINET

Robert D. Rodriguez is Chairman and Founder of the Security Innovation Network™ (SINET) — an international community builder whose mission is to advance innovation and enable global collaboration between the public and private sectors to defeat cyber security threats. SINET connects the ecosystems of the entrepreneur, academia, science, private industry, investment banking, system integration, policy, innovators, venture capital and the federal government to include the civilian, military and intelligence agencies. After serving 22 years as a Special Agent with the United States Secret Service, Robert retired. He currently serves on the Board of Advisors for The Chertoff Group, as Director Emeritus for the San Francisco Kraft Fight Hunger Bowl and the National Cyber Security Hall of Fame Board of Directors.

A member of Gurucul's Executive Advisory Board, Robert has provided invaluable consultation in the company's journey through its dynamic growth and evolution of predictive security analytics. He lends his qualified insights into the innovations and developments in cyber security along with behavior analytics' invested future in it.

Overview

In this module, Rodriguez observes the recent trends in cyber security and the impact of hybrid cloud adoption on cyber security requirements. As a solution element of these challenges, he observes past behavior's predictive utility in identifying future anomalies. This solution factor is most effectively incorporated when the realities of establishing and managing identity in the environment are optimized. Strategies for managing excess access are also discussed. Program trends for insider threat detection are examined as it is weighted against the challenges of balancing the human effort against the critical mass of growing data. Rodriguez also shares his insights on the solution optimization trends targeting today's security gaps. Rodriguez provides his analysis on why advancements in cyber security are incremental and lack dynamic innovation. He concludes with his perspectives on private companies' partnership with government agencies and behavior analytics' place in that relationship.

Recent trends in cyber security

Since 2011, we've seen CISOs sharing more information than ever before. They're collaborating with a spirit of partnership in their own trusted communication channels and environments. The focus on the importance of holistic enterprise risk, versus compartmentalized risk, has been part of that dialog. Boards of directors and CISOs are having constant communication. If cyber security is not number one, it's in the top three priorities of every board of directors meeting.

CISOs with multiple strengths in demand. These CISOs have moved from being primarily a technical leader, to an executive leader role, able to articulate to the executive management team, along with the CEO and board of directors, the issues and priorities relative to cyber. Compensation and demand for talented and qualified CISOs has grown markedly. The job shortage has also increased. Instead of filling these important roles, we're seeing larger gaps and voids because of the lack of qualified talent.

Research and investments on the rise. The research and development community, the academic community, and the grant opportunities on cyber security, have all increased significantly over the last five years. The dynamics of mergers and acquisitions has also grown significantly. In addition, the amount of venture capital for the last five years has risen to massive amounts. Many changes have taken place over the last five to ten years, even from the policies perspective.

Government's priority focus on cyber security. Part of the policy evolution and change includes the national framework we now have, with the creation of the White House's role of Cybersecurity Coordinator in 2009, and Michael Daniels currently holding that post. The numerous information sharing bills, the security versus privacy bills on Capitol Hill, and the debate of cyber security versus privacy — Apple vs. FBI — are part of the security industry's response to the changing face of cyber security in the world today.

Data overload in today's environments. The amount of data overload is staggering, crippling some organizations. The bottom line is we simply can't afford not to have innovative solutions address this challenge. It's impossible to keep up with the deluge of data. Imagine all the military drones sending photographs of rocks in the middle of the deserts of the Middle East, to the analysts — millions and millions of photos. Which one do they pay attention to? The technology needs to be able to say, "This rock moved, and that's the one we need to focus on and prioritize."

A haystack of needles. The same circumstances of overwhelming data are true with present-day cyber security in hybrid cloud environments. We've moved from finding the needle in the haystack, to finding the needle in the haystack of needles, and then prioritizing and making that information actionable.

> *We've moved from finding the needle in the haystack, to finding the needle in the haystack of needles...*

Enduring importance of insider threat. Regarding insider threat, during my tenure with the Secret Service, studies were done in 1999 through 2002. *CSO* magazine and the Secret Service collaborated, interviewing chief security officers to understand the emerging threat plane. Insider threats were the chief concern. It's still either number one, or at the very least, in the top three today, and it's not going away. From the malicious component to the non-malicious, mistakes by people just trying to do their jobs, insider threats are a constant priority concern.

Big data solutions meet the challenge. Virtually all security experts say the amount of data and the growth of that data has become so exponentially high that security organizations can no longer keep throwing headcount at the problem. Qualified and experienced companies like Gurucul, with big data user behavior analytics solutions, address this challenge by delivering the ability to closely monitor anomalous human behavior, providing predictive risk scores to detect access risk and unknown threats. These advanced analytics, empowered by innovation, driven by advanced machine learning, and plugged into big data, are critical to provide a comprehensive part of the behavior-based solution.

UEBA minimizes human touch points. It's acknowledged you can never eliminate humans from the security equation, nor would you want to. While they must remain a critical part of the process, security teams can no longer completely cover the gargantuan expansion of manually managing the data. We must minimize the amount of touch points by humans because it just doesn't scale. That's the importance of UEBA and IdA technology as part of the solution.

Best-in-breed solutions and reliable results. Forward-thinking CISOs know they have to utilize the best from this new breed of solutions which are coming out today. These solutions can bring the needles to the top of the haystack, as well as pick out the most critical ones, and send them off to the specialists who need to take a closer look.

The impact of hybrid cloud adoption on cyber security

The impact has been seismic on the security industry. This move between traditional on-premises solutions to cloud-based solutions has changed the rules of engagement. Organizations continue to adopt some sort of a cloud-based play — from AWS, Office 365, Box, Dropbox, or solutions like Salesforce.com, and a range of SaaS, PaaS, IaaS options — so that the security challenge has transformed into a different scale and complexity than ever before. Not only do you have to continue to perform your on-premises security in the way you were, but you now also need to understand your cloud worlds and integrate effective cloud security in each one. Then, you must seamlessly stitch it all together.

The inevitability of expanding cloud adoption. It's interesting to look back to 2010. The conversations were all about, "Can we trust the cloud?" Today's discussions observe that data might be even be more secure in the cloud. Yet the provocative question persists, "But, *really*, how secure is the cloud?" While that debate continues, the trends tell us we've swung the pendulum of the word 'trust'. The government and other commercial entities are entrusting their data in the cloud. Anyone who looks at ASW — Amazon

...the trends tell us we've swung the pendulum of the word "trust." The government and other commercial entities are entrusting their data in the cloud.

— knows they're dominating the web services market. Their revenue growth indicates there's definitely a path moving forward in the IaaS direction and it will continue to change the dynamics of all cloud solutions. This is especially true for the rising importance of targeted cloud solutions offering unique values over others.

Cloud innovations add security requirements. Cloud definitely brings a wave of innovative concepts that have been game-changing influences for some companies. Their growth has enabled them to turn the corner of success. No longer do companies need to overpay for infrastructure resources they're not utilizing. Instead, cloud's new options of utility empower flexible growth to match the entire spectrum of how fast or how slow an organization might go. Cloud's elastic pay-as-you-go provisioning reduces CapEx and maximizes the value of OpEx expenditures. These cloud innovations deliver greater efficiencies and effectiveness while reducing cost. Nevertheless, hidden within the agile complexity of the cloud's advantages lies the fundamental requirement to reliably protect everything in the environment.

Outdated security strategies fail to secure the environment. In the past, some CISOs were unable to understand the concept of the paradigm shift in proper perspective because they remained ingrained with the perimeter concept of security for the corporate environment. At the time, the domain was so secure that they knew about anything coming in or going out, while on the outside it was the wild world. This had been the standard model of focus: protect the perimeter and give support to keep the bad guys out and the good guys in. But now with cloud, that old solitary concept has no place in the minds of forward-looking CISOs.

The potential threat of employee devices. This new normal compels security leaders to retool their thinking when they examine their on-premises environments, with people coming in and out, there are a completely new set of factors to contend with. Employees are bringing their own devices (BYODs), IoT (the Internet of Things) is expanding, and people are jumping the perimeter all the time. Most are good people, with legitimate behavior —

...people are jumping the perimeter all the time. Most are good people, with legitimate behavior – but not all – and that's where the danger lies.

but not all — and that's where the danger lies.

The goal: hybrid cloud as secure as on-premises. An additional factor CISOs should keep in mind when considering their evolving security requirements is that the typical tenure of an employee has declined markedly. It has shrunk from multiple years to a few months in some cases. One or two years are quite common nowadays. In the past, companies used to have people work for decades within a single organization. This gig economy circumstance creates a situation where organizations must keep giving new people access to data, yet also make sure all of that remains secure, just as it has traditionally been with their on-premises environments. That is the CISO's goal and challenge: to make their hybrid cloud solutions as secure as their on-premises solutions were. As CISOs start to rethink the right way to approach this objective, some are also seeing that the way cloud is managing security might even provide some of those innovations for their on-premises environments. These new capabilities allow customers to pay a cloud fee for an identity management as a service (IDaaS) solution, meaning elements of on-premises security requirements are eliminated with a significant cost savings.

Past behavior's role in identifying future anomalies

Beyond what the potential cloud security solutions offer, the variable that needs to be taken into account is an individual's behavior within the network. We're all creatures of habit. Just think about how you operate every day, or every week. How you type. That's intelligence, and that's also a critical part of identity which is defined by behavior. I have a colleague in the UEBA space who likes to say: "You can steal somebody's credentials, but you can't steal their behavior." That's the giveaway right there.

Behavior defining identity. Here's what's behind identity through behavior: when you see someone comes into work every morning, badges into the building at 9:00, logs onto his computer at 9:10, checks emails at 9:15, makes morning calls, interacts with a certain category of documents, uses cloud services in a certain way for a particular purpose — he has a distinct behavior pattern. This is all part of that person's identity defined by their behavior.

The fingerprint of behavior. At times, while someone else might succeed in stealing someone else's credentials, their ability to mimic that person's behavior is next to impossible. The distinct behavior for access and actions are like fingerprints that give away the attacker. It quickly flags the action as an anomalous behavior, ready for the next step, risk scoring. The anomalous behavior pattern is conspicuously outside the baseline behavior profile established by the user's earlier use patterns as well as those of his peer groups.

> *The distinct behavior for access and actions are like fingerprints that give away the attacker.*

Balancing priorities of identity management with UEBA. While there is a rising awareness of the benefits of user and entity behavior analytics, and its importance in emerging technologies, an equally important element of security success relates to identity management. Too often, identity management is in the purview of IT departments while security monitoring belongs to the SOCs, creating two separate silos of responsibility. This disconnect represents a serious vulnerability.

Establishing and managing identity in the environment

Identity management in cyber is a persistent challenge. It's becoming more acute while account compromise continues to grow as an effective method of penetrating an environment. Along with organizations having a solid identity analytics solution in place, one broader idealized concept would involve not only having a national identity management enrollment and authentication program, but a global program. If you consider that we register vehicles, and we're able to get a driver's license, a social security card that enables us to get a passport, we need to get there. Until we do, we'll have a higher level of risk, which lowers the level of correct and timely attribution. We need to know, with the highest level of precision possible, who's out there on our landscape.

A call for more comprehensive identity standards. Some privacy advocates may disagree, but we need, at a minimum, to have national identity management and multi-factor authentication to include biometrics. Therefore, whatever that consists of needs to augment identification and to make it the most robust and user-friendly technology advance to identify who's who. In my previous career with the Secret Service, I was issued something called the commission book. In my commission book, I had a badge, a photo, and a document certifying I was a United States Secret Service agent. The only way to get it was to undergo a thorough background check, polygraph, and dozens of interviews. You still have to go through that because the nature of the job enrollment was extensive. We need an element of this process to get proper identity management. In an ideal world, having a global or even national identity, would address quite a few challenges.

The complexity of a single identity in many systems. Looking at the realities in present day hybrid network environments, nothing's ever this simple and straightforward. When we look at any corporate environment there are so many different systems, so many different infrastructures. Sometimes, just to establish identity becomes tricky because there are so many handoffs, so many proxies, so much masking, and all the required procedures to make sure you are able to have the

> " Sometimes, just to establish identity becomes tricky because there are so many handoffs, so many proxies, so much masking, and all the required procedures to make sure you are able to have the right attribution. "

right attribution. All of this is to assure, "This action is being performed by this person, and based on their behavior profile built in correlation with peer groups, and other data, we can see that what this person is doing is normal."

Strategies for managing excess access

Organizations must think seriously about access and how they grant it. In the past, some IT groups issued access to a new employee based simply on cloning the access of someone else who happened to be on the team the new hire is joining. The hazard is that the IT group might end up giving far too much access to this person than their position requires. Elimination of cloning access and rubber stamping certifications should be a first order of business for security leaders.

Too much access. The following scenario exemplifies the problem. Bob has been in a tech company for nineteen years. He went from engineering, to support, to special projects, and after almost twenty years he accumulated a great deal of access which was never properly closed off when he moved from department to department. He's currently in special projects. Then, a new person joins the team and IT says, "Okay, just give him Bob's access profile." What IT did at that point was provide this new person too much access, much of which he won't pay attention to while he is primarily focused on his new special projects activities. Every piece of unwarranted additional access an organization gives represents an access risk which could be hacked or compromised. Multiply this scenario, and a host of others where privileged access entitlements are granted and unaccounted for across a global enterprise, and the scale becomes staggering.

> Every piece of unwarranted additional access an organization gives represents an access risk which could be hacked or compromised.

Excess access elimination. The goal is reducing this access risk plane, including eliminating excess access, or access outliers, as requirements. It can be achieved by implementing two methods. One involves using identity analytics for a risk-based approach to identity access management (IAM) removing excess access, cleaning up the access plane to reduce access risk. A second involves the creation of intelligent roles from machine learning models that reverse engineer role access from the entitlement level back into peer groups. Intelligent roles replace legacy roles defined by manual processes and rules. Going forward, from a clean access plane status, risk-based certifications and access requests and approvals keep things in check.

Insider threat detection program trends

Here's a testament to the importance of analytics. If you look at the number of companies that have been funded and grown over the last four years or five years, the number one area that's covered are the analytics-based companies because knowledge is king. Intelligence trumps all. Whether it is business intelligence, or threat intelligence, or market intelligence, people pay a great deal of money for that specialized, timely and accurate information.

Unmanageable data overload. Based on the growing challenges facing organizations today, you can't understate the importance of innovative analytic technology solutions to help advance the field. It is a new normal of total, massive, unmanageable data overload of digital exhaust. This data excess is continuing to get worse. Only solutions with advanced analytics, powered by machine learning and leveraging big data for context, can provide the visibility into identity risks and the monitoring of user behavior for unknown threats that is needed across all an organization's hybrid cloud environments.

> *Only solutions with advanced analytics, powered by machine learning and leveraging big data for context, can provide the visibility into identity risks and the monitoring of user behavior for unknown threats that is needed across all an organization's hybrid cloud environments.*

Resiliency and recovery priorities. The cyber security trend is also moving toward the importance of resiliency. CIOs and CISOs know the bad guys will get in and they can create harm. Now they need to ensure they can operate if harm comes. This circumstance reflects an attitude that the likelihood of a breach occurrence is high. For security leaders it's just a matter of, "What severity will it be, and how do we respond to it?"

The challenges of balancing human efforts against the growing data

A starting point for addressing the new approach is with the recognition of the overwhelming volume of data that can no longer be realistically analyzed by humans. In some quarters, however, a bias remains that this is still a viable option.

Vested interests in the status quo. An illustration highlighting some of the characteristics embedded in the challenge of innovation adoption is exemplified by system integrators, the SI model. It's designed as a billable service model. A number of business minds are locked into that framework as a sensible, profitable, and sound business approach. Yet when you have a billable service model, it's inherently designed to suffocate innovation while inflating budgets.

Lower efficiencies and higher risks. A number of organizations today, as well as the People's Republic of China, are inclined to throw headcount at a challenge like this. That's simply the wrong approach, with diminishing returns in efficiency. The further anyone ventures along this strategic path in a setting of such rapidly evolving technology and complexity, the more unnecessary cost and risk they instill.

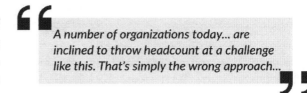

A number of organizations today... are inclined to throw headcount at a challenge like this. That's simply the wrong approach...

New technology model required. To evolve successfully, organizations must move from the 80% bodies and 20% technology model, to 80% technology and 20% bodies. Today's cyber security requirements simply no longer scale with the majority of the work being performed by humans. The imbalance is growing daily. It will not solve our hard cyber security problems. It can't give us the intelligence and knowledge we need to effectively do our job and deliver the appropriate levels of security.

Priority focus on data. As security leaders come to accept that technology is needed to support their needs, they also begin to identify their wish list of features and capabilities. My colleagues in the security industry have observed how CISOs are increasingly saying they want their cyber security analysts, their data scientists, or any of the intelligent people in their organization, to focus only on the right data. They want technology to help their specialists pick out exactly what that data is. They should not be bound by chasing down alerts that ultimately turn out to be low priority or false positives. That results in the analysts missing the forest from the trees when it comes to the criticality of assessing priority anomalies efficiently and being unable to keep on top of details that require the most attention.

Solution optimization trends targeting today's security gaps

While automation of different sets of tasks has been widely recognized for its advantages within different security solutions, this advancement represents the first building block of empowered efficiencies within a holistic environment.

From automation to orchestration. A critical recognition among many CISOs is that of the need to move from automation to orchestration to facilitate more effective central decision-making. This means having the ability to integrate all of the varied automated components of an advanced analytics security solution, supplying simple transparent holistic controls to enable monitoring, analysis and response from a comprehensive solution with flexibility for future needs.

Emerging requirements for remediation and attribution. The orchestration capability helps the CISOs do their job to assure comprehensive remediation. Eventually, some form of attribution should be included because a number of industries and corporations are battling with this challenge. Nevertheless, in order to do proper attribution, it must become clearly mandated within the cyber security industry.

Larger organizations are early adopters. While a few vendors are developing these solutions, it is an area that needs to trend upwards, with wider customer adoptions, which supports solution capabilities development for a broader base of customers. The select companies that are currently in need of this generation of solution tend to be the larger organizations with the budget. The size and complexity of their hybrid network environments warrants the development and adoption of this kind of solution. While a wide range of organizations could benefit from these solutions, lower awareness of the proven value, and budget constraints, are currently inhibitors to wider adoption. This is a hard problem to solve, and an important one at the same time, especially with certain government agencies. The challenge too is that the solution must be viable and scalable.

More innovation needed in cyber security. In terms of other trends, the restraining factor is the frustrating limitation of the conservative incremental advances of innovation. It is disappointing that we are not seeing more disruptive innovation in cyber security. I haven't seen anyone discovering fire or the light bulb. Meanwhile, it's a cat and mouse game. Sometimes we're staying ahead of the adversary, and other times we're not. What's needed are solutions that reflect thinking from an intel perspective, with components reflecting an understanding of weak points of defense, attacker strengths and likely scenarios.

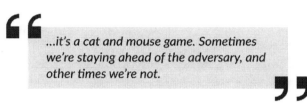

...it's a cat and mouse game. Sometimes we're staying ahead of the adversary, and other times we're not.

Why advancements in cyber security are incremental and lack dynamic innovation

First and foremost, we essentially built an information highway, as a DARPA (Defense Advanced Research Projects Agency) project, which was not originally designed for critical business or financial utilities. It was not constructed to be ultra-secure, but instead to facilitate exchanging and sharing information. Its architecture was ad hoc and designed to be resilient. Over the decades, there was never a real master plan, and for better or worse, its structure grew organically as the use cases for it continually changed and evolved with remarkable speed. By the time we arrived in the nineties, it was identified as a future cornerstone of commerce. Because it's so porous, we're now trying to re-frame, strengthen and shore up the digital highway.

Absence of original plans intensifies challenges. In an ideal world, the infrastructure for this digital highway would have been built with high quality ingredients in the first place — the best cement and asphalt available. There could have been standards established determining the requirements and regulations to assure the highest grade materials were used to provide a safe, resilient, robust, strong, secure, trusted freeway. It could have been planned and developed by seasoned civil engineers working with a unified purpose and vision. But organic and dynamic innovation does not always work that way. Use cases rise in popularity, evolve and change drastically, as has been demonstrated by the original Facebook model and what it has become today. Multiply that dynamic phenomenon exponentially, and you have today's internet. Now we're trying to go back in and fix a framework that has too many porous holes in it. Moreover, we're chasing a moving target. Better cement and better asphalt will always need to be developed.

A higher calling motivating innovation. This uncharted development legacy makes inspired leaps of innovation in cyber security difficult. Nonetheless, entrepreneurs dream. They dream of flying to Mars. They dream of solving the world's hardest problems. Most of the cultures of these entrepreneur companies are wonderful, very mission focused. They have a sense of purpose and commitment and sometimes of collaborating with the government. They realize that we all have a shared hard problem to solve. They're entrepreneurs who are making solutions that are perfecting the national security and economic interest of our respective nations. There's a lot of personal commitment. Because of national interests and economic interests, as well as privacy and personal rights, we all have a higher calling. That certainly motivates innovation.

Conflicted priorities inhibiting progress. Some companies often funded and backed by private or venture capital, may be too focused on making money at the expense of dynamic innovation. In addition, it seems at times that when capitalism comes into play it can get in the way of the path forward towards productive game changing dynamic innovation. These people start thinking about their exit strategy early on versus solving the real hard problems. Frankly, these players are rarely a source of dynamic innovation.

Additional factors stagnating innovation. Another factor influencing a stagnation of innovation is about how people tend to be scared of changing, or making wholesale modifications. While you have a new and completely different solution which might seem to meet current needs, people may still be cautious. They feel, "This is my security portfolio and I'm turning it upside down. There could still be unseen liabilities with it. It's probably best if I wait and see later versions of the solution to be sure it addresses all my needs. Then I'll think about adoption." This hesitant cautiousness in a community considering forward-looking solutions stifles innovation.

Accepting some level of risk in new solutions is required. A fundamental reality remains: we must move from being conservative, or too risk averse, to taking risks. We need more early adopters in the buyer community. If we don't take risks we'll never really truly be able to rebuild this digital highway or to alter the world. That's one

> If we don't take risks... we're going to continue to fall further behind the adversary.

of the challenges of not taking risks: we're going to continue to fall further behind the adversary. The buyer community is also a partner in this. I'm looking for change agents who are not afraid to lead change, but to embrace change, and move forward with it.

Factors influencing early adoption in security technology

Inherent risk takers, versus risk-averse people that depend on legacy systems, are early adopters. These change agents are willing to take that risk. They drive the spirit of early adoption. Part of the challenge, however, and especially in the government, is that there's no reward for failure. There is no profit margin or shareholder value, no driving motivation to deliver more for less. As a result, there's no reward for taking risks. So the culture there is different than in the commercial world.

Organizational pain defines urgency. An additional factor that might influence someone who was originally inclined to be a late adopter, to ultimately become an early adopter, is that they may have gone through a compromise or a breach. It boils down to the amount of pain the organization's suffering. If there's a lot of pain and uncertainty about the quality of a system's security assurance, and if the existing solutions clearly are not addressing the pain, CISOs need to adjust their strategy.

Regular exposure to innovators strengthens insights. Another influence is when CISOs are exposed to and surround themselves with the innovators, the risk takers, the early adopters. Those change agents are a key influence. Listening to and understanding their forward-thinking, and the way they approach challenges, is part of building a platform of strategic change targeted on the needs, goals and objectives of an enterprise's next generation of security assurance solutions.

Fast-tracking knowledge via experienced communities. In Sydney, Australia, SINET is taking U.S.-based forward-thinking CISOs to share insights from their innovative projects with the Australian CIO and CISO communities, as they exchange their knowledge in turn. Thought leadership means sharing at a high level. The U.S. CISOs have different perspectives towards the big problem involved with hybrid cloud challenges based upon their years of hands-on experience with cloud. With the country's recent 'cloud first' mandate, Australia's CISO culture is undergoing an unprecedented and accelerated nationwide adoption pattern with unique insights apart from the U.S. culture in terms of state-of-the-art cyber security technology and practices. The takeaway in this context is that this is a group of security leaders who know they can gain knowledge from colleagues who've already gone through their own versions of trial and error adoption cycles. In doing so, U.S. and Australian peers' experience helps each other streamline their own paths to adoption of certain solutions,

> ...a group of security leaders... know they can gain knowledge from colleagues who've already gone through their own versions of trial and error adoption cycles.

with knowledge and processes that have been proven in the field. Moreover, adoption of best practices developed elsewhere can speed implementation at a lower cost.

Newer infrastructure encourages earlier adoption. In this context, it's also interesting that with their cloud first mandate, Australia is moving much faster than the rest of the world. The adoption of cloud services in Australia is growing rapidly with compound annual growth rates (CAGR) of 23-24 percent (per Melbourne IT study) against a global average of 19.4% (per Forbes.com). It appears that because they were newer, and some other adopters before them have established a number of proven best practices, that they have less to lose, or risk. This might be one of the factors causing them to be adopting at a quicker pace. Experts observe the benefits Australia will experience with these solutions represent a possible 30% savings for taxpayers in government spending.

More legacy physical infrastructure complicates adoption. One additional perspective on that idea is when we look at physical infrastructure. Changing our telephone systems in the United States was difficult to go from landlines to mobile. On the other hand, we are seeing other countries where there was not as much infrastructure already in place. They're adopting mobile phones at a much quicker pace because it's easier to set it up, as opposed to the legacy technology solution of digging trenches and managing other cumbersome infrastructure requirements.

Individuals, not industries, determine solution trends. While some wonder if there are any specific industries that encourage early adopters, aside from organizations depending on legacy systems which would compel late adoption behavior, it essentially depends more on the individual security leader than it does the sector. In today's world, these sector independent security leaders drive innovation and adoption.

UEBA, IdA and perspectives on private companies' partnership with government agencies

When I transitioned from the public to the private sector in 2004, I rebooted to become an entrepreneur and a venture capitalist on a mission. As an entrepreneur, I became focused on advancing innovation to defeat global cyber security threats and providing a platform for the business of cyber to take place. I founded SINET (Security Innovation Network) as a super connector. We connect the investor, the builder, the buyer and the researcher.

Shared interests and goals. Part of my mission and activities also included a deep involvement with the Secret Service Electronic Crimes Task Force (ECTF). ECTF is a nationwide network of participants who provide support and resources to field investigations of crimes such as bank fraud, virus and worm proliferation, access device fraud, telecommunications fraud, internet threats, computer system intrusions and cyber-attacks, phishing/spoofing, identity theft, and more. It's more of a human model, a collaboration model, than technology. The beauty of it is when you bring together investors and government, security professionals, entrepreneurs, and large corporations, the opportunity to collaborate on shared hard problems increases dramatically. It's a great alternative to working in silos, and only focusing on your own respective path in society.

The value of a public/private partnership. The ECTF model has proven to be highly successful. It's based on trust. It's based on a community and a sense of purpose and commitment that we all have a hard problem together. The public/private partnership is essential to the success of that model. Nevertheless, the private sector needs to lead. The mandate is on industry, the owners and operators of critical infrastructure. The onus is on them to take more of a leadership role and facilitate more participation in these collaboration models.

Innovation leadership from the private sector. The government can't do everything. The participation by small, medium and large companies several years ago, and with the DHS (Department of Homeland Security) supported by the White House, formed a security cooperative. It started in various cities like Washington DC, San Diego, and a number of cities in Texas, that participated in building out the framework on the Internet of Things. Their topics of interest addressed cloud as well. This organizational framework provides a well-reasoned, foundation for possible regulation — a precursor to official government regulation — that has already been developed and vetted by a national group of recognized and qualified security experts. Indications are that the market will be regulated. Like the path of the automobile, the automotive industry at least had input on that framework,

> ...the White House... formed a security cooperative... that participated in building out the framework on the Internet of Things.

and on those policies, versus the government working with no input from the private sector.

Proven experience in on-premises and hybrid cloud required. A last point is quite important in terms of the ecosystem of a public/private partnership. We must promote an awareness of innovative solutions that could ultimately protect the military command and control systems and our nation's critical infrastructures. Innovation, in its most simplistic form, is just having an awareness that comes with predictive security solutions from enterprises like Gurucul that exist so that it can better society.

CONCLUSIONS & TAKEAWAYS:

Implementing productive change in predictive security strategies

Observing that the internet has evolved in an organic way, by spurts of innovation, taking it in new unforeseen directions, Robert Rodriguez notes its original design was not created to service the robust business applications and sensitive information being managed and transmitted across today's networks and within hybrid environments. Factoring in the rapidly multiplying digital exhaust, which doubles every year, he states it is time to recognize the need for change in security strategies.

Government has responded to these concerning trends, establishing new initiatives to cope with the new challenges, including the White House's role of Cybersecurity Coordinator. All the while, the data overload in today's environments continues to mount. Rodriguez observes: "We've moved from finding the needle in the haystack, to finding the needle in the haystack of needles, and then prioritizing and making that information actionable." As this circumstance endures, it does so with the recognition that the issue of insider threats, whether malicious or not, has had an enduring sense of importance for both government and private organizations. Rodriguez calls for the need of machine learning to handle the sprawling digital exhaust, which is now far beyond human capabilities to manage. The impact of cloud adoption and the emerging growth of hybrid environments have made that urgency even more acute.

Yet innovation within government is not driven by the same profit motives as private enterprises, and risk-taking is not rewarded. Advancements in cyber security in both the public and private sectors are incremental and too often lack dynamic innovation. Outdated security strategies fail to secure the environment as some organizations continue to see the business case as a systems integrator model, and to futilely commit more human resources to the challenges. As attackers continue to innovate, Rodriguez calls out the need for private and government organizations to find more common collaboration points to partner and strengthen strategies and security solutions. A critical component of this initiative is to promote solution development targeted more at the 20% human engagement and 80% technology ratio, where he observes the reverse ratio is prevalent in too many organizations today.

At the core of success in these future initiatives lies the requirement to achieve a single identity risk profile across all systems, as well as the comprehensive management of identity through a risk-based approach. Achieving these goals facilitates the significant reduction of the access risk plane. Without this, and machine learning with big data to draw from, effective user and entity behavior analytics programs cannot be realistically effective to detect unknown threats. For those who have adopted the next generation of predictive security analytics, they are looking toward the automation of various security analytic functions along with the optimization of the entire solution across a hybrid environment. The leaders for adopting these next-generation solutions are ultimately found among those whose acceptance of innovation is part of their personality versus their organization profile or a particular industry they might work in.

With the need for a new approach in security being recognized, the next chapter examines the evolving technology of machine learning and big data which makes predictive security analytics possible. The next *Borderless Breach Flashcard* portrays an instance where, faced with clear signs that they were a ripe target for a major malicious attack, they chose instead to focus their strategies on developing new products and easy-to-use services, instead of bolstering their security. This decision resulted in what some experts described as the largest breach in history.

BORDERLESS BREACH FLASHCARD	
Notoriety on Steroids	
CATEGORY	Stolen user data – one of the largest breaches of its kind in history.
WHO	**The target:** Yahoo and its customers.
WHAT	Hackers allegedly backed by a "state sponsored actor" compromised over 500 million passwords and other information from Yahoo's server.
WHEN	2016
WHERE	USA, online.
WHY	Economic gain and notoriety.
HOW	In July of 2016, notification that vast amounts of personal data originating from Yahoo were posted online for sale. Yahoo responded by investigating their network to see if indeed any claims of these might be true. They discovered that over 500 million of their customers' personal information had been compromised. The final count surpassed one billion. This breach occurred four years following the massive Aurora cyber assault by Chinese military hackers, who breached a number of prominent high tech companies, including Google. Unlike Google, who prioritized security to a high level, Yahoo instead focused on developing new products and services, placing security at a lower priority. Yahoo saw security more as an inhibitor of customer retention, where products were slower and more difficult to use (the internal name for Yahoo's security team was "The Paranoids").
HOW BAD?	Named by some as the largest intrusion into a company's network, Yahoo is subject to FBI and SEC investigations. The company also faces a number of lawsuits. One specifically cites Yahoo for reckless disregard for not strengthening its security when it had promised to do so, and knew it was a prime target for attackers. The cost per remediation of each breached identity is estimated at $232, representing an astronomical cost. In addition, Verizon was in the middle of acquiring Yahoo for $4.8 billion dollars. The final status and acquisition price of that transaction, if it goes through, is now in question.
HOW COULD IT HAVE BEEN AVOIDED?	Yahoo was clearly forewarned of their company's risk, and did not have a mature UEBA-IdA solution in place. If it had, the anomalous behavior would likely have been identified, allowing their SOC team to respond effectively years ago to remediate the threat. The cost of doing so would have been a fraction of the cost of remediating this in 2016.

Discovering the Unknown:
Big Data with Machine Learning

Machine learning's road through big data to predictive security analytics

Why was predictive security analytics comparatively late to the game in machine learning?

Eric Schmidt, Executive Chairman, Google observed: "From the dawn of civilization until 2003, humankind generated five exabytes of data. Now we produce five exabytes every two days... and the pace is accelerating." While a number of experts quibble with the accuracy of that statement, it still rightly calls out the rapid speed of the expanding world of big data. The PBS special *The Human Face of Big Data*, and its accompanying teaching materials, portray the vast range of new possibilities emerging from big data. Elephant seals equipped with antennas on their heads help to map the oceans. Satellites target mosquitoes to support a better understanding of malaria. An SMS (system maintenance service) solution prevents the sale of counterfeit medicines in Ghana. Smartphones predict you're going to get depressed. Credit cards know two years before you do that you are headed toward divorce. Pills transmit information directly from your body to your physician.

Joe Sullivan, CSO of Uber observed in an earlier chapter, "As I researched it more deeply — seeing that every company was storing increasingly more data — I came to realize that the future was in big data." But big data is nothing without machine learning. Big data is something like a vast field of wheat that needs the farmer to harvest, the mill to process it, and the baker to mix the flour with the right ingredients and then bake it to produce a gourmet pastry you might consume at a coffee house. Big data is the raw material. It is nothing without the right tools and process. Machine learning is like the diamond lane on the information superhighway.

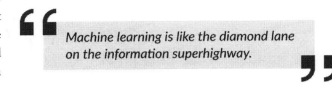

Machine learning is like the diamond lane on the information superhighway.

From 1952, when Arthur Samuel wrote the first learning program to play checkers and improve the more it played, the 'game was on'. The research and scientific applications are well-acknowledged for their importance. Since then, the evolution of machine learning witnessed a shift in the 1990s, where the knowledge-driven approach shifted to a data-driven one, and the business applications in machine learning began to offer an entirely new world of potential. In business, machine learning analytics driven by algorithms have been adopted with great effect and value, in a range of market verticals including finance, manufacturing, marketing, and, of course, behavior analytics.

The benefits machine learning delivered to all these endeavors are:

- Accelerated time in model development, model testing and delivery of actionable insights
- Delivery of an optimal balance between predictive accuracy, performance and cost
- Utilization of streaming data to deliver real-time analytics
- Reduction of risk with enterprise-grade machine learning
- Acquisition of best insights in model performance and outcome

The age of advanced analytics had arrived, which meant organizations had solution capabilities that were much less reliant on human knowledge to build and maintain the solution. This solution set gave organizations the ability to detect patterns and predict outcomes across a wide range of variables far beyond human capabilities. This delivered a capability to analyze vastly greater amounts of data, which included unstructured data alongside traditional structured data found in transaction application systems. This unstructured data included elements such as text, log, social and machine data. Within this sea of raw information, machine learning has provided the ability to adapt to changing conditions through continuous learning.

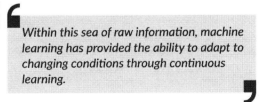

Within this sea of raw information, machine learning has provided the ability to adapt to changing conditions through continuous learning.

Financial organizations, such as FICO, have used it in fraud detection where their solutions employ an input layer (with the raw data), 'hidden' layers that process and link the inputs, and an output layer that produces a score indicating fraud risk. Machine learning (ML) use cases extend into property, casualty, life and health insurance and more. Manufacturers have used ML to facilitate resolution of machine outages or assembly line disruption. Utility businesses use machine learning to manage service interruptions to their customers. Businesses have employed ML to enhance the logistics of delivering goods and services. Sales and marketing organizations leverage ML to analyze a massive number of factors contributing to a consumer's purchasing considerations, such as demographic and location data. This data, along with purchase and browsing history, helps predict a consumer's preferences and buying actions. Included in this capability, ML analyzes vast repositories of disparate data found in social sources, web logs, transaction systems, and geospatial sources to deliver a scalable predictive solution that provides distinct advantages for today's marketing and sales requirements. Internet giants like Amazon Web Services (AWS) now offer their own ML solution. All have used ML to bring together disparate information to deliver accurate forecasts which had before been impossible to render.

Predictive security analytics had a steeper curve to climb for one simple reason: accuracy. The challenge to accurately identify verifiable risk amidst a sea of complex data in near real-time defined its core requirement. If errors occurred in marketing analytics, or logistics in manufacturing or service deliveries, it represented an inconvenience or diminished productivity. Predictive security analytics had a higher bar for proving value. Failures in security analytics held the potential for impacting an organization's bottom line due to data exfiltration, espionage or regulatory fines. Security teams needed to see the unassailable proof points and were hesitant to adopt unless relevant solid results could be shown. Their requirement was the highest detection rate with the highest validation. For example, noisy alert systems delivering 5 detections out of 100 high scoring alerts, versus 8 out 10, were considered to have low value to security teams.

Predictive security analytics had a higher bar for proving value.

The other issue of requesting absolute proof in results drives analysts to use rules of known threats versus uncovering the unknown with machine learning. To be predictive and absolute in results is something of an oxymoron.

As recently as 2010, some analysts created a misperception that predictive analytics, powered by machine learning, was not feasible for the foreseeable future. Generally, their concerns boiled down to a few areas:

- **_Outlier detection_** – With machine learning considered better at identifying similarities than finding outliers, outlier detection was viewed as a classification problem. The lack of a perfect model of normality was a constraint.

- **High cost of errors** – With intrusion detection, the cost was too much noise. Administrators in turn, dialed it down. Factors like spam detection generated a highly unbalanced cost model creating unacceptably high false negatives or misses.

- **Semantic gap** – The challenge of transferring results into actionable reports and the problem of defining the difference between abnormal activity and attacks were considered unresolved.

- **Diversity of data and network traffic** – Basic characteristics such as bandwidth, duration of connections and application mix, exhibited immense variability, with large bursts of activity being common, were considered too large a challenge to overcome.

- **Difficulty with evaluation** – Where evaluation of the data produced was considered more difficult than building the detector because of data difficulties.

While this may have been the perspective of some doubters in 2010, concurrently the market leading vendors in UEBA had already been making significant inroads in their solutions, working at all of these quality challenges. 2014 was a breakout year for the advanced development of these solutions. Decisive strides were achieved in establishing this next generation of proven and reliable UEBA capabilities with mature machine learning. Evolution continues. Leading vendors in the UEBA space are targeting new challenges, to strengthen their prescriptive user and entity behavior analytics capabilities into platforms. It is instructive, however, to consider the evolutionary context in the development timeline of UEBA and IdA, to have an understanding of how the UEBA venders addressed the analysts' concerns of 2010.

- **Outlier detection** – Reliable models of normality have become well-established through self-learning and self-training models of users and entities over the course of 30 to 35 days, and much faster with ingestion of existing history of users. Linking their behavior with static and dynamic peer groups further refines the modeling and eliminates the issue of bad behavior in baselines. Identity analytics (also using ML) has helped to drastically reduce the number of unaccounted for access risks.

- **High cost of errors** – The comprehensive ability to classify users, entities and their behavior across the

> " The comprehensive ability to classify users, entities and their behavior across the broad spectrum of hybrid environments, applications and devices has robustly addressed misclassification issues. "

124

broad spectrum of hybrid environments, applications and devices has robustly addressed misclassification issues. False positives and negatives have also been demonstrably reduced, with critical context from big data and increasing the number of models for specific use cases.

- **Semantic gap** – The gap between UI (user interface) and API (application program interface) has been closed by virtue of numerous innovations. The UI experience has become enhanced with color-coded graphics which include business and user friendly descriptions of anomalies that facilitate speed and ease of use. Accurate and normalized risk scores (0-100), with thresholds for specific alerts, in a number of categories within a UEBA solution, provides precise actionable intelligence and clearly defines the difference between abnormal activity and attacks in a range of relevant categories. Analytic response codes (ARC) with risk scores, instantly categorize what type of anomaly it is, and its severity, communicating directly to the solution in the API relationship, facilitating accuracy and optimal automated risk response times.

- **Diversity of network traffic** – Mature solutions have migrated to big data supporting both structured and unstructured data. They include predefined data connectors for ease of data ingestion. They enable customization and addition of new attributes with flexible metadata. In essence, a mature UEBA solution can ingest any data for any desired attributes.

- **Difficulty with evaluation** – The advancement of the normalization and correlation of data has enabled shorter proof of concepts, along with using historical data to speed-train models for faster time to value for the use cases of UEBA and IdA. More mature UEBA solutions with experience in hybrid environments have learned on-premises data is often more varied, as well as 'dirty', however, while cloud data is less varied and cleaner.

While machine learning may have arrived late to the game of advanced analytics, its journey has been filled with initiatives making the solution more mature, comprehensive and robust. It now stands in a position of delivering extreme value in a broad range of security use cases. Our expert contributor Leslie K. Lambert, CISO at large, with a vast range of first-hand experience in information security, will share her seasoned insights on machine learning and its benefits in user and entity behavior analytics and identity analytics.

BORDERLESS EXPERT INSIGHTS

Leslie K. Lambert*
CISO at Large

Former CISO for Juniper Networks and Sun Microsystems, Leslie K. Lambert, has over 30 years of experience in information security, IT risk and compliance, security policies, standards and procedures, incident management, intrusion detection, security awareness, threat vulnerability assessments and mitigation. She received *CSO* magazine's 2010 Compass Award for security leadership and was named one of *Computerworld's* Premier 100 IT Leaders in 2009. An Anita Borg Institute Ambassador since 2006, Leslie has been mentoring women across the world in technology. Leslie has also served on the board of the Bay Area CSO Council since 2005. Lambert holds an MBA in Finance and Marketing from Santa Clara University, and an MA in Experimental Psychology.

The chair of Gurucul's Executive Advisory Board, Leslie has supplied instrumental support in the company's planning, development and strategy for the organization's solution development and market approach. In this chapter, she provides her expert insights on machine learning in predictive security analytics.

Overview

In this module, Ms. Lambert observes the impactful way in which machine learning is reshaping security. She explores the manner by which machine learning helps meet the challenge of social engineering attacks and she provides insights into low and slow insider threats and how machine learning detects abuse by trusted users. She also lends critical insights into data exfiltration through remote access malware and the detection of IP theft with machine learning. As misconceptions of machine learning are common, Leslie provides real-world perceptive context on this topic, especially in reference to UEBA and IdA. Common UEBA utility scenarios are provided which are followed by real-world case studies in UEBA, empowered by machine learning. These brief case studies include citing the distinct benefits security leaders see with this caliber of security solution. At the conclusion of her section, she explains notable misconceptions around machine learning in predictive security analytics, as well as shares thoughts on the future of it.

Machine learning is reshaping security

At the 2016 RSA Conference in San Francisco, it was virtually impossible to find a security solution vendor not claiming to use machine learning. Both new and

---

* The views and opinions expressed by Leslie K. Lambert in this book are her own, and do not necessarily reflect those of her current, or any of her previous employers.

established companies are touting machine learning as a major component of the data science being used in their products. What is machine learning? Is it really reshaping cyber security?

The pervasiveness of machine learning. We'll define machine learning as the science of getting computers to act without being explicitly programmed. Over the past decade, machine learning has enabled self-driving cars, practical speech recognition, effective web search, and it has vastly improved our understanding of the human genome. Machine learning is so pervasive that we use it dozens of times a day without knowing it. Many researchers believe machine learning is the best way to make progress towards human-level artificial Intelligence (AI). The incredible power of machine learning and its application to analytics is reshaping cyber security, as we know it.

Machine learning and UEBA. In particular, applying machine learning to user and entity behavioral analytics is profoundly improving our ability to make sense of the volume of data generated by security products in the enterprise. When machine learning concepts like automated and iterative algorithms are used to learning patterns in data, we can probe data for structure, even if we don't know what that structure looks like.

...applying machine learning to user and entity behavioral analytics is profoundly improving our ability to make sense of the volume of data generated by security products in the enterprise.

Relationships in data nodes. In the past, security products attempted to correlate data to discern patterns and meaning. We now know better. Instead, today we perform link analysis to evaluate relationships or connections between data nodes. Key relationships can be identified among various types of data nodes or objects, things we might think of as organizations, people, transactions, and so on.

Extracting meaning from digital exhaust. Machine learning is what enables us to bring together huge volumes of data which is generated by normal user activity from disparate, even obscure, sets of data — digital exhaust — to identify relationships that span time, place and actions. Since machine learning can be simultaneously applied to hundreds of thousands of discrete events from multiple data sets, 'meaning' can be derived from behaviors and used as an early warning detection or prevention system.

Iterative data reprocessing to discover patterns. The ultimate test for a machine learning model is error validation on new data. In other words, machine learning is looking to match new data with what it's seen before, and not to test it to disprove, reject, or nullify an expected outcome. Since machine learning uses an iterative, automated approach, it can reprocess data until a robust pattern is found. This allows it to go beyond looking for known or common patterns.

Machine learning and social engineering attacks

How can analytics prevent IP theft after a successful account compromise? Real-world use cases from Verizon's 2016 *Data Breach Digest: Scenarios from the Field* illustrate potential ways machine learning can be used to detect or prevent similar incidents.

Industrial espionage discovery. In one example, a manufacturer's designs for an innovative new model of heavy construction equipment were stolen following a social engineering attack. The company was alerted when a primary competitor, located on another continent, introduced a new piece of equipment that looked like an exact copy of a model recently developed by the victim company.

Targeted spear phishing. The attack employed a scenario familiar to forensic network security analysts. The threat actors identified an employee who they suspected would have access to new product designs they were after — the chief design engineer. They targeted their victim via a spear phishing campaign based on the fictitious LinkedIn profile of a recruiter. The attackers began sending emails containing fictitious employment opportunities to the victim. One contained an attachment with a malware file embedded in the document. When opened, the malware began beaconing to an external IP address used by the threat actor. The attackers then installed a backdoor PHP (hypertext preprocessor) reverse shell on the chief design engineer's system. From there, exfiltration of all the pertinent data the threat actors required was achieved.

Security breach forensics. When viewing this scenario from a perspective of maintaining the goal of stopping the breach before the damage is done, an InfoSec analyst would seek to identify what intercept points might have been used to uncover the anomalous behavior occurring with the chief engineer's account. One is the presence and availability of multiple log files containing rich information about what data had been transferred, when, by whom, and to where. This data is available from intrusion detection logs, NetFlow data, DLP logs, firewall logs, antivirus and malware reporting. Because this data was underutilized, the victim company left itself wide open to several types of compromises.

 Because this data was underutilized, the victim company left itself wide open to several types of compromises.

Correlating expanding unwieldy data. It is an unfortunate fact that not all organizations are capable of making sense of complex data from multiple sources. The volume and speed at which this data is produced can seem unmanageable. In addition, the ability to correlate dissimilar data in a normalized and comparable manner may be unavailable to an organization. When this situation occurs, it's time for more advanced analysis with sophisticated mathematical support. This entails data normalization, analytics, and the application of machine learning.

Comprehensive visibility of data and user behavior. Using machine learning in circumstances like these can provide a more holistic view of the combined log data and expose suspicious activity. In addition to revealing malicious command-and-control traffic, machine learning models reveal who is accessing, storing and using data in uncharacteristic ways when compared to normal and peer group behavior. However, according to Sommer and Paxson's *Outside the Closed World: On Using Machine Learning for Network Intrusion Detection*, detecting account compromise via machine learning also poses unique challenges.

Outdated security methodologies and tools. Security professionals typically expect an extremely low false positive rate from network security tools. This has given rise to the popularity of 'whitelist' and 'blacklist' approaches which are too rigid to adapt to account compromise threats like the one described above. When scaled to an enterprise of 2,000 users, a one percent daily false alarm rate per user translates to 20 false alarms a day. Eventually, a tool generating this many false positives will be ignored. That's basically what happened with the infamous Target breach referenced earlier.

Analysis accuracy strengthened by proven techniques. When an account is compromised, bad logins are typically sparse and mixed with good behavior in such a way that an algorithm or human operator may miss bad behavior among the preponderance of good logins. The expectation maximization (EM) algorithm approach addresses this problem by treating the compromised account as a two-user model in which sessions may either be produced by the original user or a new user. This method causes benign sessions to fall out of the likelihood calculations, so they do not sway a mix of good and bad sessions toward being evaluated as good overall.

Security gaps without machine learning. In this particular incident, if the victim company had employed machine learning to analyze the data already in hand, they likely would have been alerted to several suspicious activities including who was accessing the designs, where the files were being stored, how and where they were being moved, non-typical access to sensitive data repositories, and several other possibilities.

...if the victim company had employed machine learning to analyze the data already in hand, they likely would have been alerted to several suspicious activities...

A valuable supplement to security strategies and practices. Most organizations have multiple security tools in place producing meaningful log data. Applying machine learning algorithms to these information sources to profile user access and behavior is a logical next step and will certainly deliver critical security data.

Low and slow insider threats: Detecting abuse by trusted users

In the preceding section, I discussed how machine learning could be used to detect phishing-based account compromise attacks using a real-world use case from the 2016 Verizon *Data Breach Digest*. Here we'll examine how to detect insider threats using similar techniques.

Insider spying with 'borrowed' credentials. This Verizon example involves an organization in the middle of a buyout that was using retention contracts to prevent employee attrition. To find out what other employees were being offered, a middle manager acquired IT administrator credentials from a colleague who was also a friend. He used these credentials to access the company's onsite spam filter and to spy on the CEO's incoming email. The abuse didn't stop there. The same credentials were also used to browse sensitive file shares and conduct other unauthorized actions.

Compromise leads to multiple breaches. This scenario is rife with information security issues. These include social engineering, unauthorized and inappropriate use of privileged access credentials to access files including the confidential email archive on a spam-filtering appliance. Why wasn't the company able to detect this activity until an after-the-fact forensic investigation, despite having ample data to support its clear and direct discovery?

Flaws in privileged access security policy. It's apparent the victim organization was unaware of the illicit activities of this specific IT administrator. In fact, they were not monitoring the access patterns and behaviors of elevated privileged accounts. While it's unclear what the IT administrator's specific job function was, we know the access privileges assigned to his user account were wide-reaching and powerful, spanning the gamut of file shares, from email archives to spam filtering infrastructure. Meanwhile, the access privileges were poorly configured, as he was able to traverse several different types of systems with just one set of credentials.

Context criticality. What makes it difficult to detect insider threats like this one is context, or more accurately, the lack of it. The mind-numbing volume of log files and outputs from security tools are typically standalone, siloed sources of data. Rarely are these rich sources of intelligence correlated with one another to achieve greater understanding of what access and activities have taken place.

> *What makes it difficult to detect insider threats like this one is context, or more accurately, the lack of it.*

Leveraging existing data for critical insights. Security teams need to be able to examine these access patterns and behaviors in a way that allows them to see important relationships between multiple sets of activities, possibly taking place in different locations concurrently. This is where data science and machine learning is invaluable. In this case, machine learning could have been used to analyze the data already in hand.

This would have revealed suspicious activities including accessing inappropriate files (that belonged to others), how and where they were being moved or copied, and non-typical access to the spam filtering infrastructure and confidential email archives.

A new normal for IT and SOCs. IT technology and know-how has moved far beyond verifying the simple heartbeats of IT applications and infrastructure servers. Organizations need to know who, what, where and why, and they must know it virtually in real time. Machine learning overcomes the seemingly insurmountable challenges of creating links between mountains of dissimilar and disconnected data sources. In this case, being unaware of the online activities within an organization, and not monitoring access credentials in a vigilant manner, reflects a lack of ownership for the basic responsibilities of security professionals. It demonstrates a deficiency of due diligence for the organization they support.

Mandated security procedures deliver results. In contrast, within Lockheed Martin's *Cyber Kill Chain*® model, the "Exploitation" phase is where security professionals are mandated to perform systematic examination of rich data sets that exist inside the organization. What better way to do this than via link analysis techniques used in machine learning that enable us to proactively detect and prevent persistent threats?

Data exfiltration through remote access malware: Detecting IP theft with machine learning

In this section, we'll look into how remote access threats can be exposed with the machine learning techniques we explored in earlier sections. I like to call it catching a RAT (Remote Access Trojan) by the tail.

Phishing email delivers stolen credentials and privileged access. In this next Verizon example, a manufacturing company experienced a breach of a shared engineering workstation in its R&D department. A phishing email resulted in a RAT backdoor being downloaded onto the system, which enabled the threat actors to escalate privileges and capture user credentials for everyone who had used the system. By the time the breach was discovered, a significant amount of information had been leaked out via FTP to a foreign IP address.

Evolving cyber-attacks bring greater risk. Most companies understand that data breaches are inevitable. It's no surprise that spending on cyber security tools has expanded from traditional 'prevent and protect' technologies to include post-breach 'detect and respond' solutions in an attempt to control and manage unavoidable cyber-attacks. In addition, cyber-attacks

> *...spending on cyber security tools has expanded from traditional 'prevent and protect' technologies to include post-breach 'detect and respond' solutions...*

are becoming more targeted, resulting in companies experiencing more damaging compromises that have a bigger impact on their business. These attacks aren't limited to specific vertical markets, though healthcare and financial services seemed to be the favorites in 2016.

Compromised identity a growing concern. The Identity Theft Resource Center (ITRC) has been tracking security breaches since 2005, looking for patterns, new trends and information to educate businesses and consumers on the importance of protecting identities and personally identifiable information. From 2005 through April 2016, the ITRC recorded 6,079 breaches, covering 862,527,023 identity records. That's a lot of compromised identities! Moreover, these are only the ones reported!

Attackers favor identity theft. Today's attacks compromise identity as a primary vector to pull sensitive information from an organization for both financial gain and social notoriety. These attacks are sophisticated, better funded, more organized than ever before, making it imperative for organizations to immediately analyze potential threats and risks related to anomalous and suspicious behavior.

A range of data sources to monitor. In addition to monitoring how identities are being both used and managed, other critical data sources within an organization's computing environment should be examined to provide more context beyond who and what. Some example data sources include network access, event and flow data, DLP data, sys logs, vulnerability scanning data, log files from IT applications, etc. In many cases, this data may already be consolidated into a log event management or SIEM solution.

Rich context needed for security analytics. This vast array of data, when combined with information on how identities are being used by both humans and machines, creates a rich source of context that can be mined using threat analytics and anomaly detection. When we view identity as a threat plane, hundreds of attributes can be modelled in machine learning algorithms to predict and remediate security threats.

Rules no longer apply. Machine learning is a force multiplier. Rules-based detection alone is unable to keep pace with the increasingly complex demands of threat and breach detection. This is primarily because rules are based on what (little) we know about the data, and in turn generate excessive alerts. Since humans lack the ability to predict what future cyber-attacks will look like, we can't write rules for these scenarios. In contrast, machine learning and statistical analysis can find anomalies in data that humans would not otherwise recognize or detect. For example, they can leverage useful and predictive cues that are too noisy and highly dimensional for humans and traditional software to link together.

Pervasive RATs. Going back to our Verizon *Data Breach Digest* example, let's consider how machine learning could detect a RAT. First, let's clarify what we're talking about. A Remote Access Trojan is malicious malware software that runs in the background on a computer and gives unauthorized access to a hacker so they can steal information or install additional malicious software. Hackers don't even have to create their own RATs; these programs are available for download from dark areas of the web. Trojans have been around for two decades. The term 'RAT' is relatively new.

Masked downloads install malicious malware. RATs usually start out as executable files that are downloaded from the internet. They are often masked as another program or added to a seemingly harmless application. Once the RAT installs, it runs in system memory and adds itself to system startup directories and registry entries. Each time the computer is started, the RAT starts as well.

Machine learning's ability to detect atypical activity. How can machine learning help here? RATs generate anomalous data conditions from several system resources. Machine learning algorithms would detect this activity as atypical, since they represent system services or resources that are not 'normally' running. In this case, machine learning algorithms can perform anomaly detection for machine-, not user-, based access and activity. Machine learning models can even compare 'self-versus-self' and 'self-versus-peer group' access activity for machines and users. They do this by using historical baselines to determine anomalies with high accuracy. If it's not a normal condition, it's an anomaly, and machine learning will uncover it and catch the RAT by the tail!

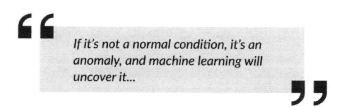

> If it's not a normal condition, it's an anomaly, and machine learning will uncover it...

Misconceptions of machine learning

While numerous UEBA vendors tout their machine learning capabilities, their ability to demonstrate this in a POC (proof of concept) might be problematic for a number of reasons. The first is if the POC is short-term, for example five days, and the customer wants the solution vendor to find a smoking gun with the presumption it will be done via machine learning. Real ML, however, takes time, needs context and is deeply data adjusted. The models must train with baselines to do the work. That takes time for the models to self-learn and self-train — a lot more than five days.

Threat hunting vs. demonstrating ML in POCs. If the objective is to find anomalies in this short term, the only likely way a vendor will be able to do that is by threat hunting, to run a collection of rules and causalities, and they may indeed succeed in finding anomalies. But that's not machine learning, nor is it repeatable. Anything that shows up within a few days is almost certainly rules-based.

Use cases demonstrate machine learning capabilities. More mature customers of UEBA and IdA are learning to ask for use cases where only machine learning can solve a problem, such as finding access outliers or privileged access risk and abuse. The main use cases require risk scoring of entitlements that could be in the millions and far beyond human capacity. If customers understand the benefits of ML, and plan to adopt it for its long-term value, they must give the solution a true ML test. This means commit the time required to vet the worth of the solution and the breadth of its capabilities. As the old adage goes: "A shortcut is the fastest way to get somewhere you don't want to be." Short-term threat hunting simply can't provide any meaningful insight into a vendor's ML capabilities. In some cases, vendors say they have machine learning, when they really don't. They have merely rebranded their solution to respond to the awareness trend of ML's popularity and perceived value in predictive security.

Self-learning models that optimize in a month. Contrasting the rules-based model, user behavior-based machine learning uses clustering to find outliers or anomalies from the normal for self-versus-self, self-versus-static peer groups, and self-versus-dynamic peer groups (where the machine learning determines the peering for more accuracy in outlier detection). Once an anomaly is found, predictive risk scoring machine learning models factor in time-based norms and deliver feedback to score accurately, with low false positives. These models are self-learning and self-training. They optimize over 30-35 days of data ingestion to create baselines for behaviors. Access to historical data can speed the learning curve of models to a few days. Keys to success are the magnitude of access to ingest data sources into big data infrastructure,

as well as, the proven compute scale for the data science math within the machine learning models and the resources provided.

....historical access data can speed the learning curve of models to a few days.

Context from big data lakes. The causality scenarios demonstrate that more context is crucial to get a useful perspective of the total risk in the hybrid environment. Here, machine learning evolves on context and it integrates effectively with big data lakes to provide the critical ability to analyze data over a length of time, not just an instance. Visibility extends across both on-premises and in the cloud.

Holistic visibility of accounts, entitlements, access and behavior. Machine learning comes in various disciplines. Identity analytics focuses on identifying access risks, excess access and access outliers. UEBA, on the other hand, focuses on anomalous behavior from insider threats, data exfiltration and access abuse. Both disciplines use clustering and outlier ML analysis, however for different outputs. These outputs can be used holistically together for improved security. For example, and as previously noted, to detect privilege access abuse, you must know where the privileged access is with identity analytics. This is a critical solution element, since industry experts cite over 50% of privileged access entitlements lay outside an organization's directory and vaults. If the UEBA ML does not know where to look, or is missing 50% of its target, it can't be effective. To address that challenge, IdA uses ML to provide holistic visibility of privilege access risk and runs in concert with UEBA models to look for abuse.

Common utility scenarios for machine learning in security

The following three examples represent familiar, yet risky, circumstances for a majority of enterprises today. These scenarios illustrate common identity-based access risks and threats, which highlight the importance of combining machine learning with contextual behavior analysis that includes peer group access and activity comparison, cloud access and activity monitoring and the ability to correlate access and activity against identity data stores like HR applications, IAM solutions, directories, and more.

Data exfiltration with departing employees. A sales employee plans to leave the company to take a job with a competitor but has not yet made his intentions known. Before resigning, he wants to gather as much competitive information as possible. This is information the employee would normally have access to for their job role. However, the new actions of downloading more data than usual are suspicious. When compared to that individual's dynamic peer groups, they are shown to be the only sales person performing this volume of activity. The machine learning risk models give the identity a high score for the recognized anomalies, indicating the actions must be investigated.

Stolen credentials from phishing attacks. A set of login credentials belonging to a customer support representative of a financial company are stolen in a phishing attack. The attacker logs into the on-premises support application account with all of the authority of the original genuine user. The intruder accesses many of the same contact and support account records as the legitimate user normally would do. However, the attacker does this with more frequency and with increased volume of data downloads than for a normal customer support analyst. This activity is quickly spotted as something outside the norm, and the company is able to suspend the account until an investigation can be conducted.

> This activity is quickly spotted as something outside the norm, and the company is able to suspend the account until an investigation can be conducted.

Misuse of unmanaged cloud resources. A contract worker had been working with a company for many years. He worked at home and performed his job via VPN for remote access. For all practical purposes, he acted like an actual company employee, with the access rights and privileges of an employee. When his contract was terminated, he was deprovisioned in the HR systems. Nonetheless, login credentials for Salesforce.com were overlooked for termination. He still had access and continued to login to siphon off customer information to provide to a competitor. This behavior was detected through analysis of the current HR data correlated to the contractor's current activities.

Case studies in UEBA machine learning: The broader benefits

While the scenarios above represent common events many organizations might face where UEBA and machine learning are engaged to provide a fundamental security solution, the use cases below present a deeper insight into how UEBA and IdA combine to deliver broader crucial benefits to an organization. These field cases are from Gurucul's portfolio of customer delivery success stories.

Organizational security fortification through risk scores. An insurance customer needed to disrupt external intruders by adding step-up authentication based on machine learning risk scores for user behavior. When a user logs into an account, the authentication system performs a real-time call to the user behavior machine learning solution that provides a current risk score. This risk score is fed into the authentication system which then determines the authentication challenges for the user. A high risk score can result in two or three security challenges to successfully login while a low risk score may result in one or no challenges to login. If an account has been compromised, the external intruder is highly likely to raise the risk score due to abnormal behaviors as compared to the normal user. The high risk scores result in additional authentication challenges which the external intruder may not be able to provide thus locking them out for the present time. The employee may also become more security aware by seeing an increase in the number of authentication challenges required to access their user account.

Attack surface reduction enhanced with targeted identity roles and privileges. A financial services customer employed machine learning models to analyze access and activity for employees to highlight excess access. With this intelligence, they reduced accounts and entitlements by 83%. This lowered the vulnerable surface area of identities open to phishing and social attacks. Machine learning models enabled the determination of the right person, data, time and place with more accuracy than human processes could, reducing both group and role proliferation. Machine learning also produced new intelligent roles for eleven departments, replacing legacy roles created from manual processes and rules. Gartner analysts estimate that machine learning models will determine 50% of roles and privileges in the next two years.

Rapid discovery of industrial espionage via compromised credentials. A leading manufacturing enterprise was concerned about protecting intellectual property, knowing that unethical nation states and espionage are common threat vectors exploited in their industry to gain technology advantages. The customer had modern security defenses in place for known bad threats using signatures, patterns and rules. They understood that targeted phishing and social engineering attacks could compromise account credentials. The customer deployed a user behavior analytics machine learning model solution, which extracted historical access and activity data to accelerate analysis by the models. On the second day of use the SOC team detected two highly privileged research accounts that had been compromised. Further analysis revealed an unethical nation state as the intruder. What the enterprise suspected came to light in a few days using machine learning to detect abnormal account behavior that common security defenses looking for known bad indicators had missed. Without machine learning, normal patterns of discovery and response cycles for this type of attack would be in the range between months and years, with standard intruder dwell time cited by most analysts as well over 150 days.

> " Without machine learning, normal patterns of discovery and response cycles for this type of attack would be in the range between months and years... "

Self-audit feature flags nefarious activity. An insurance company sought to raise security awareness by providing employees with self-audit reports once a week which furnished risk-scored access and activity data from machine learning models. One employee spent a Wednesday out of the office to be in support of a sick child. That employee did not access her high privilege accounts on that day. The following self-audit report she received on Friday, however, revealed account login and activity for Wednesday. Having her own unique context, the employee quickly recognized this was not possible. Upon investigation by the security team one of the high privilege accounts was found to have been compromised for over 3.5 years by an external intruder. The context of the self-audit report with machine learning risk scores and visibility into access and activity data added new eyes beyond the SOC team's capabilities where they would have likely overlooked this activity. Machine learning models aggregate multiple accounts, access and activity under one identity for an employee to quickly assess their activity and any possible risk-scored anomalies, much in the same manner as reviewing a credit card statement.

Clear benefits delivered by machine learning and UEBA. All four cases above were Gurucul customers who experienced clear-cut benefits to their businesses, along with numerous enhanced security monitoring efficiencies that have continued long-term.

Perspectives on the future of machine learning in security

As I mentioned at the beginning of this module, a majority of UEBA security vendors are touting their solutions as being driven by machine learning. However, *caveat emptor* — let the buyer beware — not all machine learning is created equal. There's more information in Chapter 8 of this book on the range of machine learning in UEBA solutions as well as the specific requirements for machine learning in mature UEBA solutions.

Machine learning's continuing evolution. The important thing to keep in mind is that while its impact as seen in other industries has already been profound, we are just getting started with machine learning in security. The new realities in today's expanding hybrid environments require its support now. Continuing to employ the inefficient, ineffective, futile human efforts using rules, patterns and signatures to cope with a growing amount of data that is doubling year over year can no longer be considered a feasible strategy for security experts to detect the unknown. Data science is needed and machine learning is the answer.

CONCLUSIONS & TAKEAWAYS:
Machine learning's continuing journey in predictive security analytics

The age of big data has arrived, with machine learning supporting analytic processes across science, business and a range of other settings and applications. Its irreplaceable value provides higher accuracy, delivers substantial cost savings, offers broader performance capabilities far beyond human scale, and many more benefits. Machine learning's arrival at predictive security analytics has been somewhat slower than other channels of analytics due to the high-stakes importance of reliable accuracy. 2014 represented a breakout year for machine learning's capacities on a broad array of functionalities. Now, analysts view machine learning as providing an invaluable contribution to an organization's complex security risk prevention capabilities.

Award-winning CISO at large, Leslie K. Lambert observes how machine learning is reshaping security. She also notes, however, that all machine learning (ML) is not alike. While some vendors claim their solutions are ML, they are in fact manually driven by a rules-based process, dealing entirely with known bads. On the other hand, mature machine learning uses automated and iterative algorithms to learn patterns in data, and probes the data for structure that may be new and previously unknown. This enables machine learning to perform link analysis to evaluate relationships or connections between data nodes, things such as organizations, people, transactions, etc. This complex iterative data processing discovers patterns and extracts meaning from the vast ocean of digital exhaust. As a result, machine learning identifies relationships that span time, place and actions, on a potential scale representing millions of access entitlements within an organization.

Instances of real-world breaches are examined where machine learning might have discovered the behavior anomaly associated with the malicious activity in a timely manner. They include an industrial espionage case where targeted spear phishing was employed to compel the victim to open a file containing a malware file embedded in the document. Another case depicts an insider using 'borrowed' credentials to spy on executives through their email accounts. This was an instance of privilege access abuse that was poorly monitored by the victim organization's security team. The final scenario cited involved data exfiltration through remote access malware — a Remote Access Trojan (RAT). All of the cases examined by Lambert were well within the capabilities of machine learning and predictive security analytics, drawing from big data via UEBA or IdA, to neutralize a potentially severe risk.

Lambert goes on to observe how compromised identity is a growing concern, as attackers favor identity theft to compromise account credentials. To address this challenge properly, a broad range of data sources must be monitored comprehensively and with a responsive speed to inhibit attacker dwell time as much as possible. With the rich context, this machine learning process produces required security analytics.

Lambert then examines misconceptions of machine learning and how some vendors strive to demonstrate their value during POCs with swift threat hunting, and showing results. Mature machine learning, however, takes more time to ingest data to be able to produce valuable results. The best method to demonstrate machine learning capabilities is through use cases, which employ both self-learning and self-training capabilities. This is a marked contrast to manually driven threat hunting driven by rules and causalities that may not be sustainable over time.

Finally, Lambert presents three examples of common utility scenarios in machine learning for security. These are: data exfiltration with departing employees, stolen credentials from phishing attacks, and misuse of unmanaged cloud resources. She then cites four case studies from Gurucul's solution delivery roster which have delivered definitive value for their customers. They are: enterprise threat detection through risk scores; identity access surface reduction for accounts and entitlements; rapid discovery of industrial espionage via compromised credentials; and a self-audit feature flags nefarious activity. Lambert then shares her observations about the future of machine learning in predictive security analytics, which is growing and evolving, keeping pace with emerging technologies and attacker innovations.

The brave new world of hybrid environments, with users and entities connecting from countless wireless devices, from anywhere in the world, 24/7, is the new reality for a majority of enterprises. The next chapter explores this, along with the insights of one CISO who is well along the journey to secure his company's hybrid environment through predictive security analytics. The next *Borderless Breach Flashcard* portrays a case of wide-scale unethical activity within a bank, where employees created millions of accounts without customer knowledge.

BORDERLESS BREACH FLASHCARD	
The Virtual Boiler Room	
CATEGORY	Company-wide high privileged access (HPA) abuse.
WHO	**The target:** Wells Fargo Bank and Wells Fargo customers.
WHAT	Over 5,300 employees were fired from the bank for creating millions of unauthorized checking, deposit and credit card accounts, without the customers knowing about it.
WHEN	2011 to 2015
WHERE	North America branch offices.
WHY	Greed. Overaggressive sales targets? Management pressure?
HOW	To meet aggressive sales targets, a large number of employees engaged in an abuse of their privileged access to customer account information to open over 1.5 million unauthorized deposit accounts and 560,000 credit card accounts in customers' names. This was done without customer approval or their knowledge. A large number of these accounts incurred annual fees, interest charges and overdraft protection fees which accrued over time. The bank hired a consulting company to investigate after this activity only after it faced a massive law suit from the City of Los Angles for these shady practices.
HOW BAD?	At least one class-action law suit (City of Los Angeles). The damage includes over $185 million in fines, and the largest penalty fee in the history of the Consumer Financial Protection Bureau (CFPB). The states of California and Illinois have suspended bond investment in Wells Fargo, representing billions of dollars. The two top executives have been stripped of tens of millions of dollars in pay, with the CEO being forced to step down. Serious brand damage includes compromised trust of the institution in the market place. The magnitude of damage, and customer flight, continues to be assessed as a number of criminal investigations are pending.
HOW COULD IT HAVE BEEN AVOIDED?	Since they hired a consulting firm to discover the problem, the bank did not have a working or effective UEBA-IdA solution in place. If it had, the pattern of opening multiple accounts for customers with HPA accounts would register anomalous behavior and would have created timely alerts about the questionable behavior.

Cloud and Mobility:
Unknowns for Identity Risks and Misuse

Strategies for addressing the evolving unknowns

If you haven't been impacted by cloud, when will you? And if you have been impacted, what are the significant adjustments?

One way to look at this challenge is to view the old traditional security strategy as something like what Joe Sullivan observed, how on-premises environments were originally like building a castle, with a moat for protection. That thinking parallels, in ways, with the traditional waterfall model applied to software development, which was popular many years ago. Like castle building in the physical environment, this production model has a highly formalized and unidirectional work flow and promoted monolithic, inflexible development. One way to look at it is in the figure below.

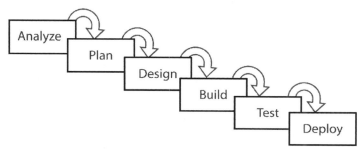

Traditional Waterfall Methodology Model
Figure 7.1

Contrast this model with the newer Agile and DevOps nonlinear methodology which is gaining increasing adoption and popularity. Various graphic conventions have been developed to portray it. The one below distills the concept.

Agile-DevOps development model
Figure 7.2

The obvious difference between the waterfall model and the Agile-DevOps approach is that once the development cycle is complete, it immediately begins anew, initiating a new phase of improvement. Gary Eppinger observed in Chapter 1 how his approach in security solution adoption is not to try to get it perfect, since once it's in place, elements of it will already be out of date. The important objective is that the solution works as planned. Both he and Jerry Archer discussed the benefits of a phased approach. Because of the smaller solution components being implemented, this approach is more budget friendly, and also takes into account the factors of both continuous technology evolution and attacker innovations. Once a phase of a solution has been adopted, it needs to be measured against the original design goals. You must also perform an assessment of the solution against the emerging requirements in the environment.

> ...his approach in security solution adoption is not to try to get it perfect, since once it's in place, elements of it will already be out of date. The important objective is that the solution works as planned.

Success in today's hybrid cloud environment demands the acknowledgement that requirements are changing, evolving. Like machine learning, CISOs must be continuously self-learning and assessing their environment's needs and responding with insightful and impactful responses. Adopting this strategic mindset is key to managing the broad array of factors that comprise the unknown unknowns in the security leader's world.

Once that perspective is adopted, the fading perimeter becomes less of an amorphous threat. The prospect of dealing with all the variables of unknowns for identity risks, compromise and misuse become more tangible and workable. Factors like terminated employees with active access rights and privileges, insiders wandering networks collecting data and exfiltrating it, and compromised accounts logging in from multiple locations, all become focal points of a practical predictive security analytics solution that delivers reliable and actionable results. Initiatives like radical reductions in accounts and entitlements due to excess access, access outliers, plus group and role proliferation, producing a net effect of reducing the attack surface area for identity, become a matter of standard best practices and manageable due diligence.

Solutions will be in place for scenarios like cloud users downloading confidential information, concealing it on their devices, and then exfiltrating it from the company network. This is often seen with soon-to-depart employees leveraging a hybrid environment to evade detection. Gaps in visibility, with SIEM (security information and event management) being on-premises and CASB (cloud access security broker) and IaaS (infrastructure as a service) being in the cloud, with limited connection or unified visibility, will be addressed.

Once this paradigm shift in perspective and strategic thinking is achieved, and mature best-of-breed UEBA, IdA and cloud security analytics (CSA) solutions are adopted, CISOs will be able to field and answer the tough questions like: How does cloud expand access risks, compromise and misuse to employees, business partners or customers? How do you ensure you cover all the bases for on-premises and cloud for unknown risks and threats? How is data access and use changing with cloud and mobility? How does cloud and mobility change visibility for defenses? How does the importance of identity access change with cloud applications? What changes for data exfiltration detection are required with cloud applications? How is identity managed to reduce access risks in the cloud? If cloud identities are compromised, what detects compromise or misuse?

> " *Once this paradigm shift in strategy thinking and perspective are achieved... CISOs will be able to field and answer the tough questions...* "

The hybrid environment — bridging on-premises and cloud, along with mobility, BYOD (bring your own device) and IoT (Internet of Things) — currently represents the embodiment of the new frontier of Borderless Behavior Analytics. An early adopter in cloud security analytics, along with UEBA and IdA, Gary Harbison, CISO of Monsanto, is a pioneer in utilizing advanced predictive security analytics in both cloud and on-premises environments. In the following section he shares his seasoned experience in information security and insights on the benefits of CSA, UEBA and IdA.

BORDERLESS EXPERT INSIGHTS

Gary Harbison, CISO*
Monsanto

As the Chief Information Security Officer for Monsanto, a leading global agriculture company, Gary Harbison leads the Information Security Office (ISO) with global ownership of information security, IT risk management, and protection of Monsanto's critical data. Gary's organization is responsible for the Global Information Security Strategy, IT risk management and compliance, security education and awareness, cyber threat and intelligence, business continuity planning, and governance of the IT Security Controls and Privacy program. Gary and the ISO are focused on managing Monsanto's risks and cyber threats globally, and enabling the business with pragmatic security solutions. He is also a member of the IT Leadership Team helping to define and drive Monsanto's global IT strategy. Gary has over nineteen years of IT experience, with seventeen of those focused in the information security domain. This has included multiple global Fortune 500 companies, as well as public sector experience with the US Department of Defense.

A member of Gurucul's Executive Advisory Board, Gary has provided instrumental guidance for the company's path through the ever-evolving and complex path of challenges of facing the company's emergence in the field of UEBA and IdA security. He shares his seasoned in-depth insights into the challenges in emerging world of the hybrid cloud security and machine learning's place in it.

Overview

In this section, Harbison begins with his depiction of the fading perimeter of enterprise environments as a model for securing a company's network and the importance of Borderless Behavior Analytics within this context. He then discusses the challenges with transforming into hybrid cloud security from legacy platforms and also how cloud and mobility changes visibility for defenses and perimeters. On the critical topic of data exfiltration, Gary explores comparisons on change and impact with cloud application security versus on-premises security. Relating to legacy processes, he discusses the future for signatures, rules and patterns within cloud security. He then investigates the impact of cloud API transparency challenges in the corporate network. Employee and user identity in reducing access risks in the cloud, as well as the detection of compromised cloud employee and partner identities in cloud hybrid environments, are examined. Harbison then delves into how machine learning discovers unknown access

* The views and opinions expressed by Gary Harbison in this book are his own, and do not necessarily reflect those of Monsanto, or any of his previous employers.

risks, account compromise and detection of unknown threats. He summarizes by giving his observations on the CISO's role with cloud and mobility trends and balancing business goals with network security priorities.

The fading perimeter and Borderless Behavior Analytics

The fading perimeter has been going on for some time. For years companies have had contractors, third parties or partners in their environments, configuring and installing systems. These outside parties might even have had devices plugged into the environment that were not managed by the enterprise IT groups. Security experts have observed this kind of perimeter erosion over the last few years.

Perimeter multiplication and de-evolution. More recently, as capabilities in the cloud became more prevalent, this erosion became even more pronounced. A major influence was the proliferation of devices in terms of numbers and type (including BYOD), as well as the increasing number of different infrastructure environments that now form a company's 'virtual perimeter'. It is this blurring, eroding border, and the lack of effectiveness of the old 'one border' perspective that has accelerated the mindset of CISOs. It reflects profound implications for those changes. This is important, because enterprises must now contend with an increasing number of multiple perimeters and borders in the future.

Moving from legacy platforms to hybrid cloud: The security challenges

As companies migrate platforms to the cloud, the key for security teams is to understand they still need the same capabilities, controls, visibility and protection as on-premises. This objective may consist of the same approach or the same controls. However, it might require entirely different controls, a new approach, or a completely different thought process.

The challenge of visibility across varied environments. In the past, we relied on egress points and standard areas in the network to get visibility. With cloud environments, however, we may not have the same opportunity. As more applications and systems move off premises to the cloud, employees may not always VPN back into their network to access resources. So how do we continue to get the visibility we need and the comprehensive monitoring we require?

The need for innovative resourcefulness in security. With the expanding range of enterprise cloud adoptions, we no longer have one perimeter. This means multiple entry and exit points. The challenge is in understanding how to consistently have the same

> The challenge is in understanding how to consistently have the same baseline security assurance in each of those environments.

baseline security assurance in each of those environments. Achieving that same protection, outcome and value — between Amazon Web Services (AWS), Microsoft Azure and Google's Cloud IaaS environment — requires creative thinking within security organizations. As part of the planning process, security design teams will also take into account that with infrastructure or platform as a service (IaaS or PaaS), a majority of the security will be managed by the provider. In this context, a company's security team will serve in a security assurance role, ensuring the controls are in place.

Redundant duplication and rebuilding controls. On the infrastructure side, there is no easy way today to consistently apply control across an AWS, Azure, or Google mixed cloud environment. Security teams often find themselves duplicating and rebuilding controls several times based on what IaaS/PaaS environment they're migrating to. A benefit of going to the cloud, however, is that automation provides the opportunity to ensure all of an organization's servers (workloads) are configured properly and have passed automated security checks. Segmentation can also be achieved within IaaS/PaaS environments more easily than adding segmentation in traditional on-premises environments.

> *Security teams often find themselves duplicating and rebuilding controls several times based on what IaaS/PaaS environment they're migrating to.*

Cloud's scaling flexibility. One of the variables impacting this new perspective is the ability of speed to deliver infrastructure environments and the agility to scale up and down. This contrasts with the traditional model of building capacity to peak loads on-premises, and having it stand idle when not at that threshold. The cloud's scaling flexibility can also help maximize budgeting dollars.

Innovative security tactics. Security experts are discovering innovative methods of utilizing the capabilities of the cloud to benefit them. An example is refreshing workloads every 48 or 72 hours pulling from the known gold standard build images. From the persistence standpoint of an attacker seeking extended dwell time in their target's environment, this represents a challenge to gain and maintain access for a sufficient period of time to find and exfiltrate the data they're after. This security tactic increases the likelihood of attacker mistakes, which enhances the probability of detection by machine learning models and SOC teams. This method is not foolproof if an attacker succeeds in stealing valid IT administrator credentials through social engineering or other means.

How cloud and mobility changes visibility for defenses and perimeters

As data has become much more portable, and as enterprises adopt cloud-based storage and file sharing/collaboration services, identity and access management becomes critical in maintaining the user experience through federating authentication and using those credentials across the various cloud environments, mobile devices and other entities. Migrating this functionality into this complex collection of systems and elements is a core CIO and CISO objective. This is necessary to provide employees the ability they need to have a more seamless and frictionless experience using the environment.

Achieving visibility across all environments. This functionality is also an important factor in terms of security teams maintaining visibility. As IT systems are spread across those environments, the commonality SOC teams use to correlate comprehensive and reliable visibility is the identity. As long as IT and security teams have implemented a strong federated single sign-on solution with consistent identities across cloud platforms and applications (e.g., Amazon Web Services, Salesforce, Microsoft Office 365 or email, as well as an IT system on an internal network), security teams can then use that identity model to correlate their visibility across those environments. This is where fuzzy logic and nearest neighbor algorithms develop an identity associated with its accounts, access and activity. Orphan and dormant accounts are also called out for remediation.

> " As IT systems are spread across those environments, the commonality SOC teams use to correlate comprehensive and reliable visibility is the identity. "

IdA and UEBA empower hybrid environment threat analysis. Going forward, cloud providers continue to offer better and more robust capabilities for the monitoring of access and activity through APIs and CASBs. In parallel with this, security teams will empower a big data platform with IdA and UEBA machine learning models as they consolidate it centrally to correlate, analyze and identify access risks and unknown threats across all those environments. They'll have an excellent picture of an employee, entity or partner's access and activity, even though it may actually be spanning across five or six different IT cloud environments or on-premises systems, located anywhere in the world.

The impact of mobility and BYOD with DLP transition from on-premises to the cloud

The need to understand the movement of critical data remains unchanged. It goes back to the original function DLP (data loss prevention) provided: visibility into the flow of our data — where it's being sent, how it's being used in the environment, and where it's being saved. It has also allowed us to take proactive control to stop sensitive information from being sent out, or from being copied and removed from our IT infrastructure and endpoints.

Limitations of unconnected DLP. While some cloud vendors have begun to build in DLP capability in their environments, it's only a partial element of the solution. The real challenges emerge as you have on-premises DLP through your endpoint, and DLP integrated with a cloud storage environment, but they aren't connected. As a result, your team must write policies multiple times for the multiple scenarios. This is where cloud security and integration requirements grow in complexity, challenging efficiencies. Unless the vendors start to open up their products and DLP capability to integrate with other products, this drawback will persist. The need to tie DLP together only increases as environments become more complex.

> *The real challenges emerge as you have on-premises DLP through your endpoint, and DLP integrated with a cloud storage environment, but they aren't connected.*

Embedding controls in data. Beyond DLP, the other part of the transition challenge is the need for data protection as it moves through the various cloud infrastructures, endpoints and devices. This is known as containerization, and includes encryption and rights management. CISOs are asking, "Can we reach a point where controls really follow the data as it moves throughout all those different endpoints?" The ultimate objective is to embed those controls (e.g., print, save, access, open) into that unstructured data file so controls stay with the data file as it is in transit throughout the various hosting and infrastructure environments.

Varying BYOD policies for different organizations. Each company will have to determine their own risk profile and policy as BYOD and mobile becomes more of a need and a standard. With mobile devices, you can implement mobile device management and ensure you are able to securely wipe the device. Containerized solutions also keep all the data on a mobile device, or even a laptop, in a controlled secure encrypted container. Without standards and controls in place, BYOD can become a sieve with respect to controlling data.

BYOD functionality evolution. Some security solutions allow you to use applications in the cloud (with a proxy-based CASB), but they can prevent data from being stored locally, downloaded, or copied locally. You can use those enterprise applications within a mobile browser; you just can't save data via downloads. It's all evolving, but within the BYOD space, it will boil down to how much risk a company wants to take on. In addition, the corporation must determine if employees want to use their own device or possibly see this as burden where they must buy and support their own device. Either way, data on the device must be protected.

BYOD access context determining risk levels. Context and scale are other critical factors in assessing BYOD security policy. It's not one size fits all. For example, security teams may allow more flexibility around BYOD within their organization's sales group, versus a product development team or an R&D group dealing with intellectual property. They may not offer the same types of enablements because of the difference in risk. Determining who has access to the data becomes critical.

> Context and scale are other critical factors in assessing BYOD security policy. It's not one size fits all.

Data exfiltration: Change and impact with cloud application security versus on-premises environments

Similar to other traditional security controls, as we transition into the cloud, detection of data exfiltration may require a different approach and mindset to be successful. For example, the methodology remains the same to understand data movement in each environment — what 'normal' looks like and what is authorized, versus seeing data activity that doesn't make sense or is an anomaly. Behavior modeling and baselining a user's typical usage patterns, rates, and thresholds, on how much data is accessed and downloaded through those environments each day, helps surface anomalies for users and within peer groups. This offers the ability to quickly investigate those anomalies with rich contextual insight that alleviates false positives — data use that might be atypical, but which is in fact legitimate and required for an employee's work.

Digital exhaust hampers efficiencies. The older, manual ways of approaching security visibility, or non-automated ways, slows security teams down. There is so much digital exhaust to monitor that any realistic prospect of security assurance simply cannot be expected. In this new normal of the hybrid cloud, machine learning and big data are essential to deliver accurate and timely insights to the security analysts. They can quickly understand what actions are required so they can execute appropriate remediation in an expedited manner. This is a critical key in security for successful cloud adoption.

> In this new normal of the hybrid cloud, machine learning and big data are essential to deliver accurate and timely insights to the security analysts.

Revelations from deeper data. While enterprises strive to draw the full value from their hybrid environment's data, they invest in security products providing controls and visibility today, where too often it's too little too late. After a SOC analyst sees an alert fire on an incident, and digs into the data, they find the missing clues of what they should have seen was going on for some time. In collecting all the data without user and entity behavior analytics, organizations are not driving the insights they need, when they need them; and they're not getting the full value from their existing investments. UEBA provides analysts with

> *UEBA provides analysts with the deep data insights they're not getting today, yet which allows them to drive additional value from their existing data sources.*

the deep data insights they're not getting today, yet which allows them to drive additional value from their existing data sources.

A force multiplier required for complex hybrid environments. Over time, the industry is learning that to be truly effective at proactively 'hunting' for threats, you must have the right tools. Traditional patterns, rules and signatures are not able to detect more advanced attacks, and 'throwing people at the problem' simply does not scale when you consider the amount of digital exhaust is doubling year over year. A force multiplier is required to pick up the human nuances of behavior that ultimately flag anomalous activity. Machine learning leverages useful and predictive cues that are too noisy and highly dimensional for human experts and traditional software to detect. It has the ability to find high-order interactions and patterns in data for complex problems such as insider threats, compromised accounts and fraudulent cyber activity. Machine learning is the force multiplier whose time has come to support the mounting data volume and variety in hybrid environments for access risk and unknown threats.

Efficient security analyst utilization. With the high demand and shortage of quality talent to detect and respond to advanced threats, it is important that organizations do everything in their power to drive the most value from each employee on the team. Every second those highly talented and qualified resources spend engaged in manual data crunching and correlations, means the true value of their expertise is not being realized. The hazards of data fatigue loom and the security team specialist may grow increasingly dissatisfied with their role and responsibilities. From a CISO's perspective, while they can't fully utilize that resource, the SOC team won't be catching attacks as quickly and as comprehensively as required.

The future for signatures, rules and patterns in cloud security

Signatures, patterns and rules will continue to maintain a role in network security for the foreseeable future, to block the known bads. Most companies face varying types of attackers. Some of the less sophisticated ones will continue to use a selection of the more dated attacks that could trigger a signature. These signatures still play an important role in 'cancelling noise', thus increasing the ability to detect more sophisticated attacks.

Innovative intruders persist. This concept is more focused on the fact that sophisticated attackers watch the security industry very closely, and they have observed a continued focus on stopping malware. For this reason, they are shifting tactics to rely less on malware, and pivot to the use of valid employee credentials (preferably privileged access accounts) that allow for lateral movement in the environment and data access that looks like legitimate employee activity.

Machine learning baselines normal behavior. This is where user and entity behavior analytics plays a critical role. When machine learning understands the normal behavior of an account, it will see when someone else may be using that account for non-legitimate purposes through behavior anomalies. Security teams are observing the rising hazard of the insider threat and of data leaving their environments. This could be a disgruntled employee or a cyber-espionage kind of attack where employees are targeted to try to gain their credentials. Finding that insider attack, using UEBA, requires baselining the employee's and peers' normal behavior and then identifying when they're trying to access data and systems which are either not part of their job or that they typically don't use.

The inevitability of compromise. Most CISOs agree, they can't guarantee there will never be a compromise or a breach of IT systems. To help defend against that probability, security teams need to lower the threshold of noise it takes to detect an attack or an account compromise. Reducing the entire surface area open to attack in a proactive manner also reduces the profile of excess access and access outliers. As a result, an attacker is forced to work harder. They become more frustrated trying to gain access, and in the process they are more likely to generate noise and make a possible mistake. Security analysts will see this occurrence with behavior analytics and be able to address issues early on. It's a two-sided approach of lowering the ceiling of noise for detection and raising the difficulty of access attack infiltration. UEBA and IdA are key disciplines to achieve this goal.

> *....security teams need to lower the threshold of noise it takes to detect an attack or an account compromise.*

Reducing intruder dwell time. A success metric security teams should consider is the dwell time. The quicker SOC analysts see the account compromise occur, the shorter the dwell time. This means that it will be less likely these intruders will be able to succeed in getting data out of the environment and resulting in a breach. While signatures and rules will still maintain a supporting role cancelling noise of known threats, security experts recognize they must expand their capabilities to find the problems quickly, and leverage UEBA to fill the gaps for unknown threat detection, and IdA to reduce access risk.

CASB solutions provide shadow IT visibility and controls

It's important to understand new tools, like a cloud access security broker (CASB), and understand how it fits into your security architecture. Along with delivering functionality in visibility, compliance, data security and threat protection, they provide opportunities to achieve similar capabilities implemented for on-premises environments through a proxy or secure web gateway. In other words, a CASB provides a 'funnel' for centralizing monitoring of cloud environments by forcing traffic entering the environment through a CASB proxy gateway. You can also get visibility and monitoring from a CASB using an API deployment for access and activity of SaaS applications with APIs. Another benefit of forcing some of your egress traffic through a CASB is to gain a deeper understanding of cloud usage and greater visibility into unsanctioned cloud applications, or shadow IT.

CASB form factors. Three types of CASBs exist. They give their customers a range of options for visibility and to control a larger set of cloud applications. They are:

- *Reverse proxy* – Deployed as a cloud gateway, this mode sits in front of a SaaS application, to provide visibility into identity, to authenticate who the users are and where they are going. This monitoring includes data moving in and out of the environment.

- *Forward proxy* – Here the CASB provides a forced control choke point on-premises, in most instances, by routing all endpoint traffic through it, and then updating endpoint DNS settings. Visibility for instances such as BYOD are then monitored by a reverse proxy where DNS settings remain unaltered. On-premises solutions may deploy software agents on endpoint devices.

- *API mode* – This mode enables users to operate on any device at any location with no modifications. It analyzes access and activity via API integration with SaaS, IaaS, PaaS and IDaaS. This mode provides organizations access to native SaaS features, to perform log telemetry, policy visibility and control, as well as, data security inspection on all data at rest in the cloud application or service.

Multimode CASBs. When all the operational modes described above are available in one solution, they are referred to as multimode CASBs. All forward or reverse proxy-based CASBs are important data sources which expedite the delivery of rich context for machine learning models. Cloud, however, is only one data source, and if unincorporated with what users are doing on-premises, this allows machine learning in only one silo and represents limited visibility. To facilitate the breadth of risk scoring needed for accuracy, comprehensive monitoring with hybrid visibility across both cloud and on-premises is required.

API transparency challenges in the hybrid cloud environment

For UEBA and IdA, the importance of APIs relates to the access and visibility they provide into logging data and other information involving movement to the cloud, mobility and other initiatives. Empowered by advanced machine learning, UEBA pulls all the data together. It then centralizes the data so it can be utilized from a comprehensive analytic standpoint. These analytics then deliver the ability to unlock new and broader insights from the data, enabling security teams to see things they had not been able to see before. This delivers the full value of the data.

Empowered by advanced machine learning, UEBA pulls all the data together. It then centralizes the data so it can be utilized from a comprehensive analytic standpoint.

Uniform visibility across systems and users. The reality of most organizations, however, is that visibility is achieved through many different vendors, partners and infrastructures. While the APIs expose rich data, which can be consumed by those platforms, the challenge is this information from multiple sources needs to be accessible in a simple-to-use, centralized and orchestrated way to truly unlock the value. Vendors and cloud providers are progressing and getting better with that capability. This goal would be further enabled if the industry had an open API standard SaaS applications could adhere to. This would help ensure seamless integration between SaaS applications and behavior analytics platforms. As time goes forward, and network speeds increase, the proxy options of a CASB becomes less attractive. However, for now, it provides SaaS application visibility for those cloud applications lacking an API.

Security solution criteria. As you review most enterprise security architectures deployed at companies today, you will likely still see controls and products provided by various security vendors. Though CISOs have desired a simplified vendor landscape and more integrated product stack, the fact is that to achieve effective controls, a 'best-of-breed' approach is still largely used to achieve success. There's always some work required to integrate the various products and unify the visibility. It becomes even more difficult as you go to the cloud environment where you must rely on the application, infrastructure or platform (SaaS, IaaS and PaaS) provider to expose the data to you. CISOs always have to ask, "Does the solution have an API? And does the data available from the application and infrastructure expose the right mesh required with the data from other providers? If not what's missing, and how do I get it? Am I getting the data I need for security and behavior analytics in my custom environment?"

The importance of identity in reducing cloud access risks

In the future, as enterprises' cloud adoptions expand, recognition occurs that the inside and outside of the network has begun to blur. At this juncture, identity becomes critical for security assurance. This is not just user identity in the traditional sense of how security teams think about it. It's also the identity of employees, partners and third parties, the identity of the endpoints they're using, as well as the identity of different keys automating authentication in the environment.

Context in identity, trust and access. CISOs must start making security decisions based on identity and the context around how much we trust that identity, versus, determinations based on IP addresses and where someone is entering from. If you look at the traditional model of a perimeter where everyone who is inside is trusted — and there may be some segmentation internally — we often make decisions on trust based on what network users were coming from. In the future, enterprises will not have one big perimeter, but many perimeters. For example, each SaaS provider or the cloud hosting environment is itself a perimeter. SOCs can no longer make security and trust decisions based on which network users are connecting from. People will have always-on connectivity, via mobile devices, and as a result, a more mobile workforce will exist, even on their laptops. It becomes critical to make trust and access decisions based on identity and the context of what we know about that identity.

Numerous factors determine context. The following are examples of how UEBA uses context. If Gary Harbison is logging in, is this the normal time Gary logs in? Is he logging in from the work laptop he always uses? Is he logging in from a geo location based on his IP address which he normally uses? Is he trying to access a system he normally uses? Answering all these questions gives us the context that either increases or decreases the level of trust a SOC correlates with this identity. It's no longer just, "Yes this is Gary because he gave the right password and username." It's also, "Do these things look right? Or instead should more information be required to validate it's Gary (e.g., step-up authentication)?" Or should a SOC analyst use this data to understand the context through UEBA and IdA risk scoring and possibly highlight it as a potentially risky connection? In addition, it's not uncommon for an outsider threat to first manifest itself within an environment as an insider threat due to account compromise or hijacking. SOC teams must constantly assess these potential scenarios.

> **....context... either increases or decreases the level of trust a SOC correlates with this identity.**

Changing trends for establishing identity with passwords and usernames

No one in the security industry would say they're happy with the level of security and assurance provided by usernames and passwords. As attackers continue to target valid credentials, more and more CISOs are moving to multi-factor (MFA) authentication. Single passwords continue to be compromised. With the more sophisticated attackers, their goal is to attain valid credentials to help them move laterally in an environment and access the data they want. Using passwords only to establish trust for an identity is no longer a reliable approach.

Validating identity with context. While two-factor and multi-factor authentication are important, the focus now must also incorporate the context — the broader and richer context in which you validate trust in the identity. Username and password is one way to validate the identity and gain trust. But there is additional and critical activity context to consider around the circumstances of any instance of access to an asset as referenced above. For example: What time is the employee using it? How often or how normal is it that the employee logs into the application? Where are they logging in? What machine are they logging in from? What type of data are they accessing and how long are they using it for? Context details like these aid security teams in truly determining the validity of the individual using the identity. UEBA and IdA provide the force multipliers by assessing this large amount of access and activity data and delivering predictive risk scores to focus security analysts' attention.

Multiple elements determine trust. All the factors above come into establishing trust. It's also possible to take the step-up authentication approach where you may ask for different levels of verification. This means your system starts by asking for a username and password if a lot of the context matches the normal baseline profile. However, if the system sees abnormal behavior, like logging in from a different machine, a different time, or from a different location, or high risk score, you may then ask for a MFA, or some other validation to assure the person is who you think it is and you can trust the identity.

The endpoint and identity. UEBA providing a risk score via API integration with an authentication system can automate step-up authentication and alert security analysts as required. Meanwhile, increasingly, our security focus zeroes in on the identity and the endpoint to drive trust. This is the direction hybrid cloud security priorities are headed.

> *...increasingly, our security focus zeroes in on the identity and the endpoint to drive trust. This is the direction hybrid cloud security priorities are headed.*

New modes of establishing identity for cloud gateway

An increasing number of creative solutions are appearing that capitalize on the fact that people always have their mobile phone (or phones) with them. So whether it means having a token or a SMS (short message service) message sent to them, or whether it's where the phone is within proximity of the machine they're accessing data from, the options are expanding. There are even solutions looking at how people use their phones, or how they enter in information on the phone to validate whether it's actually the owner.

Evolving variables impacting identity in the environment. New products, features and capabilities continue to evolve that will determine the validity of who, what, why, when, where and how. This context around what is normal is an irreplaceable component and makes a big difference in determining how much you trust someone is who they say they are. For example when you log into Facebook, they have 80 plus different variables analyzed by big data machine learning to determine who you are, as they assume your password and phone are likely compromised.

Detection of compromised identities in a hybrid cloud environment

Suppose an attacker successfully gains access to a valid identity, begins to use it in the environment then tries to access data and systems the employee usually does not access. This should be something highlighted by user and entity behavior analytics and require investigation by the security team. It may turn out there's a legitimate reason for the user's behavior when the team investigates it. Advanced machine learning is the key to this capability of highlighting anomalous behavior. With machine learning, this previously unusual behavior would then be correlated into the user's baseline use patterns. This in turn helps to define a unique and living contextual 'persona' of the user and likely will not trip a priority alert for the same behavior in the future.

Accounting for all identities in the environment. All identities in the environment, such as system accounts that aren't tied to one person, and including cloud access keys and similar elements, should be included in monitoring through UEBA and IdA. Moreover, in order for business partners and third parties to provide value to an enterprise, they must also have an identity within the organization's environment. They might be connecting through a secure VPN through a limited subset of systems they are providing services for. Alternatively, they may be logging into more of a virtual desktop environment, so they have segmented access. With UEBA and IdA, they will all have a valid identity in the environment, which is established with a baseline normal behavior within their defined business roles and responsibilities. In some cases, customers may be included on their identity and roles within the organization as well.

UEBA's predictive risk score alerts. When the employee or partner's credentials and identity have been compromised, and there's an attacker moving through the environment in a way that does not match the employee or partner's baseline behavior, the SOC will be alerted to see high UEBA predictive risk scores. The critical importance of delivering a singular and comprehensive picture of a user's identity and behavior across all environments and peers is vital for security. UEBA and IdA have an irreplaceable role in successfully reducing access risks and detecting these identity compromises.

How UEBA and IdA integrate to discover unknown access risks, account compromise and behavior anomalies

One key point should always be kept in mind, which relates to both the CIO and CISO's mandate. That is to facilitate company goals and employee productivity, and balance that productivity with security. Here, as well, identity plays a crucial role. Fifteen years ago employees had ten different passwords to access systems in the different environments they worked in. If that was still the highly inefficient workflow model today, employees would be frustrated to no end. Identity access management (IAM) is the key to maintaining that integrated kind of frictionless experience for employees, to be able to access the system in the way they need to do their jobs and enable the business. There is a benefit to utilizing IAM, from an enabling perspective where it helps employees' quality of workflow and productivity. Its benefits in today's environments, however, are no longer as comprehensive as they used to be in traditional environments.

The gap in security assurance. When it comes to effective monitoring and control strategies, however, one issue relates to how certain organizations handle their threat intelligence mandate. It represents a gap in their approach toward security assurance. This gap concerns the policies these organizations have adopted between their IT infrastructure, IAM access side, and the security monitoring threat detection side. At times, far too many unnecessary accounts and access entitlements are permitted to grow unchecked on the IT side. This only increases the threat exposure.

> At times, far too many unnecessary accounts and access entitlements are permitted to grow unchecked on the IT side. This only increases the threat exposure.

Big data and the threat plane. For any large organization, the data lake represents a serious set of challenges. Data haphazardly pushed into big data can create an unwieldy data swamp, thus creating a challenge for UEBA solutions to detect unknown threats and anomalous behavior due to poor context. However, amplify that with an unmanaged growing number of orphaned, dormant, and inactive accounts, plus excess access and access outliers, and it will unnecessarily multiply an organization's access risk and threat plane by sobering magnitudes. The result is that the core requirements for comprehensive and reliable timely monitoring become much more difficult to achieve.

Siloed inefficiencies in organizations. Security experts have observed how in the past some operational sides of an organization remained separate. Their functional perspective reflected that the responsibility for identity comes from the IT infrastructure side, or the IAM and access side, where access is given to employees, business partners and customers. The security side remained focused on monitoring the existing environment for threats. The two group's policies lacked coordination to view identity as a threat and access risk plane.

Inadequate and risky identity management. Industry awareness of identity as an attack vector continues to grow while excess access risks, access outliers and shared privileged accounts are recognized as critical elements of this challenge. Account compromise and misuse are at the core of modern threats. Having a poorly managed identity access plane exposes excess attack surface area for phishing and social engineering threats. By leveraging IdA machine learning, defined intelligent roles, risk-based profiles and dynamic access provisioning, organizations radically reduce the access surface area. This minimizes risk dramatically.

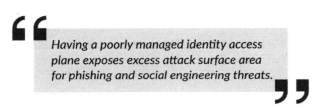

Having a poorly managed identity access plane exposes excess attack surface area for phishing and social engineering threats.

IT and security strategy coordination. Understanding where your most sensitive data is, who should have access to it, and how to control that access properly, helps assure you've built the right security into the environment. When IT and security teams coordinate their strategies with a risk-based approach of identity access management, utilizing risk-based certifications, requests and approvals, the identity surface is greatly reduced. SOC analysts can observe access and activity more closely around employees' behaviors due to a minimized privileged environment. At any time the right focus is applied to the highest risk and highest value assets in an organization. This provides an optimal methodology and capability for effective security control.

UEBA as a platform for on-premises and hybrid cloud

From the UEBA and IdA perspectives, the solution allows enterprises to correlate wide and deep sets of data with a focus on user behavior and their identity for multiple accounts, access and entitlements. The solution set's optimal capability provides a broader view correlated across various devices and hybrid on-premises and cloud environments. If you can stitch together identity, accounts, access and activity, within applications on-premises, SaaS cloud applications — as well as high privileged access to

IaaS, or PaaS environments, to correlate these events and logs all together across all of those various environments and perimeters — then you're approaching the threshold of comprehensive security visibility and the 360-degree context. This capability begins to let organizations maintain a holistic view by pulling in big data that's available to start monitoring collectively as one perspective across the identity.

Expanded visibility and monitoring. UEBA and IdA also empower enterprises to maintain and extend visibility, and drive value, because they leverage baseline behavioral profiles and identity access with big data through machine learning. This allows security teams to expand the context of their monitoring, and not just rely on the known bad detection of the signature-based world. This threshold is where security teams begin to truly understand their employees' usage patterns and behavior throughout a normal day and gain insight into where the patterns changes and why. As hybrid environments expand and grow with complexity, the *only* way to achieve holistic user and entity behavior analytics is through the power of proven machine learning models. This leverages big data with validated UEBA and IdA models, to reduce access risks and detect high-risk behavior anomalies. Recognizing that IAM needs machine learning is often overlooked by security teams solely focused on detection and response. For some organizations, IAM needs to be cleaned up and revamped to fully address the issues of identity as a threat plane.

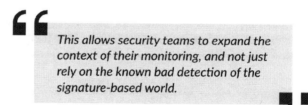

This allows security teams to expand the context of their monitoring, and not just rely on the known bad detection of the signature-based world.

Network security priorities: The CISO's role of balancing business goals with cloud and mobility trends

There is a range of clear benefits in cloud and with mobility, and for some enterprises they represent a decisive factor for their success in the market. These innovations enable strengthening of their position against the competition. Adopting these new technologies and capabilities, empowers a company's ability to compete in the digital marketplace and meet the needs of their customers. For enterprises to stay competitive, CISOs must be the partner in managing these new risks and deciding what risk is acceptable to the company. For an enterprise to continue to gain share, CISOs must make sure they're able to adopt those types of capabilities in a safe manner that properly manages the risk.

Business goals and security requirements. As technology progresses more quickly than it ever has, the challenge for the CISO is

....the challenge for the CISO is to continue to understand the values and benefits to the business and weigh them against the security requirements.

to continue to understand the values and benefits to the business and weigh them against the security requirements. This entails understanding the rapidly evolving landscape of capabilities, how they impact the network, and figure out how to employ a holistic and flexible security program that manages the evolving risk properly and enables the company to move forward.

The expanding role of CISOs. Even though security is a specialized technical space, CISO's can't discount the critical importance of understanding the business. They must understand what it takes to run the business, what it takes for the enterprise to succeed within its industry and to gain market share. The more security people maintain this business acumen, as well as support an understanding of what employees and leaders are trying to accomplish, the better security leaders can effectively think through that risk within its proper context.

Experienced insights on security risk. There's also a maturity that occurs over time as experienced security professionals come to better understand the threats. With that comes the knowledge of how security controls are integrated together into an ecosystem to manage those threats. This experience helps develop a contextual perspective to assess the actual risk to the company. Experienced security leaders weigh factors in the right balance while someone newer into the space might lack that full understanding.

> " There's also a maturity that occurs over time as experienced security professionals come to better understand the threats. "

Risk-averse perspectives. Security professionals newer to the field are often more risk averse because of their concerns about taking on risk in general. They lack the perspective to weigh the impact of an adverse event, and the likelihood of the event occurring, so they lean more to 'no'. A more experienced security leader will apply their perspective to assess how bad it would actually be if this risk materialized, and how impactful it would be to the company. The CISO must ask and answer: "How likely is it to materialize when we compare it against if we don't do what's being requested? What's the impact to the company?"

Security's partnership with business. Security leaders must understand why a project is needed, why it's important, what it means to the company, and understand the risks. They can evaluate those risks holistically, and think creatively about solutions that can be put in place to minimize the likelihood of the security risk occurring. First, a CISO's role should always be as a partner to the business and enable the business to succeed by continuing to innovate and move forward, enhance productivity, and gain market share, while properly managing and balancing risk. That's where experienced CISO's will succeed with cloud and mobility going forward.

CONCLUSIONS & TAKEAWAYS:
Addressing the evolving unknowns of hybrid environments

As technology evolves, so too do the processes involved to implement them, from those emulating the traditional waterfall methodology, to the Agile-DevOps development model. Instead of unresponsive monolithic development, the Agile-DevOps model prescribes continuous improvement, with cycles of explore, design, install, adopt and review, and then begin the process anew. With an ever-increasing ratio of cloud adoptions within organizations, this phased development model is best suited to the emerging hybrid cloud environment.

Monsanto's Gary Harbison observes the perimeter has been fading for some time. More recently, with increasing cloud adoptions and the use of mobile devices by a wide range of individuals to access hybrid environments, the security implications are profound. The old 'one border' perspective no longer has a place in forward-looking CISO thinking. Yet the goal to maintain a hybrid environment with the same security assurance as legacy systems remains the same, however, it is challenging across multiple cloud environments, with various controls. Here, the need for innovative resourcefulness in security comes into play.

Where the clear advantages of cloud adoption deliver scaling flexibility, increased productivity and cost savings, the security requirements to accommodate this often involve redundant duplication and rebuilding controls. Included in these challenges are how cloud and mobility changes visibility for defenses and perimeters. The requirement is to achieve comprehensive visibility across all hybrid environments. Both UEBA and IdA deliver that capability, along with hybrid environment access risk and threat analysis, driven by risk-based scoring.

More protracted challenges exist as well, with the impact of mobility, and BYOD, along with DLP transitioning from on-premises to the cloud. With BYOD, different organizations will be required to define their specific security policies in relation to the level of risk they are willing to take on in their environments. With DLP, an innovation involves embedding controls in data to help protect it as it moves through various cloud environments.

The challenge of data exfiltration remains on the forefront of security leaders concerns as the impact on cloud application security versus on-premises environments becomes more clearly understood. While digital exhaust hampers efficiencies, the revelations that can be derived from big data, and the context gained by deeper data analysis, is why machine learning is required. The depth and breadth of these analytics are far beyond human capabilities. As a result, critical data too often resides within a system that could flag nefarious activity. Without the force multiplier of machine learning, it remains hidden. The risk persists. This class of solution also maximizes valuable security analyst resources.

Signatures, patterns, and rules are being complemented by the use of machine learning, analytics, and the ability to detect behavioral changes and drive insights. CASB is a new cloud-based way to achieve a number of these goals. The CASB form factors are: reverse proxy, forward proxy and API mode. These three offered in single CASBs are referred to as multimode CASBs. For UEBA and IdA, the importance of cloud APIs relates to the access and visibility they provide into SaaS, IaaS, PaaS and IDaaS. API-based CASBs provide access and activity data critical to deliver machine learning model context. CASB proxies themselves are also a data source for UEBA and IdA machine learning.

As all the experts observed in preceding chapters, Harbison also calls out the critical importance of identity in reducing access risks, especially in cloud. Contextual baselines in identity establish trust and provide risk-based access. This context can include where a user is logging in from, with what device, when they are active, and what systems are they accessing. Are they all normal? It's no longer a matter of providing just the right password. This is an example of where risk-based scoring is involved. As new products, features and capabilities continue to accentuate that impact on organizations, the ability to determine the: who, what, why, when, where and how factors that help determine risk become more urgent and essential. These evolving variables will continue to influence the development of identity and access management in hybrid environments.

Harbison also observes the challenge of silos within an environment and an organization. With IT and security, sometimes their mandates lack awareness of each other. IT is focused on providing access, while SOC teams are hunting for threats often caused by compromised access. What lies between is an access awareness gap in IAM, along with a privileged access discovery gap in PAM. These unaccounted for gaps represent a serious access risk plane. This is compounded by organizations that might adopt feature-specific UEBA solutions, tied to a CASB, IAM or SIEM. The combined UEBA-IdA solution, however, provides a platform where the two sides holistically work together, as exemplified in the privileged access abuse use case.

With the critical mass of our experts' insights presented in the first seven chapters, we next examine the requirements for successful UEBA-IdA and CSA solutions, employing advanced machine learning and drawing from the context of big data. Following that, Chapter 9 provides a guide to predictive security analytics use cases. The following and final *Borderless Breach Flashcard* depicts an episode of a very public, yet avoidable, breach which may have influenced the presidential election of United States of America.

BORDERLESS BREACH FLASHCARD	
Backroom Secrets Spotlighted	
CATEGORY	Political hacktivism, breach of internal communications, or Russian hack.
WHO	**The target:** Democratic National Committee (DNC).
WHAT	First, Julian Assange and WikiLeaks released sensitive internal communications, allegedly from the hacker Guccifer 2.0, of the DNC to the public, which caused widespread embarrassment and a political shakeup. A second release, directly from Guccifer, revealed sensitive information on DNC donors.
WHEN	July and September 2016
WHERE	Washington D.C., or possibly transnational hacking.
WHY	Influence political change.
HOW	The original collection of breached information included over 19,000 emails and 8,000 attachments from the DNC. The exact method of exfiltration has been a matter of heated debate. Some claim it was the product of Russian hacking, while others (including Assange), strongly suggest it was an insider breach. Forbes reported it was from a compromised password and login. Embarrassing disclosures about activities of the DNC were revealed, specifically exposing the DNC's leadership bias for Hillary Clinton over Bernie Sanders, her principal Democratic competitor for the party's presidential nomination. A second release revealed details of DNC donors, their finances, as well as the information technology set up to protect the DNC's sensitive data.
HOW BAD?	The chair of the DNC, Debbie Wasserman, and other top officers, were forced to resign. Allegations of bad faith with the DNC's work against Bernie Sanders, a leading Democratic candidate for President, were revealed. Trust in the DNC's integrity was damaged.
HOW COULD IT HAVE BEEN AVOIDED?	With a political organization of such prominence, both nationally and internationally, it only makes sense to perceive their environment as being a prime target for hackers. Add to that, the intense focus on one leading candidate's relaxed policies on computer security only amplifies the urgency of risk from hackers. If the DNC had an effective UEBA-IdA solution in place, the anomalous activity of accessing sensitive files would alert the security analysts to respond appropriately, and there would have been no mystery about who actually committed the breach.

Requirements for
Borderless Behavior Analytics

Qualifications for predicting risk, now and into the future

Once an organization recognizes the advantages of adopting machine learning with big data for predictive security analytics, and are seriously considering that option, how do they choose the right solution and the right approach?

The other questions security leaders will ask to determine the above will include: What does it take to enable this solution? Is my organization prepared to adopt this class of solution? Do I have all the data in place? What use cases make the most sense? Are all the resources available and is it the right time to adopt?

Part of managing this challenge involves defining the makeup of an organization's infrastructure, its maturity, and what magnitude and phase of change are being considered within their systems. A young organization adopting and integrating new evolving technologies, such as cloud and SaaS, will have quite different concerns and priorities than an established global organization with a pre-existing legacy infrastructure for IAM, SIEM, DLP and in-house applications. One size does not fit all. What are the strongpoints? Where are the gaps? Included in this assessment is understanding where elements of the infrastructure needs to be upgraded, replaced, or supported with new technology solutions to ensure a system is up-to-date on all the supporting operational required fronts. Proper timing of adoption is another serious consideration given the wisdom and experience reflected in the preceding chapters.

Different environmental states for on-premises and cloud within an organization include:

The big picture

- ***Mostly legacy environments*** – With an infrastructure heavily based in pre-existing on-premises systems, many system elements are often siloed. Large, well-established banks and some monolithic insurance companies can be examples of this class of environment, including Jerry Archer's environment at his major financial services company. Here SOC teams experience too much signal-to-noise ratio, with a preponderance of false positives from DLP and IDS/IPS. Challenges they face often consist of a preexisting IAM access risk plane with extensive opportunities to reduce access risk. The discovery gap for privilege access is not well known, and much of it is hidden. Many legacy data sources, generating a high volume of digital exhaust, make up this category of environment. The variety of big data compounds security teams' challenges with a complex logging and event environment that is likely struggling with their SIEM deployments.

- ***Mostly blank slate environments*** – With the ability to choose and adopt the best of new emerging technology solutions, the potential for optimal efficiencies within this environment is high. These organizations did not adopt DLP or SIEM, and have not struggled with IAM projects across an organization. They are, as a result, more flexible. No cumbersome infrastructure of pre-existing IT systems of significance, along with complex logging and events, need to be accounted for. This factor streamlines the prospect for broader environmental efficiencies, something like a developing country adopting wireless communications and skipping legacy wired systems other more developed countries must contend with. Like Joe Sullivan's environment at Uber, these organizations can bypass a generation of security technologies that have hampered organizations in legacy environments. This factor empowers their potential for streamlined adoption of predictive security analytics with big data and machine learning. The challenge lies in making the right security solution choices at the start. Organizations in this category can leapfrog to big data with machine learning for user and entity behavior analytics to detect unknown threats. In addition, these solutions must address and close the awareness gap for access provided and the associated activity, as well as the discovery gap of hidden privilege access risk, to take a risk-based approach for access governance.

- ***Mixed environments, in between*** – A common scenario where legacy on-premises systems must be integrated with new cloud solutions. This is the type of setting Gary Harbison is working with at Monsanto and where Gary Eppinger is revamping Carnival Corporation's hyper-hybrid environment. As a result, cloud system frameworks considerably expand the existing complexity of the original legacy environment's makeup. The goal of these cloud solutions is lowering operating costs, increasing productivity and efficiencies, along with gaining flexibility for business enablement that legacy systems cannot provide. The risks include increased digital exhaust and a more complex hybrid environment with growing risk planes. The solution development model also entails moving from a waterfall IT development methodology to an Agile-DevOps one, with continuous iterations of improvement in planned phases, with more frequent releases. For a predictive security analytics solution to be optimized properly within a hybrid environment like this, security leaders should view this adoption not as a specific feature addition offered from a particular cloud solution, for example a CASB-UEBA, but instead from a platform perspective. In a mixed environment, the requirement for machine learning is more crucial for a higher quality of data and broader visibility. Also, in recognition of identity as an access risk and threat plane, UEBA and IdA need to work holistically together in a single platform. The use case of privileged access abuse exemplifies this point.

The technical infrastructure level perspective

Security leaders must decide whether to adopt a UEBA-IdA solution before or after IAM and SIEM projects. The advantages of adopting an IdA component before a major IAM or PAM project provides a decisive reduction of the access risk plane, plus maximizing the effectiveness of the subsequent UEBA integration. Ultimately, the traditional 'red' and 'green' scenarios — the known bads and goods — are generally accounted for with pre-existing declarative security solutions. However the vast and emerging gray zone of unknown unknowns must be managed. This is where risk-scored analytics, powered by machine learning and drawing from big data for context come into play.

Individual technology challenges where UEBA and IdA solutions add value include:

- ***New SIEM implementation*** – A need exists to reduce dwell time, focus high value 'find-fix' resources, and improve detection response ratios to lower false positives and improve incident response. Manual efforts to threat hunt or find security anomalies, via query, filter and pivot efforts remain unproven. The breadth of data to drive machine learning can be costly due to SIEM indexing fees and expenses must be monitored. When considering a SIEM adoption, security leaders must determine if the SIEM should be deployed to do what it is most proficient at for network operations and compliance, and install an open source big data lake to store data long-term for value to drive security analytics.

- ***Upgrading a SIEM solution*** – A need exists to expand and optimize existing capabilities. Adding UEBA to a SIEM improves detection and response through machine learning-based risk scoring. However, the more holistic picture should include identity analytics and a future hybrid environment needs to be considered. Like the scenario above, the option of deploying a big data lake to drive security analytics should be considered. This can be a sense of heartburn for security leaders who earlier drove the adoption of a SIEM as an end all answer.

- *A SIEM alternative solution* – Here a UEBA-IdA solution provides a leapfrog opportunity for organizations to bypass a SIEM adoption, as analysts recommend if enterprises have not purchased a SIEM, they should consider avoiding it. Their advice is to invest in a basic log and event manager (LEM), integrated with UEBA, for security analytics at a lower price. This addresses the challenges noted in the new SIEM solution section above.

- *A new IAM implementation* – Requirement to have an identity access system in place (e.g., OIM, Active Directory) to expand security efficiencies with an assumption that excess access and access outliers will be cleaned up in the process. However a growing awareness gap exists between what access rights have been provided by an IAM solution and how the rights are being utilized by users. This is a serious access risk plane. Therefore, security leaders must justify importing a legacy-defined access plane that was built on manually defined roles and legacy rules, thus putting 'garbage' into the new system. Using the same roles and same definitions makes no sense for addressing the emerging excess access and access outlier problem. Instead, the potential to reduce excess access by 50% or more exists with UEBA-IdA to start implementations on a fresh footing. IdA provides a risk-based approach for identity and access governance (IGA), and IAM, after years of compliance-driven rubber stamping and access cloning. Identity analytics closes the IAM awareness gap for access versus activity with risk-based scoring for certifications, requests and approvals.

- *Upgrading an IAM solution* – When moving from a legacy IAM solution to an off-the-shelf version, security leaders must ensure the intelligence inside the solution is accurate, to reduce access risk. Manually defined roles from legacy rules has resulted in excessive group and roles access, access outliers, and over privileging users. A new best-of-breed IAM solution may not provide all the capabilities required to move to a risk-based approach. Integrating identity analytics greatly reduces the access risk plane, and closes the access awareness gap for IAM on what access is provided and how it is being utilized. In addition, the identity analytics need to feed into UEBA to increase its accuracy and value.

- *A new PAM implementation* – This is an emerging solution, which 9 out of 10 enterprises have not yet adopted. Common features IT organizations find beneficial with PAM solutions are single sign-on (SSO), multi-factor authentication (MFA), one-time passwords (OTP), and a vault to secure privileged credentials. These components, however, lack the ability to discover privileged access risk at the entitlement level and within applications. For this reason, experts note that 50% of this privileged access lies outside of the existing lists or PAM vaults. Meanwhile, risk officers demand prudent security hygiene to address privileged access risk, inclusive of application privileges, by risk scoring at the entitlement level. Thus, identity analytics, driven by machine learning leveraged from big data, fills the awareness gap for IAM along with the discovery gap for PAM for privileged access risk.

- *Upgrading a PAM solution* – While customers may see the need to expand and optimize capabilities of their existing PAM solution adoption, the constraints described directly above remain unresolved. While an existing PAM solution may discover privileged access risk at the account level, the unknown instances of privileged access entitlements which reside outside PAM vaults will remain an open issue. Discovery of this privileged access risk and its associated access risk plane can only be resolved through IdA and risk-based scoring of entitlements, while UEBA provides risk-based visibility into access and activity of all identities across a hybrid environment.

- *Risk officer governance compliance* – This entails providing information to support governance and compliance requirements, such as Sarbanes Oxley, and aligning with IT and security mandates from organizational risk management groups. SOCs must deliver accurate and timely entitlement and access risk scores to reduce risk and deliver increased data protection. Requirements include development and support of an effective insider threat program with visibility into access, accounts and activity, with priority visibility into the unknown gray areas of the identity threat plane along with the discovery gap of unaccounted for privileged access entitlements. A self-audit option may be in order for security awareness and deterrence.

The overall approach: A multistep process, to clean up access and then monitor for risk in the gray areas. First assure an identity access system (IAM) is in place, and then clean up access with identity analytics (IdA), using a risk-based approach which provides a streamlined access foundation to build upon. On the risk analytics side, harvest data into a data lake or aggregate into a SIEM or LEM. From there a UEBA and IdA solution will normalize, correlate and process attributes through machine learning models for predictive security analytics.

The customer challenge perspective
The use case areas below represent a selection of the most common encountered.

- ***Account compromise and highjacking*** – This stands as one of the top risks organizations face today, where attackers compromise access credentials to gain access and bypass existing preventative defenses. Example attacks to compromise credentials include: Phishing and social engineering. As stated earlier in the book, an identity and credentials can be stolen, however a user's behavior cannot. This scenario also applies more importantly to cloud, as access provides the keys to the kingdom. This use case is frequently included with insider threats, as early detection often appears as an insider until the compromise surfaces.

- ***Privileged access abuse*** – Given experts estimate more than 50% of privileged access risks are outside of known lists and vaults, knowing where privileged access exists is the first step for this use case, a step many UEBA solutions ignore. While account and access data is traditionally ingested from IAM, PAM, and directories, these solutions often lack identity analytics to close the discovery gap. Identity analytics are then ingested by UEBA solutions providing the accuracy for all known privileged access risks for monitoring, baselines, and anomaly detection with risk scoring. Also, with SaaS applications and IaaS (e.g., AWS, MS Azure), the potential for privileged access abuse becomes even more important for cloud as a utility.

- ***Data exfiltration*** – Considered the lifeblood of many organizations, confidential information for customers, patients, employees and partners has become increasingly difficult to protect with the broad range of systems in which it resides. Enterprise-wide insight into access and activity patterns — such as sensitive documents downloaded and copied to USB, large amounts of source code checked out from source code repositories and file uploads to cloud storage, emails to personal accounts, access to competitor and/or job websites — is required. In addition, enhancing DLP solutions with anomaly detection and advanced analytics to reduce the signal-to-noise ratio, plus prioritizing alerts to reduce volume are critical requirements. The adoption of cloud and specific applications such as Office 365 and Box also bring up customer concerns for data exfiltration in hybrid environments.

- ***Insider threat*** – Insider threat trends are solidly consistent for the last three years, and inclusion of account compromise in its definition has increased its visibility. The impact from insiders, malicious, compromised and innocent, represent a challenge that must be addressed to find high-order interactions and patterns in data for complex problems including compromised accounts, network wandering, data collection and data exfiltration. Given insiders have approved access, there is more dependence on context from big data with some solutions including sentiment from user communications.

- **_Identity access management_** – Used to monitor activity against established access rights in IAM, PAM and directories, and to identify access risks via identity analytics (IdA). This use case domain cleans up access, removes excess access, access outliers, dormant accounts, orphan accounts and provides a risk-based approach for identity access governance. Thus risk scores aid in certifications, requests and approvals, plus enable dynamic access provisioning, new intelligent roles and automated risk response such as step-up authentication.

- **_Employee monitoring_** – The combination of endpoint data with directory access and activity are primary data sources for this use case. Inclusion of this use case with a broader UEBA-IdA solution provides more varied context over hybrid environments for anomaly detection. More simplistic employee monitoring solutions with pattern matching and rules are adopting UEBA features, however they remain siloed with limited data and visibility. Employee monitoring has its opponents with privacy concerns over recording employee sessions for playback and review.

- **_Cloud security_** – The emergence of SaaS, IaaS, PaaS and IDaaS presents access risks and unknown threats for the use cases in this section, however for cloud and hybrid environments, not just on-premises. CASB solutions with proxy and API deployments are developing UEBA as a feature, however, within a silo they lack the broader data and visibility of a UEBA platform solution. Mature UEBA solutions ingest CASB data for shadow IT application usage, plus interface into SaaS, IaaS and PaaS with established APIs for visibility into access and activity. In the end, enterprises are likely to own both solutions, a CASB and a UEBA-IdA hybrid platform solution.

- **_Cyber fraud_** – Financial organizations, or departments within larger enterprises, must protect their monetary assets from the risk of cyber fraud. Some organizations deal with transactions to transfer billions of dollars on a daily basis, making human detection of anomalies that much more difficult to detect. Within a scale and setting such as this, the critical signals indicating risky behavior are too fine grained for analysis by humans. Treasury, accounting, payments and departments responsible for daily fund transfers as part of the standard operation, must have reliable security solutions to uncover the malicious actors. Comprehensive enterprise-wide big data ingestion and monitoring cyber fraud models and risk frameworks in alignment with business context are required.

[NOTE: For a complete overview predictive analytics use cases, refer to Chapter 9.]

Mapping the route through Borderless Behavior Analytics

Through the journey of this book, we have seen a number of accomplished security experts weigh in with their experiences and insights into the challenges of predictive security analytics in the rapidly evolving world of hybrid cloud environments. With the staggering rise of 390,000 *new* malware instances per day (AV-TEST IT-Security Institute's malware statistics report, May 2016), a majority of readers have likely recognized the time for change is at hand. Comprehensive hybrid security visibility and monitoring for on-premises and cloud applications is a requirement for business success and survival. User and entity behavior analytics is a key component of that requirement with its ability to detect account compromise, abuse and unknowns which existing defense frameworks cannot detect. At this juncture of their journey, the path enterprises choose defines their destination. The decision determines a route toward an effective solution, which grows with the company's evolutionary presence in the marketplace with alignment of security defenses, or it brings them to more unknowns.

The requirements are complex and exacting in a new and emerging field, where qualified UEBA and IdA solution quality and delivery experience is at a premium. Proven UEBA solution components, well-established processes and ease of use are the adoption goals. Evidence-based knowledge and actionable intelligence — drawn from rich big data context and empowered by machine learning — can help leaders prepare for unforeseen attacks against IT or information assets. Knowing the direction of future trends, many large enterprises are hiring data scientists to develop custom behavior models and risk-tuning solutions customized precisely to their needs. Other enterprises faced with similar needs, but with fewer resources, must consider a field of UEBA vendors who all represent their solution in the best light, including use cases, data sources and years of experience. However, the prospect of adopting a closed black-box solution, or developing their own homegrown solution, is a non-starter for too many prospective customers.

In the preceding chapter, Monsanto's Gary Harbison observed that while cloud adoption is a dynamic business enabler, a game changer, and inevitable for many businesses, "the challenge is in understanding how to consistently have the same baseline security assurance in each of those environments." As Verizon's 2016 *Data Breach Investigations Report* cites, the threat planes are expanding. The risks are not going away. All systems can be compromised. It is no longer enough for companies to merely shore up defenses against generally known threats with manual processes to threat hunt and employ legacy rules and roles for access. And just deploying UEBA to monitor for anomalous behavior is only part of the picture. The need to reduce excess access risks is urgent. Integrating UEBA with identity analytics provides the ability to close the IAM access awareness gap and the PAM discovery gap.

In addition, some organizations have unique requirements for use cases. Government, financial groups, and other organizations with confidential data resources and private use cases, will require the need to develop custom models as vendors cannot analyze the data and are not privy to the use cases. Having a solution with the ability to expand and customize data source attributes for new use cases, along with customer-specific application data sources, is critical. Open choice of big data lake infrastructure where the solution should compute and store on big data for faster processing and greater data variety, plus store data for long-term value, is also essential. A mature solution delivering cloud security analytics for hybrid environments, providing a combined 360-degree view for identity, and risk-scored behavioral threat monitoring, driven by machine learning, is also part of this newly recognized state-of-the-art UEBA-IdA standard. We are beyond static groups and rules, as well as, threat hunting using the known.

As enterprises must now contend with an increasing number of multiple perimeters and borders in the future, CIO at Large Teri Takai poses three critical questions security leaders must answer for their organizations: "What is the perimeter? What's protecting the perimeter? Is that protection effective?" In essence, Ms. Takai questions the existence of the perimeter itself. Meanwhile, Uber's Joe Sullivan predicts the current trends of activity will ultimately result in total fragmentation, where "increasingly more employees will be accessing sensitive enterprise data and information from more and more fragmented devices, through fragmented paths." The time for intelligent change in predictive security analytics strategies stands before the majority of organizations. Navigating that change is the challenge. In this chapter we draw from the experience of our contributing experts, Gurucul's solution specialists, and insights from leading industry analysts. With this in place, an enterprise will be well-equipped to face the new evolving challenges of BYOD, mobility and hybrid cloud worlds.

Expert findings identify the path forward for behavioral analytics

While some leaders may still consider numerous elements of the status quo in security sufficient to sustain their strategy requirements for managing risk, others recognize the fast-evolving challenges of the hybrid environment. Drawing from the collective knowledge described above, we have distilled three critical points organizations should consider with the prospect of adopting a UEBA-IdA solution versus maintaining a legacy security approach.

- ***Managing rules and threat signatures cannot uncover unknown threats*** –
  Legacy security solutions traditionally consist of comprehensive capacities for managing rules, signatures and patterns to identify known threats. They identify the 'reds' (the bads) and the 'greens' (the goods) and help keep the door closed on the known bads that may resurface. Yet today's business models have changed. Threats have shifted. Identity is the new threat vector.

Now a pressing requirement exists to know the unknown unknowns, the vast uncharted grays and their potentially nefarious activities. Behavior analytics uses machine learning-based behavior and predictive models to detect behavioral anomalies to identify access risk and unknown threats.

- *A single view of users' access and activities is mandatory* – To assure comprehensive predictive security analytics in their environment, security teams need UEBA and IdA solutions to offer actionable intelligence through machine learning. It must be able to create a single and unified view of user and entities' access and activity throughout the network, on-premises, in the cloud and across all mobile devices that interact with them. It must maintain an ability to self-learn and self-train, to assure the exclusion of false positives from feedback and to leverage the rich context provided by big data. Especially essential within hybrid environments, machine learning thrives on context, sourcing from big data in both rich volume and broad variety. Machine learning 'on a siloed diet' is simply counter-productive.

- *Context is critical* – Risk scoring with rich context is a prerequisite for successful predictive security analytics. A self-audit capability delivers risk-scored intelligence for context analysis that is uniquely possessed by employees, teams and project leaders. They have an invaluable contextual perspective that a SOC team can't possess. SOC analysts look for peaks, like someone trying to break a password or multiple logins, not low activity such as a PTO day off for an employee or user. UEBA also has an ability to rank the risk of DLP alerts and send them to project leaders who possess contextual insight into an employee's roles and responsibilities. In cases like these, the SOC team would not normally understand the context of these projects. This context is essential to help understand the gray areas to validate and provide feedback to the behavior analytics machine learning models.

Guidelines for UEBA vendor requirements

Scope the challenge correctly to invest once. Security leaders must plan their solution initiatives to address a collection of existing and emerging challenges, while at the same time, strive to anticipate, as best as possible, the future needs of their environments. Considering the requirement to implement a wide-reaching hybrid cloud solution such as machine learning for predictive security analytics, the goal of any organization considering a UEBA and IdA adoption is to get it right the first time. Within this context, assurance of effectively addressing the issue of privileged access abuse is a crucial consideration that must not be ignored. This involves implementing a set of steps at the front end of a solution adoption to ensure privileged access risks are known first from the access risk plane before machine learning monitoring for abuse.

Proper assessment of all these capabilities to confirm their compatibility effectiveness begins with performing a proof of concept (POC). This irreplaceable step in the solution adoption process ensures the solution performs as the vendor claims it should. Just as importantly, this process also involves choosing the solution capable of performing the exact desired use cases of the organization. This capability often correlates with the maturity of the UEBA and IdA solutions that provide robust machine learning and the ability to process and manage massive sets of big data for both on-premises and in the cloud. This scoping often involves cooperative consulting between the vendor and customer. This entails identifying known popular use cases and project road maps plans with the solution vendor, who traditionally has specialized and qualified insights into the challenges and solutions relating to hybrid environments, based on field delivery experience the customer might not have.

As a prospective organization considers implementing a behavior analytics machine learning solution, it helps to narrow down the field of qualified vendors as efficiently as possible to assure their solution capabilities align with a customer's challenges and requirements. Knowing where a vendor sits within the arc of UEBA maturity is one filter to apply at this stage. Well before any POC is performed, matching the vendor's strengths and capabilities with an organization's needs and requirements is a critical step in the qualification process. UEBA solution offerings are categorized in three levels of maturity in the market today. They are:

- ***First generation UEBA*** – *Tools-based analytics.* Vendors in this space first appeared over 10 years ago. Their solutions focus primarily on credit card bust out, account takeover, new account fraud, loan origination, insurance claims, healthcare fraud, tax refund fraud and government benefit programs. The solutions' tool functionality focuses primarily on entity link analysis across structured data. Users drive the analytics or they are customized by the vendors taking data converted through a comparatively prolonged extraction, transformation and loading (ETL) process, which also involves data cleansing. The objective is to have identities and entities resolved and linked. Many of the vendors in this category have developed network visualization techniques for the user interface.

- ***Second generation UEBA*** – *Progressive data integration and early canned analytics.* The majority of vendors in this second category offer automatically resolved identities and entities by virtue of their proprietary fuzzy logic and data-matching techniques. These streamline the lengthy data cleansing, resolution and ETL processes, contrasting the experience provided by first generation tools-based vendors. Users must still define underlying data models and are responsible for discovery and linkage of source data. Solution providers in this category of maturity began offering basic packaged intelligence for repeatable use cases targeted on solving cyber fraud in many of the vertical market areas addressed by first generation vendors. The primary use cases offered by both first and second generation UEBA vendors address only forensics and the investigation of theft and cyber fraud which have already occurred. This includes threat scenarios that are continuing and spreading. Predictive analytics are generally not features associated with this generation of UEBA. Traditionally, a significant amount of professional services are required to integrate and manage these solutions to assure the solution performs optimally.

- *State-of-the-art UEBA* – *Advanced predictive analytics for cyber security and cyber fraud.* This next generation of UEBA vendor innovation has been targeted at developing and delivering packaged predictive security analytics, which detect and identify insider and advanced threats. This type of UEBA solution has gained significant success, delivering notable results within challenging parameters, with a number of large corporations. UEBA solutions in this category have significantly exceeded the capabilities of the widely adopted security user monitoring applications like SIEM (security information and event) management and DLP (data loss prevention). These pure-play UEBA vendors continue to innovate in the development of their predictive analytic models. The applications will not be reliant on customer-driven analytics or inquiries of the data.

The emerging state of Borderless Behavior Analytics resides within the best-of-breed maturity class of UEBA solutions that are part of this category and the requirements described in this chapter address themselves to this class of solutions.

Requirements for state-of-the-art Borderless Behavior Analytics

Note that, even within this state-of-the-art category for UEBA solutions, various gradations of capability exist. Some UEBA vendors claim their solutions are driven by machine learning, yet as CISO at Large Leslie K. Lambert observes, "Let the buyer beware — not all machine learning is created equal." Their definition of machine learning is based on stats, rules and queries, and seeking existing known bads. Advanced machine learning, on the other hand, seeks the unknown extracted from big data via clustering and outlier algorithms, plus dimensionality reduction with risk scoring. An example of machine learning's advanced capabilities is in monitoring millions of entitlements to look for access outliers, and finding privileged access risk. Rules and queries cannot address this challenge in any way. Demonstrating actual use cases in a POC helps confirm a solution's machine learning capabilities. To assure an organization is acquiring the most advanced and comprehensive capabilities from their UEBA-IdA solutions, the following list represents a set of minimum essential requirements.

UEBA and IdA capabilities checklist:

- Hybrid visibility for on-premises and cloud applications
- Open customer choice for big data infrastructure (e.g., Hadoop, Cloudera, Hortonworks, MapR, Elastic, ELK Stack) for architectural scale
- Ability to expand and customize data source attributes for new use cases and customer-specific applications and data sources
- Ability to take any legacy data (mainframe) or new data source (CASB, SaaS application) and map desired fields into attributes without vendor assistance in using the solution
- Custom behavior model development and risk tuning without coding and minimal knowledge of data science, important for confidential data and private use cases outside a vendor's scope
- Identity analytics to reduce excess access, detect access outliers and provide a risk-based approach for IAM and PAM to close the discovery gap between access and activity
- User and entity behavior analytics leveraging peer group analysis including the use of dynamic behavioral-based peer groups to increase accuracy of anomalous outliers and eliminate the issue of bad behavior in baselines
- Cloud security analytics, inclusive of UEBA and IdA, to reduce access risk and detect unknown threats in hybrid environments
- Graphical interface and dashboards, with timelines and drill-down capacities providing a 360-degree view of an identity's accounts, access and activity
- APIs for closed-loop bi-directional deployment with other solutions for data ingestion, risk scores, analytic response codes and analytics, plus automated risk responses
- Dashboards, drill-downs, investigation workbench, open query tool, reporting and data visualizations
- Role-based access control (RBAC), data masking in UI and through workflow, plus tokenization and encryption for privacy to meet large enterprise needs around the globe, including EU privacy regulations
- Self-audits for employees, business partners, and customers providing an individual report of risk-scored access and activity
- Out-of-the-box use cases (UEBA, IdA and CSA) with supporting machine learning models noting required and optional data sources
- Rules and policy engine with step-by-step guidance for ease of use
- Case ticket management with integration for leading solutions (Remedy, ServiceNow, Salesforce) or embedded ticketing and case management feature

UEBA and IdA core components

Delivery on all the requirements above would also include a highly qualified and dedicated professional services team on-site to install the solution, train users and support the solution to assure long-term optimal utility, and future-proof compatibility for the life cycle of the solution. The vendor team's field experience should include knowledge of a broad range of data sources and hybrid environments. These delivery capabilities would include both pre- and post-sales technical support.

Third party integration requirements

To deliver value, a UEBA solution must be integrated with a potentially broad range of data sources, identity management solutions, and more for ingesting into big data infrastructure. This must be for both on-premises and in the cloud. UEBA guidelines for third party interface prerequisites include:

- *Security analytics platforms* – Ready to use connectors for popular SIEM platforms are a standard requirement. There should be an open choice for big data infrastructure. UEBA solutions should be built on popular open-source software frameworks, such as Apache Hadoop and support deployments with Cloudera, Hortonworks and MapR.

- *Data loss prevention* – UEBA solutions must provide ready to use connectors for leading DLP solutions (e.g., Symantec, McAfee and Forcepoint). These data sources are critical for on-premises data exfiltration analysis use cases. In addition, CASB solutions are increasingly adding DLP features and should also be considered an important data source.

- *Identity access management* – Ready to use data connectors for popular identity access management (IAM) solutions must be offered which also facilitate APIs providing risk-scored analysis back to these access solutions, such as automatically detecting access outliers.

- *Privileged access management* – Data connectors for popular privileged access management (PAM) solutions should also integrate seamlessly via APIs to provide risk-scored analysis back to these solutions, such as identifying unknown privileged access risks.

- *Cloud security solutions* – UEBA solutions should provide connectors for cloud access security brokers (CASBs), plus API integration for SaaS applications, identity as a service (IDaaS) and infrastructure or platform as a service (IaaS/PaaS) when possible.

- *Cyber fraud management* – The solution should provide cyber fraud detection within its capabilities, along with the ability to leverage APIs to provide risk scores to fraud and anti-money laundering (AML) solutions.

- *Endpoint solutions* – Endpoint detection and response (EDR) solutions should be available as a data source and provide risk scores and analytic response codes to trigger endpoint recording. This may also include network access control (NAC) solutions as a data source and risk-scoring feedback to enable controls.

- *Governance, risk and compliance* – In a field overwhelmed by the amount of unstructured data analysts must manage, APIs should integrate with governance, risk and compliance (GRC) solutions to provide advanced semantic analysis along with risk scores for assessments.

UEBA feature requirements

More detailed focus on the UEBA component functionality includes:

- *Diverse data collection* – Most widely adopted UEBA solutions are built on Hadoop (HDFS) and provide a flexible metadata model for structured and unstructured data sources. Ready to use data connectors that ease data source integration and data ingestion should be included. UEBA solutions should also compute and store on big data infrastructure such as Hadoop, Cloudera, Hortonworks and MapR. Also, to attain the most timely and accurate data context possible to discover access outliers, a UEBA solution providing over 200 attributes — that are both customizable and can be extended for special use cases — bring added benefits. More diverse and deep data provides better analytics while leveraging the scale with machine learning. In addition, providing a flexible data connector for legacy data sources (e.g., mainframe), for new data sources (e.g., SaaS and CASB), is critical.

- *Single view of identity* – The ability to link information to single identities is key. A single view of identity of on-premises and cloud applications, made possible by fuzzy logic to map accounts, should be a standard offering. This feature should leverage IAM, PAM, AD, Directories, IDaaS, and HR databases to self-learn and self-train on identities. Within its capabilities, orphan and dormant accounts should be identified, as well as, excess access and access outliers, to reduce access risks. Identities can be users or entities.

- *Behavior baseline pattern* – Behavior-based clustering and outlier machine learning algorithms establish behavior baselines for users, entities, static peer groups and dynamic peer groups to detect unusual behavior and access risk. The use of dynamic peer groups delivers a large reduction in false positives over static peer groups, plus eliminating bad behavior baselines. A machine learning model library for a solution should provide hundreds of models for forty to fifty use cases with the ability to optimize in 30 to 60 days. Historical data can be leveraged to reduce self-learning and training to a few days.

- ***Access control and case management*** – Internal case management capability is a standard requirement. A ticketing system, plus integration with other leading solutions such as with Remedy, ServiceNow and Salesforce, should be offered as well. In addition, data masking within the workflow, as well as role-based access control (RBAC), data tokenization and encryption, deliver distinct functional advantages to UEBA solutions.

- ***Dashboards and incident investigation*** – Dashboards with click-through drill-downs for incident investigation have become well-established as integral parts of UEBA solutions for popular use cases, risk groups to watch and color-coding to visualize risk scores. In addition, the ability to create custom reports and open queries and filters are decisively advantageous. Self-audits promote collaboration from users to view their risk-scored profiles for activities and access, to understand the context of their usage and sometimes correct unintentional misuse habits. They also provide the ability to see possible unauthorized use of an individual's identity access.

- ***API layer*** – While the UI provides dashboards and drill-downs for security analysts to act upon, more than half the value of a UEBA solution is derived via API integration with other solutions for closed-loop response, also called automated risk response. Examples include step-up authentication by risk score, automatic access outlier detection with IAM solutions, dynamic provisioning with IAM and IDaaS solutions to reduce workload, prioritized risk-scored anomalies into SIEM and DLP solutions, and privileged access abuse controls based on risk score with PAM solutions.

UEBA machine learning requirements

'Machine learning' may be one of the more over-used marketing terms currently in vogue. Nonetheless, having an in-depth contextual understanding of its place in user and entity behavior analytics is critical. One perspective to keep in mind is the nature of big data machine learning. This far surpasses what humans and software engineering can detect. It represents a magnitude of processing now coming to a state of wider understanding and adoption within the security technology community. The requirements of advanced and mature machine learning include:

- ***No rules, signatures or tuning*** – Operational independence from editing rules and signatures is a core benefit of mature UEBA solutions drawing from true machine learning. No preexisting knowledge should be required to iterate models for various use cases where data sources provide attributes for analysis. No rules or signatures are required for deployment. The focus is on data sources, data ingestion and data cleanliness for deployment. Some UEBA providers may optionally provide a rules and policy editor for customers that choose their own unique use cases and may not have a log event manager (LEM) or SIEM.

- *Peer groups creation (users, entities/assets)* – While static peer groups are a standard UEBA feature, their functionality remains limited in comparison to the next generation innovation of dynamic peer groups which can draw from over 200 attributes to create behavior profiles. The most mature UEBA solution vendors should be able to automatically create both dynamic peer groups based on behavior profiles and static peer groups based on one or more attributes for users and entities. They must provide the ability to view analysis by these peer groups in tables, charts and graphs.

- *Peer group behavior baselines* – Leveraging clustering machine learning algorithms to develop behavior baselines, UEBA solutions continuously identify changing behavior with model optimization within 30 to 60 days. In the more advanced UEBA solutions, historical data ingestion can reduce self-learning and self-training to a few days.

- *Outlier detection and scoring* – Using the behavioral baseline of the peer group, the UEBA solution maintains continuous monitoring and scores anomalies. A convention of outlier risk scoring normalized between 0 and 100 using dimensionality reduction provides an advantageous granularity of precision in scoring, and reinforcement against false positives, and should be considered a standard feature. In addition, a vendor providing dynamic peer groups increases outlier accuracy by 8-10x over the use of static peer groups.

- *Investigator feedback and re-scoring* – UEBA solutions provide the ability to send feedback via algorithm study activity or investigator feedback for time-based norms (e.g., an admin on vacation for two-weeks, or a newly accepted process or workflow). Feedback can also include data on false positives and false negatives where models will then re-score historical analysis.

Insights on machine learning: Not all UEBA machine learning is the same

Many UEBA security vendors are currently touting their solutions as being driven by machine learning. However, not all UEBA machine learning delivers the same capabilities. The following list represents criteria to look for in a UEBA solution driven by true machine learning.

- *Hybrid visibility across environments* – A number of solutions are hampered in their effectiveness because they are focused on siloed pools of data. Any machine learning associated with them is hampered as well, since it is limited to processing the data which resides only in the system concerned. This leaves a host of undetected outliers and an unaccounted for threat plane beyond the silos.

- ***Big data, big data lake*** – True machine learning thrives on large repositories of big data for increased processing and data variety over legacy infrastructure. The richer and more inclusive the source of data, the higher potential for accurate context for risk scores, along with fewer false positives. Solutions not drawn from big data have restricted processing capacity and less data variety. Solutions should provide an open customer choice for big data (Hadoop, Cloudera, Hortonworks, MapR and Elastic/ELK Stack).

- ***No rules or signatures dependence*** – While referenced in the section directly above in a different context, this point bears emphasis and deeper analysis. This issue is the most common complaint of customers and experts in the field who observe that a number of UEBA vendors have simply rebranded their solutions which are heavily dependent on rules and signatures. This is not considered true machine learning. Many of these solutions, for example, only look at limited data sources such as AD and SIEM, or some sort of nomenclature to identify privileged access, such as, tagging and naming prefixes. These solutions do not utilize true machine learning and are severely constrained by the fact that they lack any real context for analytics.

- ***Multi-vector data sourcing*** – Along the lines relating to the limitations and constraints of siloed data, a broader perspective represents the various vectors, or sources of data, that are required for broad context within monitoring. Having complete access to the comprehensive data sets to facilitate all-inclusive monitoring is essential for effective advanced machine learning and to avoid data decay. This includes the complete range of user behavior, in all environments (on-premises and in the cloud, globally, and 24/7), as well as all of the data and applications that the user might interact with, in the hybrid environment, including both company and privately owned devices (BYOD, IoT, etc.).

- ***Human analyst and automated interaction*** – Seamless efficiencies between the machine learning technology aspect and the human analyst is critical to facilitate effective, reliable and evolving (self-learning and self-training) machine learning for predictive security analytics. Many UEBA black box solutions have little to no ability to be customized so the solution might align more closely with customer organizational security goals and data sources. It may also lack the capability to integrate security analyst feedback on false positive and negatives, which is critical for model accuracy. Also, as an open solution, having the capability to customize risk weightings and create custom models for confidential data sources and private use cases, is an essential requirement for some organizations, (e.g., military, financial, federal government). A closed black box solution often lacks this functionality.

- ***Assessing known bads versus learning an environment*** – There are two types of UEBA solutions. Those that are built on rules and signatures, and those that have a foundation in machine learning with the context of big data. Where rules and signatures can show results in a few days, machine learning requires 30 to 60 days to self-learn and self-train and then optimize in the environment to show results. From there machine learning models continue to self-learn and self-train, gaining deeper context and accuracy. Rules and signatures have no growth or evolutionary capabilities as they are not built around self-learning or self-training with a feedback loop.

- ***Integration with identity analytics (IdA)*** – One industry expert recently observed, "How can you protect against insider threats if you don't understand privileged identity access and entitlements?" In today's traditional PAM environments, experts observe that over a half of an organization's privileged access entitlements reside outside of the solution's visibility. This represents a serious unaddressed access risk plane. Having the ability for IdA's machine learning to integrate seamlessly to identify privileged access risk with UEBA to monitor for privileged access abuse is essential for hybrid environments. The same holds true for the awareness gap with IAM solutions benefiting from identity analytics.

Some less forgiving experts in the security field refer to the weak substitutes supporting solutions with siloed UEBA features as 'baby machine learning'. Some solutions still appear to be in these baby step stages, which is a serious concern to any organization thinking that they are possibly protecting their environments with an up-to-date solution. These same experts also recognize that machine learning is best served by a platform or standalone solution with broad visibility for the context it provides.

A proven best-of-breed UEBA solution that draws effectively from big data, integrates seamlessly with IdA, draws from a robust set of behavior models and attributes, is a great starting point when considering a vendor for solution adoption. The POC (proof of concept) phase is where organizations then see if it all really works for them, which should be longer than 30 days.

UEBA for IAM and PAM requirements

Traditionally IAM business users have employed manual processes and legacy rules with compliance driving rubber stamping for certifications and access cloning for efficiency. IAM's complexity lends itself an optimal opportunity for machine-aided processes around managing access intelligence corresponding to users' actions and rights. Elements of the UEBA requirements for these identity and access management include:

- **Risk-based approach for IAM/PAM** – UEBA solutions provide identity analytics (IdA) via API to IAM and PAM solutions. IAM solutions benefit from risk scores for certifications and to determine access outliers, excess access and a confirmation of orphan and dormant accounts. PAM solutions benefit from unknown privileged access hidden in standard accounts and applications at the entitlement level. More and more CROs (chief risk officers) are requesting increased risk scoring at the entitlement level for these reasons.

- **Risk-based authentication** – Real-time risk scores via API to authentication solutions determine user identity context and requirements for access. The UEBA solution communicates the risk score for the user login attempt and triggers an authentication prompt or prompts based on risk level. For example, a high-risk score may result in multifactor authentication (MFA) whereas a low-risk score may only require a one-time password.

- **Risk-based IAM governance** – IdA for machine-learning-defined intelligent roles and risk-based access analytics verifies and tracks when and how a given user gets access. This greatly improves IAM governance. It can often replace manual processes and legacy roles. IdA closes the awareness gap for what access has been provided by an IAM solution, and how it is actually being utilized, enabling a risk-based approach for IAM governance.

- **PAM admin risk profiles** – UEBA solutions should provide IdA monitoring down to the level of privileged access analytics to detect unknown privileged access risk including privileged entitlements hidden in standard accounts and within applications. Privileged access abuse starts with knowing the locations of privileged access for users and entities.

UEBA and privileged access abuse

As stated earlier, industry experts have observed that over 50% of privileged access (PA) entitlements within organizations are unknown, and therefore unmanaged. This represents a sobering access risk plane. PA is widely acknowledged as a prime target of hackers, and customers employing traditional security solutions perceive a concerning gap in the discovery of unknown privileged access and privileged access abuse. Gurucul's delivery field experience has uncovered an instance of unknown access risk exceeding 70%.

Due to rapidly evolving conditions in enterprise environments that bear impact outside their original siloed solution design, PAM is currently unable to fully manage all privileged access accounts and entitlements. These solutions lack comprehensive discovery capabilities of hidden or unknown privileged access entitlements. To meet that challenge, a small selection of UEBA vendors employing advanced machine learning, have developed a solution set which integrates IdA and UEBA to create privileged access analytics (PAA). In partnership with PAM and IAM solutions, PAA delivers broad visibility providing the ability to identify and analyze privileged access across all environments, along with the capability to monitor and assess user behavior holistically.

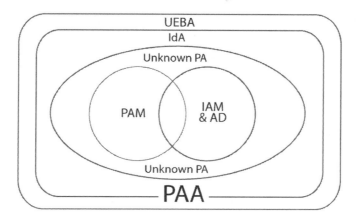

The PAA Solution Domain
Figure 8.1

Phases of privileged access risk reduction. Partnered with IAM and PAM solutions, PAA facilitates comprehensive coverage of all the phases of privileged access management. Understanding the fundamental realities of privileged access management is essential for successful risk reduction. Managing privileged access effectively entails successful implementation of the following solution phases:

- Discovery and analysis
- Life cycle management (IAM/PAM solutions)
- Access control (vaulting solutions)
- Full contextual visibility, monitoring, analysis, risk scoring and remediation

UEBA cloud security requirements

Cloud security gateways (CSGs), also known as CASBs, prevent data exfiltration as UEBA solutions expand that capability with robust comprehensive monitoring of access and activity. Core capabilities include:

- ***Cloud data exfiltration*** – A UEBA solution's integration with a cloud access security broker (CASB) solution strengthens the prevention of data exfiltration for on-premises and cloud workloads. A cloud security analytics (CSA) solution that also deploys via direct API integration, provides transparency for devices on any network by avoiding forward or reverse proxy traffic coordination. The CSA provides both enhanced IdA for access risk reduction and UEBA for detection of insider threats, account compromise and data exfiltration. The CSA also leverages proxy-based CASB solutions as a data source for shadow IT cloud activity, as not all SaaS solutions provide an API.

- ***Risk score behavior for SaaS/IaaS/PaaS*** – A UEBA solution's direct API integration with SaaS, IaaS and PaaS provides risked scored identity analytics for access risks and user and entity behavior analytics for anomalous behavior and unknown threat detection. Cloud security analytics may also provide hybrid visibility for on-premises and cloud applications in a single solution.

- ***Cloud malware application detection*** – A UEBA solution's role in understanding the behavior of cloud malware applications is critical for identifying normal data movement between cloud applications and detecting anomalies in traffic patterns. In some cases, a UEBA vendor's CSA solution enhanced capabilities are focused on behavior-based anomaly detection to predict, deter and detect cloud-based risks, threats and malware using identity as both as an access risk and threat plane. [NOTE: Industry analysts have observed the limitations of signatures, patterns and rules to detect threats and that behavior analytics provides an important new perspective on these blind spots, even more so for cloud applications.]

Proof of concept – The pre-sale project adoption objectives

As prospective customers approach the final phase of a UEBA solution adoption, the POC is the most crucial. The customer has the opportunity to assess two critical factors in their determination of the solution's suitability for addressing their challenges. The first objective is to confirm the vendor's stated claims for the solution's capabilities as they are represented in marketing collateral and the sales representatives' demonstrations of the solution. Canned demos show a product's features and functionality in their best light and under ideal circumstances created by the vendor. However, working within a live customer environment is a completely different situation, with a range of variables influencing a successful demonstration of the solution's functionality. The second objective is to assure that the solution actually works within a selected targeted challenge, or set of use cases, data sources and requirements, defined by the customer.

Any qualified vendor's field engineering services group should focus on an economical, effective and rapid way to validate key customer use cases and demonstrate specific analytic outputs with genuine metrics tied to risk issues that are meaningful to the customer's core use cases for the project. They should facilitate an understanding of the customer's potential for ROI with the adoption of the solution in consideration.

Only after a demonstration of these customized capabilities, tailored within the customer environment, can a customer be assured that the prospective UEBA solution is appropriate and a cost-effective solution for their needs. Keep in mind that staging a POC is no simple process, and the larger the organization, and the more complex the environment, and data sources to ingest, the more involved the POC. This increases staging time required to deliver the POC properly. A POC is also a trial run, of sorts, for the partnership-like relationship between the customer and the vendor, which is required for the successful delivery of both POC and the life cycle of the solution itself.

UEBA solution adoption process overview

Throughout all phases of an UEBA solution delivery, and especially in the Commitment Phase (see Figure 8.2 below), effective institutionalization of a user and entity behavior analytics initiative within an organization is a two-way process, both from the top down and the bottom up, with the core organizational goal of the solution is to protect their vital information and assets. This is especially the case with a UEBA solution involving a self-audit feature. While some information is at risk due to nefarious behavior, other information is at risk because employee awareness is low as it relates to proper best practices and risky habits that can result in data loss through that condition of unfamiliarity with the importance of and commitment to those best practices.

Part of the successful adoption of a UEBA solution includes training with all levels of users in an organization. This includes the value and utility of user self-audits — to ensure the entire organization is aligned with the best practices that ensure preservation of sensitive IP and protection of access information. The adopting stakeholders' institutionalization role is also to encourage feedback from the bottom up, to ensure the implementation is executed effectively — and does not impact user productivity. Moreover, any challenges to successful implementation are reported up, thereby assuring the smooth, continued, and evolving utility of the solution. Without this engaged and committed two-way institutionalization, a solution's prospects for success may falter.

A perspective of the UEBA solution adoption process is depicted on the S curve configuration below.

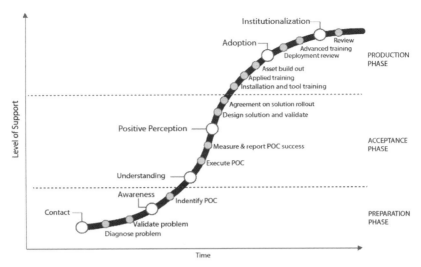

UEBA Solution Adoption Process Phases
Figure 8.2

UEBA Solution future-proofing

CIOs and CISOs, of course, view the evolution of their environments from a number of perspectives, weighing advantages of productivity and increased efficiencies that new technologies and applications offer against maintaining the security requirements to ensure the environment is protected properly. While adopting something like a UEBA-IdA solution, and its suitability for facing the current challenges, they must also take into consideration the evolving hybrid technologies and the innovation trends of future threats. As Carnival's Gary Eppinger's observes, "we maintain the strategy of continuous development and improvement, not adopt some monolithic solution that might be outdated as soon as it is finally implemented." Following on the concept of continuous improvement, Uber's Joe Sullivan shares, "These adjusted solutions must be much more flexible and robust to address the challenge." And on the cautious optimism side, there can be greater benefits in a solution adoption than originally expected. To achieve this kind optimal solution adoption, CIO at large Teri Takai notes, "the solution must supplement, and perhaps modify the access security strategy, not replace it."

Keeping an eye on the UEBA vendors who possess a proven track record of continuously developing reliable, open and flexible solutions in synch with the market demands is an important qualification to keep in mind when assessing a vendor's prospects of being able to keep pace with future rapid evolving innovations that increasingly fragment our environments.

In addition, a phased or project road map approach of implementing a solution helps customers in two ways:

- The cost of the adoption can be spread across a broader budget cycle and projects, such as privileged access abuse, data exfiltration and insider threat, offering incremental assessment of the solutions suitability and success against organizational objectives and use cases.

- The solution itself is integrated with the evolving factors of an environment taken into account. As the environment is changing from on-premises to cloud, the new phases of the UEBA solution adoption are implemented and integrated with them.

Selecting a UEBA solution partner

The final selection of a qualified UEBA solution partner is a critical decision. This entails an assessment of the solution's capabilities to address the use cases and data sources of the project, but also the people behind the solution as well. Employing a partner providing a team with a deep bench of experts in the field of user and entity behavior analytics is a key factor. This includes the SEs, project leaders, instructors, field teams, and experts in the field delivering the solution along with the support services team.

The solution partner's value is enhanced if UEBA and IdA are core competencies of the company's offerings. The UEBA team should have a holistic understanding of mobility, BYOD, on-premises, cloud and hybrid cloud environments. They must be able to articulate UEBA benefits and ROI vs. risk. In addition, the UEBA partner should have an established delivery process. Their qualifications are further strengthened if they can provide references of successful implementations that align in some ways with the prospective client's requirements.

Predictive Security Analytics
Use Cases

Introduction

Within the domain of predictive security analytics, the broadening adoption of user and entity behavior analytics (UEBA), and identity analytics (IdA), has been observed by a range of industry analysts. Drawing from big data and driven by advanced machine learning, in concert, or as standalone solutions, they deliver an effective method to manage and monitor identity-based risks and threats across all of an organization's environments. Both on-premises and in the cloud — these solutions identify and minimize excess access, establish what normal behavior is and what anomalous, possibly malicious, behavior is. The caliber and capabilities a solution vendor delivers within this niche of predictive security analytics is, in part, defined by the use cases they are capable of conducting. While some vendors may offer a limited set of use cases for UEBA, this is only one part of predictive security analytics. More recently, IdA and cloud security analytics (CSA) have expanded the breadth of use cases within predictive security analytics. These categories supported by a vendor should be one of the first factors prospective customers examine when considering adoption of a predictive security analytics solution. Customers must assure the use cases offered by a vendor align with their specific needs and varied requirements, both long-term for an initial project and long-term as a new defense. This chapter explores a comprehensive and optimal set of use cases across all the solution domains of UEBA, IdA and CSA.

Functional domains of predictive security analytics

The three solution capability categories within predictive security analytics are as follows:

- *Access analytics* – Directly associated with IdA, it involves detecting access risks, access outliers, shared HPA accounts, orphan and dormant accounts. In addition, it reduces the attack surface area for identities with machine-learning-based intelligent roles. Access analytics also reduces identity management manual processes, increases revocations, improves provisioning, and cleanses identity as an access risk plane for compliance and audits with identity analytics.

- *Threat analytics* – Aligned with UEBA, this systematic analysis deters, detects, and prevents insider threats, compromised accounts and data exfiltration with big data machine learning models. Identity is a threat plane that modern defenses miss with signatures, rules and patterns. Machine learning and dynamic peer groups uniquely uncover and monitor these holistically, minimizing false positives and enabling prompt, targeted remedial and automated risk responses.

- *Cloud analytics* – Affiliated with CSA, this category provides access and threat analytics for SaaS, IaaS, PaaS and IDaaS. It is deployed as an API-based CASB (cloud access service broker) to monitor access and activity for identity-based access risks, unknown threats or anomalous behavior. Deployments are also likely to integrate with proxy-based CASBs for shadow IT access and activity data where many SaaS applications do not provide APIs. Cloud-to-cloud connectors for popular software as a service (SaaS) applications including, infrastructure, platform and identity management as a service (IaaS, PaaS and IDaaS), ease installation and deployment to begin analytics.

Big Data Security Analytics Funnel
Figure 9.1

Predictive security analytics – Use cases

The depth and range of use cases fundamentally defines the areas of expertise and functionality for predictive security analytics vendors. A number of vendors offer only a limited selection of use cases, while others are more inclusive and comprehensive in their offerings. An optimal list of use cases predictive security analytics is found in the table below. Use cases are organized in three categories: UEBA, IdA and CSA, with PAA (privileged access analytics) use cases overlapping within these groupings. Some of these use cases are correlated and/or parented with use cases in other columns. A good example is the privileged access abuse case, which requires both UEBA and IdA, and has been discussed earlier in this book. Also keep in mind the need and ability to create custom models for private data and confidential use cases common with federal, military and private industry deployments.

Use case summary table

UEBA	IdA	CSA
• Account Compromise, Hijacking and Sharing • High Privileged Access Abuse • Data Exfiltration and IP Protection • Insider Threat Detection and Deterrence • Self-Audit and ID Theft Detection • Cyber Fraud Detection and Deterrence • Trusted Host and Entity Compromise • Stateful Session Tracking • Step-up Authentication (Adaptive Authentication) • Anomalous Behavior and Watch Lists • SIEM and DLP Risk Intelligence • Hybrid Infrastructure	• Access Outliers and Excess Access • Outlier Access Clean-up (Oracle Identity Manager [OIM]) • Risk-based Access and Certifications • Dynamic Access Provisioning • Role-Access Reconciliation • Role Mining and Intelligent Roles • Access Governance and Segregation of Duties (SoD) Monitoring • Dormant and Orphan Account Management	• Cloud Account Compromise, Hijacking and Sharing • Cloud Privileged Access Abuse • Cloud Data Exfiltration and IP Protection • Cloud Insider Threat Detection and Deterrence • Cloud Self-Audit and ID Theft Detection • Cloud Step-up Authentication • Cloud Anomalous Behavior and Watch Lists • Cloud to SIEM Integration for Alerts • Cloud to On-Premises DLP Closed-Loop • Cloud Access Outliers and Excess Access • Cloud Risk-based Access Compliance • Cloud Dormant and Orphan Accounts • Cloud Application License Metering (Account Level)

Chapter appendix – Capital Markets Use Cases.

User and entity behavior analytics – Use cases

User and entity behavior analytics use cases are focused on detection of unknown risks and threats beyond the capabilities of rules, signatures and patterns. Using machine learning models to detect anomalous behavior, minimizing false positives, these use cases result in predictive risk scores which drive alerts, actions and case tickets. To assure optimal and comprehensive capabilities, UEBA vendors' use cases should draw from big data utilizing at least 200 plus attributes leveraged in over 150 machine learning models.

This solution model should include data ingestion available via flat file, database, API, message or streaming inputs with ready to use data connectors for common enterprise systems and platforms (i.e., HR, IAM, PAM, SIEM, AD, databases, networks, vulnerabilities, DLP, threat intel, cloud applications/SaaS, authentication, physical ID badge systems, file storage and endpoints). This level of advanced solution should support an open choice for big data with Hadoop, Cloudera, Hortonworks and MapR.

Account Compromise, Hijacking and Sharing

One of the Top 10 OWASP (Open Web Application Security Project) vulnerabilities is related to the 'Broken Authentication and Session Management' scenario. Here, attackers exploit vulnerabilities through attacks such as Pass-the-Hash (PtH), Pass-the-Token (PtT), Brute Force and Remote Execution to gain access to user credentials (passwords and hash). Such attacks can be detected using the underlying machine learning algorithms tuned to inspect various parameters like timestamp, location, IP, device, transaction patterns, high-risk event codes and network packets, to identify any deviation from the normal behavior of a particular account and the corresponding transactions. This facilitates detection of any potential account compromise or hijacking scenarios based on the anomalous behavior patterns such as: abnormal access to high-risk or sensitive objects, abnormal number of activities, requests in a short time frame, activity from terminated user accounts or dormant accounts, PtH attacks and session replay attacks. Anomalies identified via clustering machine learning models and outlier analysis inconsistent with a user or peers' normal behaviors are given risk scores based on predictive analytics to drive alerts, actions and case tickets. Self-audits (reviewed below) may also support this use case.

Benefits

- Detects anomalous behaviors beyond rules, patterns and signatures for account compromise, hijacking and sharing
- Provides 360-degree visibility for user accounts, access and activity for on-premises, cloud and hybrid environments

High Privileged Access Abuse

This use case identifies high privileged access (HPA) abuse by leveraging the combination of accounts, access and activity data. Typically, accounts and access data is ingested from IAM, PAM and/or directory services platforms to identify HPA accounts and discover any non-HPA accounts granted high privilege entitlements. Additionally, the activity data is ingested from the enterprise level audit or log sources (e.g., SIEM or log aggregators) or obtained directly from the target sources. Once HPA accounts are identified, UEBA can detect suspicious behavior and misuse such as: using HPA to assign special or elevated privileges to the user's own account followed by an activity, transactions outside the window of password value checkout and check-in timeframe. This also includes access to resources and transactions outside normal behavior profiles, abnormal access to classified or sensitive documents, multiple concurrent sessions from the same account, different IPs, devices, locations, etc.

Benefits

- Discovers privileged access and provides visibility on who has the 'keys to the kingdom'
- Reduces high privileged access account abuse and eliminates shared HPA accounts
- Reduces access risks before abuse with risk-scored HPA accounts and entitlements

Data Exfiltration and IP Protection

UEBA identifies data exfiltration and protects intellectual property by ingesting data sources such as DLP and data classification to learn important data locations, access and application activity. Risk scoring DLP alerts are a primary benefit of UEBA machine learning to reduce alert fatigue and prioritize 'find-fix' resources. Analysis by UEBA includes on-premises and cloud applications for a 360-degree view of data access and activity. This approach helps customers prioritize DLP alerts investigation, as well as identify and monitor even the low severity DLP alerts associated with departing users or high-risk users. UEBA solutions traditionally provide out-of-the-box (OOTB) anomaly models which can identify known patterns such as: sensitive documents downloaded and copied to USB, large amounts of source code checked out from source code repositories and file uploads to cloud storage, emails to personal accounts, access to competitor and/or job websites, etc. Solution customers have also extended UEBA alerts beyond SOC analysts to managers, given their depth of context and relevance regarding employees, data and projects. Self-audits can also provide deterrence for data access and unsanctioned activity.

Benefits

- Baselines data access and activity for anomalous events through self-learning and self-training machine learning models
- Supports customized and unique DLP and data classifications, metadata models and big data infrastructure support to each company
- Significantly reduces DLP alerts, time to investigate and false positives through predictive risk scoring

Insider Threat Detection and Deterrence

Advanced UEBA insider threat detection and deterrence leverages research drawing from extensive insider threat databases of real-world incidents to develop, test and refine machine learning (ML) behavior models. Identifying high-risk profiles with abnormal behaviors in conjunction with data risk monitoring, machine learning and statistical analysis, reveals anomalies in data that humans could not otherwise recognize or detect. A force multiplier, ML far surpasses human capabilities and software engineering for managing large volumes and varieties of data. True machine learning also has the ability to find high-order interactions and patterns in data for complex problems such as insider threats, compromised accounts and data exfiltration. It does this by leveraging useful and predictive cues that are too noisy and highly dimensional for human experts and traditional software to detect. A 360-degree dashboard should provide visibility of an identity's accounts, access and activity for on-premises and cloud hybrid environments. A self-audit feature may support this use case providing deterrence and security awareness. Both access and activity are risk scored for anomalous events with results visible to managers and SOC analysts.

Benefits

- Delivers hybrid visibility for on-premises and cloud across access and activity with machine learning models leveraging big data context to detect anomalies and apply predictive risk scores for insider threat detection
- Highlights insider threats first and in common risk groups plus watch lists via UEBA dashboard
- Provides unique insider threat deterrence and security awareness to users and managers through self-audits

Self-Audit and ID Theft Detection

A self-audit feature deputizes users into a collaborative relationship with security analysts to provide context and relevance not found with SOC teams. This multiplier of 'eyes on glass' applies to employees, business partners and suppliers, agents in hub-spoke organizations, and in some cases, customers. All of these parties are likely to have one or more accounts with

access entitlements to critical applications and data. A frequently issued (usually weekly) self-audit report provides visibility for access, devices, locations and risk-scored anomalous behavior providing both detection and deterrence for end users. A case in point: a self-audit is implemented by a company where an employee was out of office on a Wednesday due to a sick child. This employee never logged into her accounts on that day. A self-audit report sent to this individual on the following Friday showed account activity on Wednesday when the employee knew they had not logged in. Further investigation by security analysts discovered the account had been compromised for over three-and-a-half years where the employee had high privileged access to critical applications and data.

Benefits

- Deputizes end users into a collaborative relationship to quickly identify anomalous behavior and ID compromise
- Leverages end users and managers with unique context and relevance for accounts, applications and data not easily replicated into SOC teams
- Provides an audit and compliance benefit for employees, business partners, suppliers and even customers

Cyber Fraud Detection and Deterrence

UEBA addresses cyber fraud use cases for treasury, accounting, payments and areas concerning funds transactions. Here the UEBA solution provides a flexible data model open to attributes from commercial or homegrown treasury and accounting systems to be considered for behavior analytics from machine learning models. UEBA solutions have been deployed for merchant solutions to monitor for cyber fraud and account compromise. A

real-world scenario: in April 2016, SWIFT acknowledged attackers had obtained valid credentials for operators to create and approve SWIFT messages. Over 11,000 financial organizations that use SWIFT daily to transfer billions of dollars were jeopardized by this cyber fraud. SWIFT and supporting vendors issue patches and make recommendations to detect fraudulent use. However, the data volume is overwhelming and signals are too fine-grained for analysis by humans. Ingesting data on access and activity from treasury, accounting and payments areas within organizations, UEBA allows enterprises to integrate their cyber fraud models and risk frameworks, providing significant benefit of leveraging existing investments and security models in alignment with business context. The use of self-audits may support this use case.

Benefits

- Supports the ingestion of data sources from treasury, accounting and payment systems through an open metadata model
- Detects anomalies for predictive risk scoring with feedback for false positives and negatives powered by machine learning behavior models
- Improves accuracy reflected in risk scores for data quality and relevance through risk weightings that can be customized for attributes

Trusted Host and Entity Compromise

It is well known that one of the widely used tactics to execute cyber-attacks is to compromise trusted hosts connected to an organization's network infrastructure. In addition to monitoring anomalous user behavior with UEBA, it is critical for organizations to monitor closely all the endpoints (devices and hosts) connected to the network. UEBA builds an anomaly timeline for an entity based on the high-risk anomalous events and activities performed from the respective devices and hosts. UEBA correlates a wide range of parameters associated with an entity including: endpoint security alerts, vulnerability scan results (Common Vulnerability Scoring System [CVSS]), risk levels of users and accounts used, targets accessed, packet level inspection of the requested payloads, and more. This correlation facilitates detection of any anomalous activities and events to determine predictive risk scores.

Benefits

- Detects advanced persistent threat (APT) attacks and attack vectors and predicts data exfiltration by performing entity-centric anomaly detection
- Provides risk-based dashboard for closely monitoring high-risk entities and investigation using detailed anomaly timeline based on users, accounts, alerts and activities associated with the entity

Stateful Session Tracking

In this use case, UEBA builds and tracks the user session state, even when a user navigates across heterogeneous resources or applications using different accounts and devices at different times. Leveraging machine learning, UEBA dynamically builds session correlation attributes used to build session context in order to link any subsequent activities based on a confidence factor. This enables the identification of valid IP switching due to transitions between wired and wireless networks, a workstation and a handheld/mobile device, or accessing enterprise resources from various onsite locations or remotely over VPN. UEBA's ability to track user sessions across these various parameters ensures a significant reduction in false positives while simultaneously delivering greater visibility into the sequence of events. It also provides the capability to drill down to specific activities performed by a user or entity while performing an investigation. This analysis also expedites the detection of session replay and hijacking attacks, highlighting any anomalous activity from a user session or concurrent sessions from the same account.

Benefits

- Provides greater visibility into user activities across multiple resources or applications via with stateful session tracking
- Provides drill-down and raw log views for deep event analysis at the source
- Reduces false positives due to common scenarios like IP, account and device switching while performing day-to-day activities
- Detects session replay and hijacking attacks

Step-up Authentication (or Adaptive Authentication)

The use of passwords to authorize users is core to the problem of identity compromise and misuse. Deploying multi-factor authentication takes time, resources and expenses and can impede high productivity users in low-risk environments. The concept of Step-up Authentication (also known as Adaptive Authentication) leverages the UEBA risk score of an identity or entity to determine the levels of authentication for access. A low-risk score may result in a simple password challenge while a high-risk score may result in three or four authentication challenges (e.g., password, access code and answering questions). Mature UEBA solutions support bi-directional integration with industry standard adaptive authentication solutions by using ready-to-use connectors and API interfaces. The net effect raises security awareness to end-users when they have high-risk situations. In addition, there is an increased chance of disrupting external intruders that have compromised the account at the password level only and may not have compromised the end-user's smartphone where an access code is provided. Even with Step-up Authentication, an account may still be compromised or hijacked and the use of UEBA for detection is advised.

Benefits

- Creates a closed-loop for step-up authentication with API integration between threat analytics and authentication solutions
- Raises security awareness with end users via authentication challenges when their identity shows high-risk behaviors
- Combines Step-up Authentication with self-audit as key parts of an increased security awareness program

Anomalous Behavior and Watch Lists

UEBA addresses anomalous behavior with watch lists to quickly profile and maintain an eye on unknowns and apply escalating predictive risk scores. Machine learning behavior models are designed to deliver feedback on false positives and negatives and then update self-learning and self-training models to adapt to time-based norms and conditions unique to each customer deployment. For example, a database administrator may create a

script that runs several commands with security implications at 2 a.m. each evening. This user is an innovator working to improve the enterprise's productivity. However, machine learning models will see these commands during non-business hours as an anomaly and risk score accordingly. Feedback from the models can note the situation is benign. Nonetheless, the database administrator should be put on a watch list. Watch lists also come pre-defined within UEBA for common high-risk groups like new hires, departing users, terminated users, and high-risk users. These groups should be easily accessed in dashboard drop-down menus to analyze risk scores, anomalies, accounts, access, activity and timelines. UEBA also supports explicitly adding or removing identities within watch lists.

Benefits

- Quickly profiles high-risk user groups from watch lists to monitor their risk scores and anomalies by SOC security analysts
- Facilitates profiling by audit and compliance teams of a specific person or group via a watch list to analyze their identity, accounts, access and activity
- Controls who has visibility to watch lists and for what data fields through Role-based Access Controls (RBAC) and data masking features

SIEM and DLP Risk Intelligence

UEBA addresses the alert fatigue issue of SIEM (security information and event management) and DLP (data loss prevention) solutions by aggregating the risk scores at the user and entity level, rather than generating a huge number of alerts at the transaction or event level. This allows SOC analysts to focus on the high-risk identities and the associated anomalies detected by UEBA. The result is a significant reduction in the

number of alerts. This use case employs bi-directional integration via APIs enabling SIEM and DLP data ingestion into UEBA as it provides risk scores back to these systems to allocate 'find-fix' resources. SIEM and DLP solutions provide critical data sources for additional context related to identity profile information and the corresponding access grants (accounts, entitlements), also including the activity and alerts data ingested from on-premises and cloud applications in hybrid environments.

While SIEM and DLP solutions work with known variables and identifiers via rules, patterns and signatures, UEBA detects the unknown via robust machine learning behavior models. Leveraging clustering and outlier algorithms, the models identify anomalies for predictive risk scoring. UEBA examines the data from an identity-based perspective analyzing user or entity behavior against itself and peer groups using baselines norms. As companies migrate to the cloud for applications and data, the role of UEBA becomes more essential for security events and data protection.

Benefits

- Provides ready to use data connectors for popular SIEM and DLP solutions to speed connectivity and data ingestion
- Delivers risk-scored SIEM and DLP events and alerts to focus 'find-fix' resources through machine learning behavior models
- Provides bi-directional integration via APIs and enables data ingestion into UEBA as well as the export of risk scores and identities to SIEM and DLP solutions

Hybrid Infrastructure

This use case addresses hybrid infrastructure by providing UEBA platforms for both on-premises and cloud applications, removing the need for any data transfers between environments. These transfers can be expensive and impede the use of big data for security analytics. The threat analytics side would run on-premises and provide ready to use data connectors for common on-premises applications and platforms as data sources. The cloud analytics side is an API-based cloud access security broker (CASB) that integrates with SaaS cloud applications, along with IaaS, PaaS and IDaaS, via APIs. The CASB API architecture enables direct data collection from cloud data sources while providing users a transparent access experience for any location on any network. Proxy-based CASBs are a data source into cloud analytics for shadow IT use, cloud DLP, and more. Threat, access and cloud analytics share combined processes to provide 360-degree visibility for identity accounts, access and activities in hybrid environments.

Benefits

- Enables organizations to avoid data transfer charges between on-premises and cloud (if big data was only in one location)
- Improves the context of data inputs from on-premises and cloud for each identity or entity through user and entity behavior analytics
- Ensures organizations can migrate applications and data from on-premises to cloud with peace of mind

Identity analytics (IdA)

Identity and access management (IAM) is the Achilles heel of organizations. It is quickly becoming a key concern for security leaders understanding the role of identity compromise and misuse as the core of modern threats. Identity analytics (IdA) is the proactive side of predictive security analytics, enabling the reduction of excess access, access outliers, and orphan or dormant accounts, before they are compromised or abused, plus providing risk-based certifications and defining intelligent roles. UEBA is the detection and response side using machine learning models to detect unknown risks and threats via predictive risk scoring early in the kill chain as a best use case scenario. IdA is the data science that improves IAM and privileged access management (PAM), leveraging machine learning models surpassing human capabilities to define, review and confirm accounts and entitlements for access. If the goal of user and entity behavior analytics is to profile an identity and its accounts, access and activity, then the goal of IdA is to assure this access plane is reduced as much as possible with the removal of any access risks, access outliers, orphan or dormant accounts, etc.

Intelligent roles replace manually defined roles often created from legacy rules. Group and role proliferation, plus the buildup of accounts and entitlements for employees during their career in various roles, create unnecessary access to insiders or attackers. This is an identity access plane ripe for phishing and social attacks. Implementing an intelligent roles policy redefines and minimizes an organization's access risk plane, providing the right person the right data at the right time and place.

Machine learning models provide 360-degree visibility for an identity, accounts, access and activity with the ability to compare to peer groups using baselines to determine normal and anomalous access, and nature of activity. The impact of machine learning with IdA can radically reduce accounts and entitlements for an organization. This often represents the first phase in a project plan when adopting UEBA and IdA. The objective is to clean up the access plane with IdA for access only where it should be provided. Analysis with UEBA would follow that step to detect risks and threats beyond rules, patterns and signatures. These two steps work holistically together to address identity as an access risk and threat plane.

Outlier Access and Excess Access

Identity analytics identifies high-risk systems access by consuming access entitlements (rights) data from applications and platforms. This use case identifies access that is considered high-risk including: privileged access, access improperly segregating duties, dissimilar access compared to peers and infrequent access to systems. The average user has more than 100 entitlements making certification a time-consuming process

for managers. Organizations realize managers are too often approving all certification requests without actually validating each one. Certifications are typically a quarterly or yearly process leaving organizations at risk with employees having extended access to which they should not be entitled. Using identity analytics integrated with identity access management (IAM) systems, organizations can detect access outliers leveraging peer groups of users to trigger certifications for outlier access.

Benefits

- Reduces access not associated with job responsibilities and potential account compromise risk
- Reduces the time window of access risk
- Reduces rubber stamping associated with Sarbanes-Oxley and other compliance related access reviews
- Reduces segregation of duties (SoD) conflicts for access, plus optimizes manager time with high-risk access certifications

Outlier Access Clean-Up

Identity analytics solutions can be configured to automate access clean up. Mature IdA and IAM solutions software should integrate with bi-directional APIs and with each other. The lack of APIs is a red flag of siloed data not open to analytics analysis. Discovered outlier access can be marked for removal. IdA solutions will use API integration to automatically send a de-provisioning request to the provisioning system where standard
workflows can be applied to ensure the access is removed appropriately. Removal is validated and user risk scores are adjusted when the identity analytics system receives confirmation back from the provisioning system that access has been removed.

Benefits

- Centralizes access cleanup at the provisioning system, making use of previous integration investments
- Automates access cleanup processes and eliminates the need to go to each endpoint to remove access
- Centralizes auditability; access removal is logged and captured in the provisioning system forgoing the need to consolidate logs to confirm access was removed

Risk-Based Access Certifications

Outlier access capabilities can be extended to automatically send risk-based certifications to the business when outlier access is identified. Identity analytics uses multiple parameters to drive risk-based certification, including a user's overall risk score, entitlement and account level risk score, and outlier scores from a context-rich configurable UI. Configurations may include several context points such as: access risk rating, peer group metrics, outlier risk scores and status recommendations (Keep or Remove). Mature identity analytics solutions can send built-in certifications, or use API's to integrate with other enterprise solutions to send certifications to account owners for review.

Benefits

- Enables the business (managers, data owners, role owners) to make decisions about removing or retaining outlier access to their assets
- Integrates with most enterprise certification systems and eliminates the need for training end users on a new certification platform
- Delivers a configurable context-rich UI for making decisions about access

Dynamic Access Provisioning

Dynamic Access Provisioning can be used to determine access-control permissions and restrictions based on a user's risk score. Risk scores are defined by machine learning algorithms from identity analytics. They take into account several points of context including: user behavior, resource sensitivity, the job or role of the user, access of the user versus their peers, and the configuration of the device used to access resources. Dynamic Access Provisioning reduces IT workload and should also automatically update user permissions independently without additional administrator intervention when the user's job or role changes. *Example 1*: Identity analytics determines user permissions when a user accesses a resource from their office computer versus when they use BYOD over a virtual private network. Access may be reduced if the device is considered high-risk (unknown, not patched, unusual location, etc.). *Example 2*: A user switches jobs, identity analytics software identifies the job change and new peer groups are identified. Dynamic Access Provisioning automatically updates user permissions without administrator intervention for low-risk situations.

Benefits

- Updates access to resources based on risk versus hard-coded rules
- Dynamically manages access for low-risk situations rather than depending on manual intervention, thus reducing workload for certifications, requests and approvals
- Automatically removes access when unknown devices and locations are in play

Role Access Reconciliation

Identity analytics software reviews role membership and identifies missing access, as well as, access to systems no longer in use by the role members. The solution integrates with provisioning systems to ensure all changes made to access follow the standard provisioning process, and that each transaction is logged accordingly. The system can be configured to automatically inform users and resource owners of access changes. Roles are automatically reviewed for access no longer used or needed by the role members.

Benefits

- Automatically updates users within a role to have all the access that the role provides
- Ensures access additions and removals are centrally logged with integration of provisioning or ticketing systems
- Automatically notifies role owners and business users of access changes due to updates made to role access
- Automatically adds or removes role access based on common use of systems

Role Mining and Intelligent Roles

Identity analytics can be used to review existing roles, or mine and define new roles. Unlike traditional role mining, identity analytics uses machine learning algorithms that take into account access and activity. This ensures unused and unneeded access is removed from roles during the definition process. Roles can be easily exported for consumption by provisioning systems.

Benefits

- Adds or removes role access based on common use of systems
- Analyzes existing roles for unnecessary and unused access
- Removes manual role mining processes based on legacy rules

Access Governance and SoD Monitoring

Segregation of duties (SoD) is an essential control over sensitive transactions. Role-based authorization and access often causes unknown conflicts in securing these transactions. Identity analytics automatically reviews existing roles and entitlements across systems and identifies inter- and intra- application segregation of duty risks. When these risks are identified, the

access analytics software can temporarily disable the access and send a notification to the business owner. The business owner can choose to accept the risk and allow the access, or deny the access. In both situations, identity analytics software should support configurations to send updates to the business owner and to the identity access management request system to ensure the central audit log is maintained.

Benefits

- Detects SoD rule violations within applications and between applications
- Automatically removes access from users to enforce SoD rules
- Enables business users to take action with context of what process and transactions are at risk

Dormant and Orphan Account Management

Identity analytics identifies dormant and orphan accounts. These accounts can be sent to system owners or administrators for review. Action can be taken, based on their response, to assign the account to an end user or entity, or remove the account from the system.

Benefits

- Reduces risk of orphan or dormant accounts being compromised or misused
- Automates identification of risky orphan and dormant accounts
- Enables account and system owners to take action by identifying account owners or marking the account for review
- Automatically disables accounts and notifies the owner when there is no decision

Cloud security analytics – Use cases

Cloud security analytics (CSA) utilizes an API-based cloud access security broker (CASB) architecture to deliver predictive security analytics for SaaS cloud applications, including IaaS, PaaS, and IDaaS. The advantage of API cloud integration, versus proxy-based CASB gateways, is that it provides users with a transparent experience in any location or network with any device. A proxy-based CASB has the advantage of being a chokepoint to monitor shadow IT for unsanctioned cloud applications not providing API visibility, plus cloud DLP monitoring and controls. However, device access control must be in-line for CASB proxy monitoring. CASB proxy gateways are a crucial data source into UEBA and IdA models as part of the solution architecture to deliver predictive risk scores for cloud environments where API visibility is not provided. In addition, web, email, and network cloud gateways are also data sources for machine learning behavior models.

Cloud security analytics should work on its own for cloud-only deployments and also be capable of synchronizing seamlessly with threat analytics and access analytics on-premises for hybrid environments. Having cloud, threat and access analytics holistically integrated and synchronized is essential for comprehensive hybrid environment risk analytics solution success. Cloud environments differ from on-premises, as SaaS cloud applications deliver less data variety via API. They are, however, more consistent in data quality. Whereas on-premises data variety can be much wider, the data quality is lower, and this impacts machine learning behavior models. Using a security model originally developed for on-premises requires adjustments for cloud environments.

Currently the field of UEBA vendors offering an API architecture for cloud security analytics as part of an umbrella platform addressing hybrid environments is quite small as UEBA solutions, for the most part, originated within on-premises. Separate and unintegrated UEBA features from multiple vendors restricts visibility and diminishes the ability to provide comprehensive risk scores from the full context of 360-degree visibility of an identity, accounts, access and activity. CSA, only available within a specific CASB vendor, is limited to cloud environments in the same manner as UEBA features dedicated solely to a SIEM from another vendor with an on-premises focus. Optimally, users' access applications and data in both cloud and on-premises, provides 360-degree visibility and a context, which maximizes machine learning model effectiveness and accuracy. In summary, UEBA, IdA and CSA as a platform provides the optimal visibility and context for machine learning.

Cloud Account Compromise, Hijacking and Sharing

Cloud security analytics address cloud account compromise, hijacking and cloud account sharing via API integration with SaaS cloud applications, plus IaaS and PaaS. Visibility into Office 365 cloud applications leverages Microsoft Azure visibility for cloud infrastructure and platform information alongside cloud application activity data. The same applies to other popular cloud applications in AWS cloud environments. Identity and access

management as a service (IDaaS) also plays a role for cloud environments. The benefits of big data infrastructure with a flexible data model come into play to develop API data connectors for cloud data ingestion that may mimic on-premises functions in numerous ways. Utilizing advanced machine learning behavior models, cloud security analytics leverages this capability for cloud environments to detect account compromise, hijacking and sharing on-premises. The basic concepts of clustering and outlier algorithms to find anomalies based on normal baselines of the user and peers for predictive risk scores remains consistent with adjustments for data variety and quality. The data sources differ and data ingestion is API-based for cloud environments.

Benefits

- Detects account compromise, hijacking and sharing for cloud application accounts and privileged accounts for IaaS, PaaS and IDaaS
- Detects anomalous behaviors beyond rules, patterns and signatures for cloud account compromise, hijacking and sharing
- Combines cloud security analytics with on-premises security analytics for hybrid environment visibility in one UEBA-IdA platform

Cloud Privileged Access Abuse

Cloud security analytics addresses privileged access abuse via API integration with IaaS, PaaS and IDaaS solutions. This provides visibility to high privileged access (HPA) accounts. This also includes instances where privileged access entitlements are assigned to non-HPA accounts creating a high-risk situation. SaaS cloud applications and other activity data sources, including CASB proxy gateways for shadow IT detection, enable machine

learning models to find anomalous outliers for predictive risk scoring to drive alerts, actions and case tickets. Shared HPA cloud accounts are also included in this analysis. Once HPA cloud accounts are identified, cloud security analytics software can detect suspicious behavior or misuse. This would include: using HPA to assign special or elevated privileges to the user's own account followed by an activity, transactions outside the window of password value checkout and check-in timeframe, access to resources or transactions outside normal behavior profiles, abnormal access to classified or sensitive documents, multiple concurrent sessions for the same account, however, from different IPs, devices, locations, etc.

Benefits

- Discovers cloud privileged access and provides visibility on who has the 'keys to the kingdom'
- Reduces high privileged access cloud account abuse and eliminates shared HPA cloud accounts
- Limits access risks before abuse with risk-scored HPA cloud accounts and entitlements

Cloud Data Exfiltration and IP Protection

Cloud security analytics addresses data exfiltration and intellectual property (IP) protection for cloud environments through API integration with SaaS cloud applications, IaaS, PaaS and CASBs. CASB proxy gateways, email gateways, web gateways and network gateways with DLP features are also key data sources for cloud security analytics software to analyze with machine learning. DLP in the cloud cannot always leverage data fingerprints from on-premises deployments. This makes UEBA an important platform for data risk monitoring and protection. Identity provides the 'keys to the kingdom' with cloud applications and data access so access compromise and misuse are critical to detect as early as possible. Analysis by a behavior analytics platform includes on-premises and cloud applications for a 360-degree view of data access and activity. This approach helps customers prioritize DLP alert investigation, identify and monitor even the low severity DLP alerts associated with departing users or high-risk users. In addition, CSA software should provide OOTB anomaly models which can identify known patterns such as: sensitive documents downloaded and copied to USB, large amounts of source code checked out from source code repositories and file uploads to cloud storage, emails to personal accounts, access to competitor and/or job websites, etc. Some solutions also extend risk-scored alerts beyond SOC analysts to managers, given their depth of context and relevance regarding employees, data and projects. Self-audits also provide deterrence and detection for cloud data access and activity.

Benefits

- Baselines cloud data access and activity for anomalous events with self-learning and training machine learning models
- Supports customized and unique DLP and data classifications, metadata models and big data infrastructure support

- Significantly reduces DLP alerts, time to investigate, and false positives, through predictive risk scoring

Cloud Insider Threat Detection and Deterrence

Well-developed cloud insider threat detection and deterrence leverages research drawing from an extensive insider threat database of real-world incidents to develop, test and refine machine learning behavior models. Identifying high-risk profiles with abnormal behaviors in conjunction with data risk monitoring, machine learning, and statistical analysis, finds anomalies in data that humans would not otherwise

recognize or detect. It also far surpasses human capability and software engineering for large volumes and variety of data. Machine learning also has the ability to find high-order interactions and patterns in data for complex problems such as insider threats, compromised accounts and data exfiltration by leveraging useful and predictive cues that are too noisy and highly dimensional for human experts and traditional software to detect. A 360-degree dashboard should provide visibility of an identity's accounts, access and activity for on-premises and cloud hybrid environments. A self-audit feature may support this use case where both access and activity are risk-scored for anomalous behavior visible to users and managers.

Benefits
- Utilizes machine learning models with context of big data for machine learning analysis to detect anomalies and apply predictive risk scores
- Highlights insider threats early and organized in common risk groups, along with watch lists via the predictive risk analytics dashboard
- Provides insider threat deterrence and security awareness to users and managers through customizable self-audit feature

Cloud Self-Audit and ID Theft Detection

A self-audit feature for ID theft detection deputizes users into a collaborative relationship with security teams that leverage context and relevance not found with SOC teams. This multiplier of 'eyes on glass' applies to employees, business partners and suppliers, agents in hub-spoke organizations, and in some cases, customers. All these parties are likely to have one or more cloud accounts with access entitlements to critical cloud

applications and data. A frequent self-audit report provides visibility for access, devices, locations and risk-scored anomalous behavior, providing both detection and deterrence for end users.

Benefits

- Deputizes end users into a collaborative relationship to quickly identify anomalous behavior and ID compromise
- Leverages context and relevance for cloud accounts, applications and data of end users and managers not easily replicated into SOC teams
- Provides an audit and compliance benefit for employees, business partners, suppliers, and even customers

Cloud Step-up Authentication (Adaptive Authentication)

The compromise and misuse of identity lies at the heart of modern threats. The use of passwords to authorize users is core to the problem, even more so for cloud applications. Deploying multi-factor authentication takes time, resources and expenses and can impede high-productivity users in low-risk environments. Step-up Authentication (also referred to as Adaptive Authentication) leverages the UEBA risk score of an

identity or entity to determine the levels of authentication for cloud access. A low-risk score may result in a simple password challenge, while a high-risk score may result in three or four authentication challenges (e.g., password, access code, and answering questions). This use case supports bi-directional integration with industry standard adaptive authentication solutions by employing ready-to-use connectors and API interfaces. The net effect raises security awareness to end-users when they have high-risk situations. It also provides a heightened probability of disrupting external intruders that have compromised the cloud account at the password level only, and may not have compromised the end user's smartphone where an access code is provided. Even with Step-up Authentication, a cloud account may still be compromised or hijacked, and the use of UEBA for detection is advised.

Benefits

- Creates a closed-loop for step-up authentication via API integration between UEBA/cloud security analytics and cloud IDaaS and IaaS solutions
- Raises security awareness with end users via authentication challenges when their identity shows high-risk behaviors
- Combines step-up authentication with self-audit as key parts of an increased security awareness and deterrence program

Cloud Anomalous Behavior and Watch Lists

Cloud analytics addresses cloud anomalous behavior with watch lists to quickly profile and maintain an eye on escalating predictive risk scores. Advanced machine learning behavior models are designed to find unknowns and apply predictive risk scores. Feedback on false positives and negatives update self-learning and self-training models to adapt to time-based norms and conditions unique to each customer deployment. For

example, an IaaS/PaaS administrator may create a script that runs several commands with security implications at 2 a.m. each evening. This user is an innovator working to improve the enterprise's productivity. However, models will see these commands during non-business hours as an anomaly and risk score accordingly. Feedback from the models can note the situation is benign. Nonetheless, the IaaS/PaaS administrator should be put on a watch list to monitor further innovations. Pre-defined watch lists are also provided within cloud security analytics for common high-risk groups like new hires, departing users, terminated users, and high-risk users. These groups should be easily accessed in dashboard drop-down menus to analyze risk scores, anomalies, accounts, access, activity and timelines. Cloud security analytics also supports explicitly adding or removing identities within watch lists.

Benefits

- Enables quickly profiling high-risk user groups from watch lists to monitor their risk scores and anomalies by SOC security analysts
- Provides profiling for audit and compliance teams of a specific person or group via a watch list to analyze their identity, accounts, access and activity
- Controls who has visibility to watch lists and for what data fields through Role-based Access Controls (RBAC) and data masking features

Cloud to SIEM integration for Alerts

Cloud security analytics provides a RESTful API infrastructure for integration with other security solutions on-premises and cloud, plus alerts via email or SMS (short message service). Enterprises have built detection and incident response programs around SIEMs to centrally locate SOC alerts. Deploying CSA for cloud provides the ability to send alerts for cloud identities, accounts, access and activity to SIEM solutions. While the SIEM itself may

not be analyzing SaaS cloud applications, IaaS, PaaS and IDaaS, the SIEM can be utilized for central alert notifications with predictive risks scores for prioritization. Mature CSA solutions offer a case ticketing management feature. They may also integrate with Remedy, ServiceNow and Salesforce for case ticket management.

Benefits

- Delivers bi-directional API integration with SIEM solutions for alerts, risk scores and event details from cloud security analytics
- Leverages existing SIEM detection and incident response processes for CSA, plus case ticket management
- Maintains a closed-loop for all UEBA-IdA-CSA alerts including SaaS cloud applications and IaaS/PaaS

Cloud to On-Premises DLP Closed-Loop

Cloud security analytics provides alerts via email or SMS, plus a RESTful API infrastructure, for integration with other security solutions such as on-premises DLP. Alerts, risk scores and event details from cloud security analytics software can be provided to DLP solutions to create a closed-loop for data exfiltration detection, IP data protection and data risk mining. The integration of DLP with CSA and CASB architecture is a requirement to protect data in hybrid environments with existing on-premises DLP solutions and incident response processes. Cloud security analytics provides DLP alert prioritization with predictive risk scores to make security analysts more productive and efficient with investigations and response. CSA integration with SaaS applications, IaaS/PaaS and IDaaS provides monitoring and alerting for cloud environments where legacy DLP may have restricted visibility. Advanced CSA solutions have case management features and integrate with Remedy, ServiceNow and Salesforce for case ticket management.

Benefits

- Sends on-premises DLP solutions alerts, risk scores and event details from cloud security analytics
- Leverages existing DLP detection and incident response processes for cloud security analytics, plus case ticket management
- Maintains a closed-loop for all UEBA-IdA-CSA alerts concerning data exfiltration and protection including SaaS cloud applications and IaaS/PaaS

Cloud Access Outliers and Excess Access

Cloud security analytics identifies cloud access considered high-risk by consuming access entitlements (rights) data and activity from SaaS, IaaS, PaaS and IDaaS. CSA also identifies access that is considered high-risk including: privileged access entitlements, access not properly segregating duties, dissimilar access compared to peers, and infrequent access to cloud accounts. The average user has more than 100
entitlements, making certification a time-consuming process for managers. Certifications are typically a quarterly or yearly process. Organizations realize managers are too often approving all certification requests without actually validating each one. This leaves organizations at risk with employees having extended access to which they should not be entitled. Using cloud security analytics integrated with cloud IDaaS or IaaS, organizations can detect access outliers leveraging peer groups of users to trigger certifications for outlier access.

Benefits

- Reduces cloud access not associated with job responsibilities and potential cloud account compromise
- Reduces rubber stamping associated with Sarbanes-Oxley and other compliance related access reviews
- Reduces segregation of duties (SoD) conflicts for cloud access, plus optimizes manager time with high-risk access certifications

Cloud Risk-based Access Compliance

Cloud security analytics outlier access capabilities can be extended to automatically send risk-based certifications to the business when outlier cloud access is identified. The system should be able to be configured to include several context points such as access risk rating, peer group metric, outlier risk score, and status recommendation (Keep or Remove). The solution can send built-in certifications, or use API's to integrate with other
enterprise solutions to send certifications to account owners for review.

Benefits

- Enables the business (managers, data owners, role owners) to make decisions about removing or retaining outlier access to their cloud assets and data
- Eliminates the need for training end users on a new certification platform with integration for most enterprise certification systems
- Delivers a configurable context-rich UI for making decisions about access

Cloud Dormant and Orphan Accounts

Cloud security analytics identifies dormant and orphan cloud accounts. These cloud accounts can be sent to system owners or administrators for review. Based on their response, action can be taken to assign the cloud account to an end user, or remove the cloud account from the system.

Benefits

- Reduces risk of orphan or dormant cloud accounts being compromised or misused
- Automates identification of risky orphan and dormant cloud accounts, potentially used for data exfiltration
- Enables cloud account and system owners to take action by identifying cloud account owners or marking the cloud account for review
- Automatically disables cloud accounts and notifies the owner when there is no decision

Cloud Application License Metering (Account Level)

Cloud security analytics can also provide a savings to customers by metering cloud applications at the account level, based on access and activity. Removing orphan and dormant accounts, plus rogue accounts operating under the radar for potential data exfiltration, saves on licensing fees for SaaS cloud applications. Date of last activity or inactive accounts are compared to baselines and peer behaviors to determine abnormal conditions. As

enterprises migrate to cloud applications, the licensing topic becomes more critical to minimize costs. The cloud security analytics API integrates with SaaS cloud applications, IaaS/PaaS and IDaaS to monitor identities, their accounts, access and activity.

Benefits

- Reduces cloud application and infrastructure license fees with metering based on user and entity behavior analytics
- Delivers true step-up licensing in contracts based on normal behaviors, not peak loads or abnormal use
- Provides license metering along with self-audit and step-up authentication provide ROI and raise security awareness

Capital markets – Use cases

Enterprises engaged in trading transactions face a unique challenge to assure the inviolability of trades is assured. To support that objective, a number of predictive security analytics use cases are aligned to address the various challenges these enterprises face.

Trading surveillance

- *Pre-Trade Surveillance* – Pre-Trade Surveillance, prevention of regulatory and compliance violations. Pre-validation to ensure both customer and personal (employee) trades fall within acceptable risk, limit, and price volatility thresholds. Monitor trade order manifests to ensure they are consistent with past requests and identify outliers.
- *At-Trade Surveillance* – Monitoring trade transactions as they occur with near real-time analysis, based on data ingestion. Identifying anomalous patterns in order flow (spoof trading, order entry) to manipulate volumes and security prices.
- *Post-Trade Surveillance* – Comparing trade transactions to historical trading behavior baseline and reviewing order/trade ratios. This process can be run across instruments and/or traders. The process uses supervised learning and rules based on previous abuse and known non-compliant trading patterns. Both customer and in-scope personal (employee) trades are reviewed. Instances of potential illegal insider trading can be identified during this process.
- *Cross-asset Class, Cross-market Surveillance* – Monitoring multiple market classes across geographies for potential abuse. This type of surveillance monitors for events in one class of asset or geography that impacts another class of asset (equities versus bonds, oil, gold, silver, etc.).

Cross communication trading surveillance

- *Trade Communication Linking* – Monitor voice, chat, and email for market manipulation. Link communications to trading patterns to establish patterns of communications before trades occur.
- *Social Media Monitoring* – Monitor social media feeds to map social media accounts of key employees. Generate an alert when someone posts information that could be considered a compliance violation (market manipulation).

Anti-money laundry (AML)

- *Misreporting* – Detect payments to a vendor by unrelated third parties, misclassification or over/under valuation of commodities and double invoicing.
- *Unusual Trading / Transactions* – Detection of repeated importation and exportation of the same high-value commodity (carousel transactions) or trades of commodities that do not match the business involved.

Customer accounts – Know your customer (KYC) violations

- *Consumer Account Breaches* – Monitoring of customer accounts for unusual account activities including slow drip attacks, account changes, and link this information with consumer reporting agencies (fraud detection agencies) such as credit freezes, and unusual account activity.
- *Fraudulent Consumer Account Detection* – Identity validation – Detection of accounts with suspicious combinations of SSN, name, address and phone. Validate information is not the same or similar to an unusually large number of other accounts. Flagged accounts require additional validation prior to allowing transactions.

Personal trading

- *Personal Trading Checks* – Pre-validation to ensure personal trades fall within risk, limit, and price volatility thresholds. Ensure trades are consistent with past behavior.
- *Insider Trading Surveillance* – Monitoring of personal trading of key employees to identify outlier behavior. Correlate personal trading pattern with available insider information.

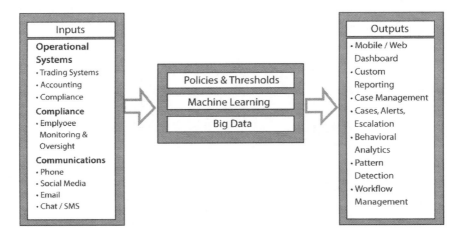

Capital Markets Use Case – Process Flow
Figure 9.2

Custom use cases – Accounting for unique and emerging requirements

At times, IT security teams need the ability to build custom machine learning models that detect identity-based threats and risks. This circumstance may be for a number of reasons including a unique requirement correlating with the individual customer's environment or user and entity profiles. It may also involve the management of very sensitive data with highly restricted access, as is the case in certain government agencies.
Other reasons for the need to develop custom uses exist as well. The fundamental requirement is for organizations to be able to create behavioral models without vendor input or involvement. This requisite would include having a step-by-step graphical interface that requires no coding, a minimal knowledge of data science and supports any big data customer choice. Additional requirements for custom use case development include:

- *An advanced analytics framework* – This custom use case capability should deliver a complete behavior-based machine learning model framework where no coding and only minimal knowledge of data science is required. Guidance should be provided at each step for attribute selection, training and baselining parameters, prediction thresholds and scoring, plus providing feedback on detected anomalies in production. Models are self-learning and self-training to optimize over time with the ability to update baselines as desired.

- ***Decoupled big data*** – Custom use case development should also support models to compute and store data from an open choice of big data infrastructures including: Hadoop, Cloudera, Hortonworks, MapR or Elastic (ELK Stack). Hybrid environments are driving the deployment of data lakes on-premises, and in the cloud, to store data for value, reducing data transfer and indexing fees. Hybrid models, with 360-degree visibility of an identity, accounts, access and activity for anomaly detection and predictive risk scoring should be supported.

- ***Flexible data connections*** – This aspect of custom use case development enables any custom or unique data with desired attributes to be ingested for custom model development. This capability provides the ability to access data with known methods to map fields to attributes. A flexible meta-model allows the customization or addition of new attributes. Popular scenarios are for mainframe data, new SaaS applications, or CASBs as desired data sources for machine learning model analysis.

- ***Analytics response code*** – This capability provides a numerical value alongside a predictive security risk score for bi-directional API integration with other security solutions such as authentication, data loss prevention, security information and event management or identity access management solutions. The numerical value also links to a business-friendly risk and threat description for security analysts to view. This facilitates the growing demand among customers for a closed-loop bi-directional API deployment for automated response when possible. Popular uses are step-up authentication, risk-ranked DLP and SIEM alerts, and access outlier certifications.

- ***Model optimization per environment*** – This functionality enables the development of custom models for UEBA, IdA or cloud security analytics inclusive of hybrid behavior analytics. Customers can develop multiple model variations in a lab environment to determine which model detected the anomaly, see which models risk score, adjust risk weightings, provide model feedback and review behavior profile comparisons. The most effective models can be moved to a test environment for staging into production. This process also validates data source continuity, as well as cleanliness and quality between environments. Often, special lab projects require privacy in production. Here, this capability provides roles-based access and data masking through workflow, plus tokenization and encryption of data.

Customer use case applications – User profiles

Depending on their roles and responsibilities, different members within an organization have varied use and interaction with predictive security analytics use cases.

- ***End user*** – With the Self-audit feature, end users have the opportunity to view their activity and behavior for self-analysis. They can view risk-scored access and activity, device inventory, and geolocations, through convenient and regular reporting. This enables them to participate in a collaborative partnership with their organization to protect assets and their identity. End users have the value of context not easily transferred to SOC analysts, making their detection lower for false positives. The self-audit feature is also used with partners and customers, and in some cases it has been monetized.

- ***Department leaders*** – Taking a risk-based approach to IAM, with identity analytics, department leaders gain the elimination of excess access and access outliers. Security efficiencies are heightened by reducing workloads through dynamic provisioning and using intelligent roles to replace those defined by legacy rules and processes. The net result is a reduced access risk plane, increased revocations and the elimination of rubber stamping and access cloning.

- ***SOC analyst*** – Through UEBA normalized risk scoring, analysts detect insiders, account compromise, data exfiltration and external intruders. Context-aware analysis facilitates Level 1 reviews. Process empowerment is available through canned machine learning models producing risk-scored access and activity in timelines accessed from dashboards for use cases and high-risk groups. Their use also includes as case and ticket management, interfacing with solution applications such as Remedy, ServiceNow, and SFDC, plus email or SMS alerts.

- ***Data scientist*** – Driven by open architecture, they avoid black box solutions closed to customization. Mature UEBA-IdA-CSA solutions enable these valued resources to create custom machine learning models, without coding or a deep understanding of data science, in a step-by-step guided process. Also, the ability to adjust risk weightings in pre-packaged analytics and ingest any dataset with desired attributes via an open and flexible metadata model are key uses. Predictive security analytics are a strategic defense that should enable skilled resources to optimize and customize deployments.

Benefits of predictive security analytics use cases

Having a broad selection of predictive security analytics use cases provides customers with the assurance that their behavior security analytics requirements will be addressed. Assuring a vendor can support these use cases across both on-premises and cloud, as well as being vendor agnostic, provides the strongest assurance that objectives are achieved. The benefits of predictive security analytics use cases include:

- *Empowered security capabilities and quality* – With the mature capabilities of UEBA and IdA integrated together, they provide robust and optimal predictive security analytics across a range of hybrid environments, scoring the gray areas of unknowns and minimizing false positives. The result is improving the focus of 'find fix' resources, and optimizing the time of security analysts, efficiency in the SOC, making operations and people more productive.

- *Extended and optimized, discovery, monitoring and visibility* – This includes the baseline ability to view the full context of a user's access entitlement risks and anomalous activities. In addition, this also includes the prime access risk plane of privileged access with the risk scoring of privileged access entitlements and user activity for any incident in question. A mature solution also includes cloud security analytics for hybrid environments, providing a combined 360-degree view for identity, and risk-scored behavior anomalies, driven by machine learning as part of a newly recognized state-of-the-art UEBA-IdA standard.

- *Improved productivity and cost savings* – By having holistic visibility across all an organization's environments, users and devices, SOC teams' efficiencies are maximized, delivering cost savings. In addition, as enterprises migrate to cloud applications, the licensing topic becomes more critical to minimize costs. Removing orphan and dormant accounts, saves on licensing fees for SaaS cloud applications.

- *Customized and self-audit capabilities* – Through customized model development capability, all conceivable requirements and use cases within predictive security analytics can be addressed. With the self-audit feature, users are part of a collaborative relationship with security teams providing unique context to confirm anomalies with exceptionally low false positive rates, plus providing security awareness and deterrence against identity compromise and insider threats.

Conclusions

The depth and range of use cases fundamentally defines the areas of expertise and functionality for predictive security analytics vendors. This factor represents an important qualification when choosing a solution partner including a UI for analysts and APIs for bi-directional integrations. Having a broad selection of use cases provides customers with the assurance that their behavior security analytics requirements will be addressed comprehensively. Assuring a vendor can support these use cases across both on-premises and cloud, as well as being vendor-agnostic, provides the strongest assurance that objectives are achieved. The operative areas of predictive security analytics are: access analytics, threat analytics and cloud analytics. These align directly with UEBA (threat analytics), IdA (access analytics) and CSA (cloud analytics). A wide range of use cases in these categories is key to a vendor's comprehensive capabilities to ensure holistic predictive security assurance. Having the capability of developing custom use cases is a critical advantage for customers seeking the ability to develop confidential use cases outside the vendor's visibility, as is the case with government agencies and organizations dealing with highly sensitive data sources.

Afterword

The journey through ever-changing borderless domains

Where do we go from here?

New York magazine recently published an article entitled *Envisioning the Hack That Could Take Down New York City*. In it, all types of nightmare scenarios are depicted, including SUV's suddenly coopted by remote control and forced to cause automobile accidents on strategic bridges going into the city, paralyzing traffic. Victims of ransomware, hospitals' computer systems freeze up; critical information stored in the cloud is unavailable. Patients' lives are in danger. Police station computer programs lock up, making any coordinated response to accidents and emergencies impossible. Chlorine valves controlling the amount of chlorine versus water into the water system are opening and closing irregularly, seemingly at will. Global anarchists have targeted the city to make a point and demonstrate how easily a major metropolitan area could be crippled purely by digital means. A chilling portrait, it is an exercise in fiction meant to portray to readers modern culture's complacent faith in technology and political authority. So much of it reads like a movie, that it might be too easy to dismiss its message with a touch of cognitive dissonance. IT leaders may feel they have that luxury. After all, it's not their job to worry about these things. Well, in actuality, it is. IT security leaders are in actuality responsible for safety.

In his book *Future Crimes*, author, and leading authority on global security, Marc Goodman portrays the innovative and disturbing methods cybercriminals, companies, and even countries, are employing with cutting-edge technologies to compromise our digital worlds. While technological advances benefit us in countless ways, hackers are continually leveraging these advances, and those of their own innovations, that threaten our security in countless ways. Poorly protected WiFi routers, thermostats, cameras and other devices can send spam or cause denial of service attacks. Smart TVs and game consoles can take you to malware of phishing sites. iOS and Android tablets and smartphones can bring you to bad applications that can expose you to malware and websites that phish for your private information and access credentials. Today's cyber criminals steal identities, drain online bank accounts, and wipe out computer servers. As individuals, we are becoming more and more vulnerable as identity is a growing access risk and threat plane.

On a global scale, when it comes to the prospect of *Future Crimes* threatening enterprises and organizations, including government agencies, the stakes are much higher. The survival of organizations and nations is at risk. And if we were to compare today's current technology and internet as the size of a pea, with the tidal wave of scientific progress underway, in the near future it will deliver a technology boom on a scale the size the largest planet in our solar system, Jupiter, or even larger. That massive lake of big data, and the accompanying digital exhaust, is rapidly becoming a sprawling and unsettled ocean. That reality is a sobering mandate of responsibility for any CISO, CSO, CIO, CEO, board of directors or cyber czar.

On any substantial journey through unknown terrain, especially those with hidden dangers, a map or a guide is always helpful. We've shared with you the experience of a number of security experts, many of whom are members of Gurucul's Executive Advisory Board (EAB). They have provided insights into the lessons they have learned while contending with the seismic transformation of their environments. They have dealt with the disappearance of the perimeter and the journey to hybrid cloud, along with the infusion of wireless devices, BYOD and IoT into their environments. As well, we've been fortunate at Gurucul to benefit from their seasoned experience to advise us during different evolutionary phases, through the years, on our path to develop the next generation of solutions we believe are beneficial for emerging environments today. What follows is a distilled overview sharing some of our experts' insights.

Gary Eppinger – In Chapter 1, *Impact of Cloud and Mobility for Identity* – a new paradigm is observed. Everyone and everything is globally connected in a 24/7 world. Consumer IT and data is no longer behind the firewall, resulting in the loss of this critical security control point. The hybrid IT security challenge bears a direct impact on traditional defenses like DLP, SIEM and IAM. Eppinger shares his experiences of managing the 'hyper-hybrid environment' of Carnival Corporation, which has drawn from his extensive involvement with generations of security strategy and policy evolution in a range of verticals. While dealing with the complexities of environments on land, at sea, in the cloud and in constant motion, with an enterprise that manages a number of enterprise verticals within one umbrella business model, he has observed his fundamental strategies for assuring security success. This involves implementation of managed solution integration in phases for bringing unique and separate siloed environments into one centralized management approach. His strategy includes moving security closer to the data itself and with the right controls. Balancing people, process and technology, this calls out the objective of achieving reliable functionality over perfection with each phase, since technology is perpetually evolving. This phased strategy includes the integration of predictive security analytics and capitalizing on the short-term benefits, while refining the long-term goals and increasing quality over time, which can best be achieved with machine learning driven by the context of big data.

Jerry Archer – In Chapter 2, *The Compromise and Misuse of Identity* – with financial fraud trending more than double in 2015, identity is recognized as the easiest doorway and path to an organization's most prized assets. Whether leveraged as user, account, entity, entitlement, or through partners, identity is the root cause of most data theft and breaches. Managing identity properly removes excess access and access outliers open to misuse and compromise. The gap between IAM and security teams, however, is a challenge as these groups in some organizations are working at cross-purposes. The problem of excess access, privileged access, and orphan or dormant accounts is widespread among enterprises. Archer lends his seasoned perspective on the development of security solutions in the environment since the inception of the internet. Due to the radical and seismic infrastructure changes, he observes that 60% of the threat problem resides at the endpoint, an organization's weakest point. But due to the overwhelming number of endpoints, the human ability to monitor them has long passed. Archer recognizes the urgent requirement for solutions detecting anomalous behavior. This is along with the critical position big data and machine learning hold in today's security strategies to provide comprehensive and continuous visibility on endpoints. This challenge is complicated by the evolution of hybrid cloud access and the plethora of devices, a majority of them mobile, which malicious actors take advantage of by virtue of stolen credentials. Throughout addressing these challenges, the prudent security management for privileged access abuse is a core requirement which can only be achieved with solutions leveraging mature identity analytics (IdA) in concert with user and entity behavior analytics (UEBA). He also endorses a security strategy of resilient defense, making it as difficult as possible for attackers to exfiltrate the data they seek once they have gained access to the environment. Like Eppinger, Archer observes the phased approach to implementing complex changes in the environment has proven be both cost-effective and strengthens the assurance that the new solution is delivered in synch with the existing environment. Metrics behind any solution initiative for executive management review, and having a framework in place for resilient recovery from any breach, are also heightened priories.

Joe Sullivan – In Chapter 3, *Insider Threats, Account Compromise and Data Exfiltration* – blind spots in the environment are identified as where the unknowns reside. These unknowns translate directly to risk. How do you detect what you do not know?

Sullivan's experience with highly sensitive customer accounts, with a broad array of insiders who have access to them, has provided him with insights into solutions and policies that help assure the integrity of the enterprise, while protecting the privacy of customers in a vast and global online environment. In one report by CMU's CERT program, 93% of the insider breaches studied exploited inadequate access controls. This problem is exacerbated when business units striving for more productivity and flexibility, adopt cloud solutions outside IT's purview, sometimes putting CIO and CISOs' priorities at cross purposes. The resulting complex hybrid infrastructures underscore the constraining challenge of traditional threat hunting with known bads, using rules, patterns and signatures. Sullivan observes that these outdated defense models are inadequate. It is a new frontier for security, after decades of declarative defenses. With limited skilled resources, budgets and time for insider threat detection, allocating more humans to security challenges will not solve the problem. That time has passed. Processing the signal-to-noise ratio and the related data volume has grown far beyond human capability. Managing unknowns today is only possible from behavior analytics utilizing advanced machine learning to derive value from big data. The rich context delivered from big data provides lower false positives for identifying the anomalous behavior of insiders. One of Sullivan's strategic approaches to address this challenge is with behavior analytics and includes a three-part security program consisting of securing applications, locking down identity, and having visibility into how authorized identities are using applications. As dwell time for malicious insiders remains near 150 days, new solutions leveraging machine learning no longer need exact attack signatures. Instead of having a significant volume of false positives from IPS and DLP systems, big data is leveraged for context to score access risks and anomalous behaviors. Sullivan also observes that the future holds more and more complexity. Employees accessing data from more devices, applications and paths will eventually result in total fragmentation of the environment.

Teri Takai – In Chapter 4, *Identity, Access Risks and Access Outliers* – two core observations are made. The first is the recognition of a new reality with the borderless perimeter. The second is that identity as an access risk has become a primary threat plane for attackers. The mathematics of this challenge is straightforward: *Data + Access = Threat Surface*. While organizations must provide access to whoever needs it, when they need it, as well as the level of access required, they must also be able take it away whenever necessary. This recognizes two primary concerns. The first is the separate functional silos numerous organization maintain between IT and SOCs, and the critical importance to bridge those. The second entails the recognition that manual processes and legacy roles driving IAM (identity and access management) solutions (including PAM) are no longer adequate to manage identity effectively or comprehensively. This creates too many open doors. Those gaps in management are a serious access risk plane and privileged access abuse stands at the top of this hierarchy of unaddressed risks, where over 50% of organizations' privileged access entitlements are unaccounted for. Included with the insider threat, partners, customers, devices, entities and applications must be accounted for in prudent identity management strategies. With the gargantuan data expansion in modern environments, legacy security strategies cannot cope with evolving cloud and mobility technologies. Robust identity management can only be achieved by employing identity analytics, with a risk-based approach, which draws from big data for context, supported by advanced machine learning. One result and value of adopting this kind of solution reduces the identity access surface area by as much as 83% by removing excess accounts and entitlements as an example.

Robert Rodriguez – In Chapter 5, *We Need a New Approach – Key Drivers* – sobering trends from Verizon's 2016 *Data Breach Investigations Report* (DBIR) cite a sharp rise in financial motives for malicious activities, while insider threat metrics remain consistent and strong. With IDC Research projecting data growth to expand from 4 zettabytes in 2013 to 44 zettabytes in 2020, Rodriguez calls for the urgent need of a new generation of cyber security solutions. While research and investments are on the rise for analytics, some resistance to adopting this next generation in cyber security remains in place. Some of it stems from legacy institutional thinking and bias. Other influences are ingrained business policies that involve adopting a system integrator model of people-intensive responses to security solutions. However, with the sprawling amount of data overload in environments, overwhelming security teams, this approach simply no longer scales. He recommends that for organizations to evolve successfully, they must move from the 80% bodies and 20% technology model, to 80% technology and 20% bodies. While Rodriguez voices the desire to see leaps in innovation of security technology, he recognizes other influences at work, one of which is a reluctance to take costly risks. Incremental solution development is the norm, not monumental, and this involves developing solution components that have the ability to evolve with existing environments. Rodriguez observes how behavior analytics effectively and efficiently minimizes the human touch points, and how behavior defines identity. Recognizing the complexity of a single identity in many systems, Rodriguez observes how identity analytics helps mitigate that challenge. Without proper identity management, excess access is inevitable, as these unmanaged identities and entitlements drastically increase the access risk plane. With the impact of the hybrid cloud, this imperative challenge is amplified by sobering degrees of magnitude. He also observes how numerous forward-looking industry change agents have promoted new insights into the next generation of cyber security along with encouraging productive change. He notes the model in Australia where organizations are adopting cloud more quickly by mandate, leveraging best practices, lessons learned by other colleagues in global security, along with hands-on experience of their peers in North America.

Leslie K. Lambert – In Chapter 6, *Discovering the Unknown – Big Data with Machine Learning* – the age of big data is acknowledged. With its arrival, the only method to successfully leverage that paradigm shift is through advanced machine learning (ML) by extracting meaning from digital exhaust through iterative data reprocessing to discover patterns. For predictive security analytics, however, the early path was slower than other disciplines to deliver value due to the requirement to accurately identify verifiable risk amidst a sea of complex data. Having ultimately met that challenge, Lambert observes how ML is now reshaping security with the support of behavior analytics and notes practical scenarios where its effectiveness applies critical value. As well, Lambert examines numerous scenarios where ML, with UEBA and IdA, deliver crucial security support in cases such as insider spying with 'borrowed' credentials, flaws in privileged access security policy, data exfiltration through remote access malware, and misuse of unmanaged cloud resources. The context of big data and continuous self-learning and self-training that ML delivers is an important component of this value. That's because without machine learning, human capacity to handle this volume of data in a timely manner is simply impossible. This also calls out the importance of recognizing the ways that big data is essential in gaining a comprehensive sense of visibility through machine learning. Four case studies of machine learning in UEBA provide deeper insight into solution value. Lambert also examined the importance of understanding that not all instances of machine learning are equal in their capabilities, and that some UEBA vendors offer solutions that are fundamentally rules and signature-based. These solutions only deal with known bads, whereas true advanced machine learning clusters big data to detect the unknown unknowns, which is at the foundational core of mature behavior analytics value.

Gary Harbison – In Chapter 7, *Cloud and Mobility: Unknowns for Identity Risks and Misuse* – new modes of security solution development strategy are explored to facilitate the transition to mobile and cloud adoption. With the waterfall methodology model representing the traditional development approach demonstrated by on-premises environments, it is contrasted by the Agile-DevOps model of continuous improvement which more aptly supports today's hybrid environments. Strengthening this strategy is the observation that when adopting UEBA, IdA and cloud security analytics (CSA) security solutions, choosing those which are mature and best-of-breed solutions is a best practice. This means they have demonstrated proven value in an array of complex hybrid terrains and in a range of customer environments. These are critical considerations as Harbison notes that, with emerging multiple cloud security environments, it's difficult to accomplish with consistency what had been realized with on-premises environments in the past. Achieving it usually requires a retooling of thinking and must incorporate the context of identity, access and trust. This includes new modes of establishing identity. Accounting for all identities in the environment is a critical requirement. As well, complicating factors like CASB convergence with traditional environments, API transparency, and the limitations of vendor-specific UEBA features, must also be taken into account for seamless hybrid security. Harbison also observed the importance of the partnership between IT and security strategy coordination, through the CIO and the CISO, to achieve optimal results in delivering on their enterprise's business objectives in the market.

All of the experts agree that maintaining a focus on emerging trends and developing technology is critical. Also, keeping a focus on what threat innovations are emerging next is also required to keep in pace with the malicious actors depicted in *Future Crime*. This policy includes using an incremental approach to adding solution components as needed within the environment, and to maintain a flexible strategy of solution development in sync with the fragmentation of the emerging environments. It is evident as well that IAM will move forward through IdA, and due to the volume of data, detection of unknown threats will come through UEBA. The *Borderless Breach Flashcards* provided insight into the range of some of these threats which are unfolding today, many employing compromised credentials and the misuse of identity to achieve their ends.

In Chapter 8, *Requirements for Borderless Behavior Analytics*, we shared the prerequisites for an effective predictive security analytics solution approach that addresses today's hybrid environments. Customer solution requirements also involve a detailed understanding of environmental states within an organization, their individual technology challenges, as well as, the problem areas reflected in use cases. With these perspectives, security leaders are better able to leverage the UEBA-IdA-CSA solution components to their best advantage. These requirements also include the need to assure that any UEBA-IdA-CSA solution's value be demonstrated in a POC (proof of concept) and be delivered by a best-of-breed vendor-agnostic solution provider, with a level of maturity that assures the solution can grow with an environment into the future. Part of this maturity entails the employment of advanced machine learning, and not reliant on rules and signatures, which some vendors have misleadingly labeled as machine learning. Another component of this solution maturity is having the ability to employ UEBA, IdA and CSA in a broad range of use cases as are described in Chapter 9.

So now, without really planning to do so, where IT used to be in the IT department, it is now in the hands of business units and business leaders. This is where mobility and cloud innovations are being adopted, putting applications on employee's phones, without informing IT, leaving them to be the spectator and sometimes the follower. The playing field has changed completely. Humanity and organizations have crossed the threshold into a brave new borderless world, with a relentless reality of ever-expanding mobility and cloud adoption. The passage into the borderless world was a reactive impulse to leverage the advantages provided from the broad array of technology innovations. While rising risks are part of the reality, we hope that with the right guidance, organizations will be able to remain focused on the rich benefits these innovations offer, all the while the business of cyber security maintains a close partnership with those goals and objectives and encompasses safety over human lives.

This book has been part of that journey. While the future will continue to deliver more fragmentation and new security challenges, along with empowering opportunities, it will be our goal to be there as well, to maximize the possibilities and minimize the risks. And while Buzz Lightyear from *Toy Story* is a whimsical character of fiction, his credo (an impossibility in geometry) exemplifies the spirit CISOs must embrace facing the constantly expanding and evolving security challenges which stand before them each day: "To Infinity and Beyond!" This is our sensibility as well.

Nilesh Dherange
Chief Technology Officer, Gurucul* – Predictive Security Analytics

* From Sanskrit, '*Guru*' = expert and '*Cul*' = group: An expert group. As a security analytics company, expertise and learning hold a very special meaning, as it reflects in our name.)

Borderless Behavior Analytics
Sneak Preview of
The Second Edition

The continuing journey in borderless domains

So is that all there is? Is this book all there is to know about Borderless Behavior Analytics? Certainly not.

The resounding support for this project in the CISO and CIO community has been impressive, encouraging and gratifying. It fortifies our perception that we're on the right track.

In fact, as a wider audience of prominent security and IT leaders have become acquainted with the book project, a number have indicated an eagerness to participate and contribute. As a result, we're planning for the near future, an expanded edition of *Borderless Behavior Analytics – Who's Inside? What're They Doing?* Two new expert interviews are already complete. More are in the works. As a parting gift, we share two selected sections of these expert interviews, which deliver additional insights into the ever-evolving world of Borderless Behavior Analytics. Two of our new contributing experts are:

- **Devin Bhatt*** – CISO & Chief Privacy Officer, U.S. Federal Government. **His topic:** *Insider Threats and Insider Programs.*
- **Jairo Orea*** – Chief Information Security Architect, Fortune 10 Company, Member Cloud Security Alliance. **His topic:** *Hybrid Environment Architecture.*

---

* The views and opinions expressed by both Devin Bhatt and Jairo Orea in this book are their own, and do not necessarily reflect those of their current, or any of their previous employers.

Devin Bhatt on:
Emerging influences impacting the insider threat

While it remains a current and ongoing discussion in the security community, it's not brand new. CISOs recognize that the border, or the network perimeter, is becoming continually more porous. The data may reside outside of a company's data center in external cloud environments. So the security focus needs to be on the data (not just on the network perimeter). Security controls should be data-centric; it is no longer sufficient to have this focus just at the border level. When the security leaders consider data-centric security, they must also ensure mature identity and access management, logging, and the latest generation of predictive analytical capabilities. They need to know who has access to what at any given time, as well as, what those users are doing with the data.

The challenges of data-centric security and controls. Security leaders require the resources, processes, and technologies to identify where all their data and assets are, and to have the visibility to effectively monitor who is accessing them and how that activity is being conducted. Is it legitimate, normal, or not? The important point is the ability to monitor behavior. Security and compliance teams often face challenges when elevated levels of security controls are required for high transactional production systems. The system administrators are concerned that if the audit logging for all events is turned on, there will be an operational performance degradation, increase in storage space, and cost. However, educating the system administrators about the risks of not capturing the required data, while addressing the other concerns, will usually be well received.

The requirement for perpetual due diligence. Even when it appears there is no resistance, or an appearance of compliance, the policy of 'trust, but verify' is essential in security. I recall numerous early payment card industry data security standards related assessments which were performed by qualified security assessors. In certain instances, when the security team requested confirmation from the system administrators that all the required controls were in place and fully operational, the team received an affirmative answer. Yet performing further due diligence and validation revealed that all the security configuration controls were not turned on. When asked for an explanation why these were not turned on, excuses were offered. When one has the technology and capabilities, but chooses not to enable and capture the important log information, then critical forensic investigation and analysis would not be possible during any incident response. It would be quite embarrassing or a career-ending situation to share the bad news with senior executives and the board of directors that the important log data was never captured. It would be ironic to be helpful to the network intruders, as they would not need to cover their tracks because the events were not logged in the first place!

'Trust, but verify' is a must for security success.

The scale of big data offering valuable insights. Today, security operations centers (SOCs) are inundated with billions of events from the company network. It's not humanly possible to review every event. That means that CISOs must use big data analytical capabilities and machine learning to analyze huge volumes of events quickly. The question security leaders need to answer is: "Can we link the data to produce actionable results?" With so much data volume, how does one meaningfully monitor this effectively and take the right action? Security teams need to perform significant and faster analysis with machine learning. These security teams are also seeking to identify all behavior indicators to fortify their monitoring strategy for insider threats. Many complex questions confront security leaders who are contending with requirements to provide access to data from anywhere, anytime, and any device. Such demands require full visibility and collection of all necessary log data. Security solutions should satisfy all the requirements instead of being standalone point solutions.

Discovering blind spots in security. This challenge is exemplified by the following classic incident of industrial espionage or theft of intellectual property. An employee at a manufacturing conglomerate tried to send an email with a huge PowerPoint presentation containing the company's five-year strategic plans. The presentation contained highly sensitive information about where the enterprise was planning to manufacture certain products overseas in 'low cost countries'. It listed which products were profitable and profit margins, including long-term strategic global marketing plans. This file was being sent directly to a competitor. The only reason the file was discovered was because the employee didn't know there was a limit on the size of attachments that could be sent during normal business hours. This IT policy was in place to prevent any delays for normal business users with email services. As a result, the email and attachment was quarantined to be sent off hours. Yet the file attachment was so large that, even during off hours, it still could not be sent. An IT specialist was called in to look at the issue, and upon examining the content, it was discovered the intended recipient was a competitor. This event raised alarms, and concern among senior executives wanting to know, "How could this happen?" Given this incident was caught by accident, what if the malicious insider had divided the attachment into four or five separate files? It probably would not have been detected, or only detected months later, well after the damage occurred. What if the insider had simply printed the entire presentation, took it home, and mailed it to the competitor? This demonstrates the need for having a much larger, holistic security analytics approach.

The CISO's enduring concerns. What keeps CISOs awake at night? There can be many reasons unique to each organization, but there are a number of common themes. Given data is no longer confined within the corporate data center, data breaches may have significant impact to brand reputation, shareholder value, loss of intellectual property, and other financial losses which can cause irreversible damage. There are likely gaps in appropriate resources, processes and technologies to mitigate these risks.

It might be easier to keep unauthorized outsiders away from sensitive data but very difficult for nefarious insiders, because they are trusted and have access. Instead of relying on declarative defenses, solutions like predictive security analytics, powered by machine learning, will help address a growing number of CISO concerns with a risk-based approach.

Jairo Orea on:
The impact of data access for cloud and mobility in hybrid architecture

Security architects are overseeing and managing a revolutionary paradigm shift in their priorities for addressing the new evolving risk and threat plane in hybrid environments. Originally, of course, all security solutions were created with the traditional on-premises perimeter in mind. It was something I call the eggshell approach. We had a hard perimeter with a soft inside. Anything inside was secure and anything outside was the wild world. The perimeter strategy was all about striving to continually fortify it, to make it thicker, stronger, and bigger. But now with the cloud and mobility, that concept has been diluted, and even more so with IoT (Internet of Things).

The new normal in hybrid environments. With the cloud, mobility and IoT, we are now putting things on the network that were originally never designed to be there. This adds a concerning factor to any comprehensive security solution strategy, where some security leaders are patching in solutions to address the immediate need as they see it. As a result, the risk aspect goes through the roof when the evolving challenges and the diminishing effectiveness of these ad hoc feature-based point solutions grow apart, lacking a platform strategy, leaving serious security gaps and a widening threat plane.

The expanding scale of data. Extrapolating on the limitations of feature-based point solutions, when security architects examine the prospect of thousands of servers, and the reality of millions of endpoints and millions of IP addresses, the issue of scalability presents its own considerable challenges in security. It represents a sprawling amount of growing data. The most realistic method security architects see to manage this kind of volume is with machine learning. Human resources cannot manage this, and the gap in security effectiveness will only grow with adherence to status quo strategies. As the perimeter continues to disintegrate, becoming increasingly porous, and the volume of data continues to rise, security architects in hybrid environments see the urgency for integrating holistic and efficient platform solutions to keep up with this challenge. Many are looking for the most effective next-generation approach for their unique environments, the majority of who see a machine learning approach as the best option for their security strategy.

The perimeter: Security strategy evolution. By necessity, the concept of the perimeter has significantly evolved for security architects. They recognize that scale, data access, and the eroding perimeter, are all directly related. One critical component of being successful in protecting the hybrid environment requires something I refer to as 'control persistency'. Controls will have to get much closer to the data. This requirement is complicated by a range of perimeter elements because of the need to get controls closer to the data in each instance. Not only do CISOs have to get closer to the data, but also closer to sensitive information they have, to ensure their controls are persistent. In addition, mobility and IoT escalates the complexity of this requirement, as users or developers access the environment from smart devices, 24/7, from anywhere. That accentuates a challenge when the original controls were primarily based on the perimeter. CISOs have to take the desired policies in each for their perimeters, with each type of supporting control, and then migrate, adapt and match them into the cloud.

Evolving controls needed. Security leaders must also ensure that their matching data controls will grow with the data itself. That's what I mean by control persistency. Regardless of connector, disconnector, on the cloud, on-premises, in the hybrid model, private cloud, public cloud, it doesn't matter. Those controls should persist in the environment of the data, no matter where that data resides and be resilient by themselves in order to protect that data. That is one main dimension to keep in mind for the concept of control persistency.

Factors influencing hybrid architectural planning. There are many issues security architects must consider as it relates to widespread and global data access. Because the perimeter is fundamentally gone, even though data is stored on certified cloud environments, it's not enough protection. Employees' own devices, microservices, or cloud services like Box, are factors intensifying the porous nature of the perimeter. With these types of services, where users can exchange data, collaborating with each other, doing that with millions of records to their phones, to their smartphones or tablets, multiplies the potential access risk and threat plane to sobering proportions. Compound that with the fact that a growing percentage of that data actually resides in a cloud environment which is owned by someone else other than the company.

Segregation: A fundamental access security requirement in hybrid architecture. The first point, regarding data access security architecture planning, is to ensure there is an ability to segregate who has access to what data, and where the data resides. To guarantee the quality of segregation for environments may include having contextual controls for the type of user or entity that is accessing the data. This could address a regular user, a service, or something like a service ID or a system ID, fixing the large amounts of data. In addition, security architects need to be able to monitor security patterns for those users and entities, so they can identify when something atypical from their established behavior patterns has occurred. This could possibly be malicious, necessitating the need to ensure SOCs are able to respond in an effective and timely manner. As a result, the need for a new generation of predictive security analytics, drawing from big data, with machine learning to gain critical context for behavior, is plainly apparent to a growing number of forward-looking security architects.

Privileged access: A two-tiered perspective. Especially in the cloud environment, security architects must think on two levels for privileged access. Privileged access has a construct level, where an enterprise's developers create, along with what IT is implementing and modeling in the cloud or with the cloud services provider. In addition, the controls for privileges of the administrators at the application level for the cloud service must be accounted for. These kinds of controls should enable the kinds of usage where the administrators can access from the host, or virtual machines, and just initiate a memory dump as required for their various roles and requirements. These controls must also account for all the data access for users with privileged access entitlements beyond the administrators in an organization. This is also why verifying controls closer and closer to protecting the data is critical. Gaining those controls contextually for the users, depending on the type of user, will help to mitigate the potential security risks in the cloud.

Complex realities of cloud tenancy. Security architects are especially concerned about the implications of living in a multitenancy environment. They must contend with this new normal condition of being a tenant in an environment where they don't own the infrastructure. They are responsible for knowing who accesses the enterprise's data in this environment, knowing that the data is encrypted, and as required, at times depersonalized. A number of technologies support this requirement, which include key management, or indexing the data in a way that involves tokenizing the data, so that core records, the PII (personal identifiable information) are rendered unusable. This makes the rest of the data irrelevant because only the application and the end user will understand how those elements are connected within the tokenization of their data. But the main focus is to have those controls close to the data. Have those controls with a deep understanding of the various factors of the privileged access user issue. Additional security control elements may also be needed. Multifactor access many cloud providers provide will deliver control data from their ecosystems, delivering addition context for behavioral analytics.

Note: In the second edition of *Borderless Behavior Analytics*, Jairo will go deeper into the concepts of data brokers, cloud brokers and identity brokers highlighted above, as services for hybrid cloud environments. Also included will be hybrid environment architectural diagrams.

We hope these additional insights are helpful, possibly providing perspective on use cases for behavior analytics. We'll have more for you in the near future! Until then, I wish you safe journeys through the borderless world!

Saryu Nayyar

ABOUT THE AUTHOR

Saryu Nayyar is a recognized visionary in the Information Security and Risk industry. Having held leadership roles with Oracle, Sun Microsystems, Ernst & Young, The Walt Disney Company, and Vaau (acquired by Sun), Saryu has over 10 years of experience in assessment, strategy, design and implementation of information security, identity and access management, and risk solutions. Saryu has served clients in several industries including telecom, retail, energy, automotive, pharmaceutical, food and beverage, entertainment, financial services, and insurance. Recognized as a thought leader, Saryu has published several white papers in the information security space.

46522848R00140

Made in the USA
San Bernardino, CA
09 March 2017